Advance Praise for

EVERY BUSINESS NEEDS AN ANGEL

"I have been leveraging angel money and experience since doing my first start-up in 1985. *Every Business Needs an Angel* would have been an invaluable resource—I wish it had been available fifteen years ago. It should be required reading for every entrepreneur. Each of my companies has benefited greatly from its association with angels."

—Philip J. Gross, angel investor, President and Cofounder of AtYourBusiness.com, and former CFO of America Online

"If venture capital were a stock, I'd be buying to hold over the next twenty-five years; with smaller government and freer markets, venture capital will boom. And as investors become more sophisticated and hands-on, angel investing is a natural. My friend Cal Simmons and his partner John May have recognized this and provide good solutions to entrepreneurs, through these words and through their life's work."

—David Gardner, Cofounder of The Motley Fool

"May and Simmons have written a must-read for every entrepreneur working to build a company. They inspire and provide insight into the company-building process."

—Rick Rickertsen, CEO and Partner of Thayer Capital Partners

"This is the 'How to Get Happily Financed' bible that any person with a business idea must buy. It's not enough just to get money (though that's good!), it's important to get the money at the right terms and from the right people. The authors show you the ropes, providing plenty of first-hand stories and insider tips that will boost your chances that you'll find an 'angel' to make your business dream come true."

—Nancy Evans, Cochairperson and Editor-in-Chief of iVillage.com

"Early in my career as a venture capital investor, I recognized that the difference between successful and so-so early stage investors was experience and the ability to recognize success patterns. John and Cal have both, and by sharing them through this book, have made a major contribution not only to angel investors, but to the entrepreneurs they will fund."

—Jack Biddle, Founding Partner of Novak Biddle Venture Partners

"John May and Cal Simmons have captured the essence of angel investing in *Every Business Needs an Angel.* It's a must-read book for anyone interested in starting a business and takes you behind the scenes of how sophisticated, high–net worth individuals evaluate new business opportunities."

—Russ Ramsey, President and Co-CEO, Friedman Billings Group (investment bankers); Chairman and Cofounder, Capital Investors (an angel investing group); and Managing Principal, Capital Crossover Partners LP (a venture capital fund)

"Every entrepreneur in search of angel funding should read this book. *Every Business Needs an Angel* is an insider's guide with real stories about real people and companies, and offering real lessons."

—Mario Morino, Chairman of Morino Institute, and Special Partner of General Atlantic Partners, LLC

"Told from the perspective of seasoned angel investors, *Every Business Needs an Angel* demystifies the angel investing process and lets the reader in on trade secrets that every aspiring entrepreneur should know. Here at the National Foundation for Teaching Entrepreneurship, we have spent the last twelve years supporting the development of over 40,000 youth entrepreneurs. This book is an invaluable resource that will help would-be entrepreneurs, both young and old, to successfully build their businesses."

—Steve Mariotti, Founder and President of the National Foundation for Teaching Entrepreneurship (NFTE)

"As a member of May and Simmons's Dinner Club, I found a great way to reduce much of the inefficiency and loneliness in my solo angel investing. They know this venture capital investing space cold, and the book is a great way to share their insider knowledge with entrepreneurs and angels alike."

—Gerald Taylor, angel investor and former President of MCI

"This is the real deal on angel investing. This book puts you in the room and enables you to learn how the wealthy make private equity investments."

—Guy Kawasaki, CEO of Garage.com

"Entrepreneurs and their businesses would be a lot more attractive to quality venture capitalists if they follow advice laid out in May and Simmons's book!"

—Art Marks, General Partner of New Enterprise Associates venture capital firm

"Angels are a crucial source of risk capital for new ventures, but entrepreneurs by and large know very little about them. John May and Cal Simmons have changed all that with *Every Business Needs an Angel,* which lifts the veil shrouding the process of angel investing. Their book is required reading for entrepreneurs who are searching for seed-stage and early-stage capital for a fledgling company."

—William D. Bygrave, Frederic C. Hamilton Professor for Free Enterprise, Arthur M. Blank Center for Entrepreneurship, Babson College

"If I had read this book fifteen years ago, our business would have grown a lot faster and I would be a lot richer and only have to read golf books today."

—Tom Messner, Founding Partner of Messner Vetere Berger McNamee Schmetterer/EuroRSCG

EVERY BUSINESS
NEEDS AN ANGEL

Getting the Money You Need
to Make Your Business Grow

John May and Cal Simmons

CROWN
BUSINESS
NEW YORK

Grateful acknowledgment is made for an excerpt from "Cities of Angels," 4/3/00, *Forbes ASAP*. Reprinted by permission of *Forbes ASAP* magazine © Forbes Inc., 2000.

Published by Crown Business, New York, New York.
Member of the Crown Publishing Group.

Random House, Inc. New York, Toronto, London, Sydney, Auckland
www.randomhouse.com

CROWN BUSINESS and colophon are trademarks of Random House, Inc.

Printed in the United States of America

Design by Lenny Henderson

Library of Congress Cataloging-in-Publication Data

May, John.
    Every business needs an angel : getting the money you need to make your
business grow / John May and Cal Simmons.
    Includes bibliographical references and index.
    1. Venture capital—United States. 2. Angels (Investors)—United States. 3. New
business enterprises—United States—Finance. I. Simmons, Cal. II. Title.

HG4963 .M348 2001
658.15'224—dc21

                                                                    2001028062

ISBN 0-609-60778-2

10 9 8 7 6 5 4 3 2 1

First Edition

Dedication

To entrepreneurs and angels everywhere working together to launch tomorrow's great companies.

And to our parents, Elizabeth and Walt Simmons, and Doris and Hugh May.

Contents

Introduction

The days when a Horatio Alger hero could go from rags to riches with nothing but sweat equity, luck, and a good mind for business are gone, probably for good. To survive and thrive, today's start-ups need more than hard work and a good idea. They need capital, and lots of it. And for entrepreneurs who have already exhausted the usual early sources of money (family, close friends, personal credit cards), the next resource is outside investors. Yet many entrepreneurs are rejecting the high demands and costly involvement of venture capitalists in favor of a new form of funding: angel investing.

Recent studies show that angels—individual early-stage investors—are the fastest-growing sector of investors. In 1999 they poured $30 billion into new businesses, compared with $12 billion from venture capitalists. Business-school experts who track investment activity say that business angels currently fund about 60 percent of new technology companies seeking $1 million or less in start-up capital. So you see, *most* every business does need an angel!

Angels are not professional investment bankers or venture capitalists. Many are ordinary citizens who have achieved a level of success in their own profession, which allows them discretionary savings for creative investing. These citizens are the unsung heroes of American business today—the "millionaires next door" who are looking to go the next step. They are the leading source of fuel for the economy's most vibrant sector—the small businesses of the technological revolution.

Every Business Needs an Angel is the first essential guide to what promises to be the most popular form of investing in the next decade. The book is intended for any entrepreneur looking for an investor, and any investor looking for a new enterprise. It was written by two people who have been involved in angel investing from the start, and who are at the epicenter of one of the country's fastest-growing angel markets. The Washington, D.C., area is now home to far more entrepreneurs and businesspeople than federal workers, and it has more start-up activity than even Silicon Valley, according to several recent reports. The quiet shift from a government-based economy to an entrepreneurial one is being repeated everywhere, from Boston to Austin to Baton Rouge. The D.C. region is just further along than most.

The book offers a blend of compelling stories, sound advice, personal anecdotes, and pearls of wisdom collected over many years of investing experience. On one side of our story are the 300,000 active angels and the 3.4 million estimated millionaires in this country who want to know how to invest creatively; on the other side are the tens of millions of businesspeople and would-be entrepreneurs who are looking for an insider's edge to get funding.

We have spent the past fifteen years advising, managing, and investing in early-stage companies. Cal Simmons became an angel after being a successful owner/operator of a business; John May's insights and expertise come from organizing and running small venture-capital funds. Together, we've been involved in more than fifty private equity transactions. Based on our experiences with both entrepreneurs and investors, and recognizing the need for a practical guide to finding angel capital, we decided to write this book.

In 1998 we helped create a new collaborative model for structured angel group investing. By early 2001, we had organized or advised four angel clubs in the Washington, D.C., region, managing over $50 million in investable assets, touching 275 investors monthly, and making dozens of investments in early-stage companies annually.

One of the angel clubs we founded is called the Dinner Club. This fund is an example of a new generation of angel investing: It is a structured organization of sixty individuals who have each contributed $80,000, creating a $5 million pool to back at least a dozen companies.

The group meets monthly to hear pitches from entrepreneurs, does follow-up investigations, and makes early-stage investments by majority vote. This group of angel investors served as a sounding board for many of the ideas related in our book. Several of the examples are from actual investments that the Dinner Club has pursued, and many of the entrepreneurs quoted received their first exposure to angel investors through this group.

Week after week, month after month, we meet with entrepreneurs out searching for funding. Sometimes they are successful; often they are not. Frequently the deals we see are good ones, but they are being presented unclearly or lack a simple key ingredient. We're constantly amazed at how naive or ill prepared many founders of new companies are when it comes to fund-raising. Having spent many years advising investors, we have developed a sixth sense for what they are looking for in an "investable deal," what it takes to convince them to write a check. In this book, we are going to share these secrets with our readers.

We will tell you *where* to find investors, *how* to prepare your presentation to them, how to evaluate whether they are the *right* partners for you . . . and then, perhaps most important, how to negotiate and structure a deal that is beneficial to both entrepreneur and investor. We'll even take a stab at explaining how to evaluate opportunities and prepare for a successful exit for both parties.

We will do all these things by sharing with our readers real-life examples of actual early-stage companies and their founders' efforts to raise outside capital. We're going to introduce you to entrepreneurs who have gone from launching raw start-ups to leading public companies—and tell you how they did it. We'll also show you some who had great ideas but failed to realize their potential. We'll examine why it is that some good companies never get funded and others, based on the strength of just an idea, are able to raise millions of dollars.

Underlying our many examples will be lessons for anyone interested in pursuing this New Economy dream . . . the founding of your own business. We will explain the subtle and not-so-subtle differences between success and failure, and we'll lay out the steps to help attract money to fledgling enterprises. The end of every chapter includes "Angel Advice" that summarizes key points.

Our book is organized in a way that allows readers to either jump around to chapters of primary interest or to read straight through from beginning to end. If you're looking for a good place to start, the following chapter descriptions should help. Feel free to dip into the book anywhere. We hope reading any one section will make you want to know more about the whole journey. Bon voyage.

In **chapter 1**, we relive an entire evening meeting of one of our dinner clubs, meeting nervous presenting entrepreneurs and angel-club members of all types. We show what goes through the minds of investors, discuss techniques used by company founders in attracting attention, and provide a window on the decision-making process of multiple angels when they pick the lucky winner of the initial dance. If you read only one chapter, we suspect you'll enjoy and be stimulated by the "dance" seen in this evening's events.

Chapter 2 is all about relationships. Angel investing varies greatly from bank financing and later-stage venture funding in that it is people to people. You get to meet, know, and bond with the check writer, not just deal with supporters by e-mail and snail mail. Since angel investing is an intensely personal experience, delivering both psychic rewards as well as possible wealth, you have to know how to understand human chemistry and how to build lasting partnerships. Go to this chapter now if you are intrigued about what "warm money" means. Be sure not to skip these insights when building your understanding of the entire angel-matching phenomenon.

By **chapter 3**, you get ready to build the business plan and to execute the strategy to have it financed by angels—and we also offer stories of entrepreneurs who weren't quite ready for angel investing. Why read the whole book or go through the heart-wrenching process of business formation if you find in these early chapters that your business concept or your personality won't appeal to individual investors? "Angel Advice" here will clearly deal with whether the angel investor world is for you.

For those on the path in search of company funding, we launch **chapter 4**'s guidance clearly at finding the *right* partner. Did you know that there was such a thing as bad money? Angels from hell? No matter how great your idea or high your hopes, they could be dashed if you find the wrong partner. We know you want specific, detailed how-to's by this stage of the learning curve on how every business needs an angel. **Chapter 5** is all about who angels are in today's market, how they are developing sophisticated structured groups in every community in the nation, and how to present to them. The presentation process is as important as your company's product or service, so learn how to prepare your elevator speech, and what are the key dos and don'ts on presentations. If you had only eight minutes to convince an angel, could you do it?

Let's make a deal! **Chapter 6** offers checklists of information you'll have to provide to angel prospects to get their confidence and see examples of term sheets (which are offers of funding). But remember, you are dealing with angels of all types, and one may well work out just in time for you. What types of business plans work with which types of angels? How will you value your company? Also, without some guidance with professionals—like lawyers and CPAs—you'll possibly have a sadder but wiser story to tell, so learn here how to deal with the financial closing process. And what a feeling when you see that check from the investors at the closing at your attorney's offices!

Once an angel relationship is begun, there is so much more than money to talk about. **Chapter 7** offers tips on how to live with your financing partner in a mutually beneficial way. If this is your key area of concern, jump to it first, then come back for the stories and insights about the entire life cycle of entrepreneurs and angels in the rest of our chapters. There are suggestions for getting better advice from your angels and outside advisers and what to do if the relationship hits a rocky patch. Having individual investor partners is like a marriage, so be prepared.

Finally, we provide stories about how the end of the angel experience can benefit entrepreneurs as well as funders. **Chapter 8** is all about the five typical exits that angels develop. Find out why acquisitions are the most likely way entrepreneurs and angels cash out—and what to watch out for in the deal. Angels and venture investors do need an exit, a way to get their money and—everyone hopes—profits back out. The whole reason we present this book to you is to explain the entire life cycle of an encounter with an angel—not only to help you determine if angels are for you but also to show you how to eventually separate and have a mutually beneficial exit.

We enjoy the entire business formation and growth process, the human drama, the stimulation of creativity and tension, and the high that comes when wild successes occur. Group dynamics of bands of angels heighten our experience and have led to many of the stories and lessons we share in this book. Each dance between entrepreneur and investor is unique—we look forward to hearing from many of you about your experiences. May each of you aspiring company founders grow to become angels in your own right and continue the evolution that we have experienced!

In future editions, we'll try to build on your comments. Please contact us at the following addresses to share your own early-stage business experiences or to react to any of the lessons in our book.

John May
New Vantage Group
402 Maple Avenue West
Vienna, VA 22180
Tel: (703) 255–4930
john@newvantagegroup.com

Cal Simmons
A.S.A.P. Ventures
1029 N. Royal Street, Suite 200
Alexandria, VA 22314
Tel: (703) 837–5150
cal@asapventures.com

1

Inside "The Dinner Club":
How Angels Evaluate Entrepreneurs

For many entrepreneurs, angel investing has a certain mystique. There simply is not a lot of public knowledge about how business angels function. In this book, we hope to lift that veil of mystery and clearly explain what it takes to obtain angel investment in a fledgling business. To do that, we will rely on firsthand accounts from both entrepreneurs and investors relating their experiences and their advice.

As mentioned in our introduction, many of our stories come from the experiences we have had as managers of an early-stage investment group called the Dinner Club. These sixty investors meet monthly to listen to pitches from entrepreneurs and then, as a group, evaluate the companies' prospects and determine whether to make an investment. New CEOs and wannabe entrepreneurs frequently ask us about how groups operate, what the meetings are like, how angels make decisions, and the unwritten rules of the game. To answer these questions, we're going to give you a "peek under the tent," taking you inside a composite Dinner Club meeting.

The surprising thing is that this process is being repeated daily in communities across the country, with structured angel groups popping up coast to coast. Yet few entrepreneurs are aware of what it takes to break down the barriers and gain access to what appears to be a "members only" environment. Throughout this book, we will show you the insiders' view and share with you secrets on not only how to find angel investors but, once you've found them, how to convince them to underwrite your great new idea.

THE MONTHLY MEETING: GETTING STARTED

It's 5:30 on a Monday evening, and rush-hour traffic has snarled all the approaches to Tyson's Corner in northern Virginia, the heart of the high-tech boom outside Washington, D.C. Members of the Dinner Club are due at a private dining room at Maggiano's Little Italy, a family-style eatery famous for large portions and noisy conviviality. As managers of the club, we're responsible for making sure the monthly meetings go smoothly, and now it looks as if rainstorm-slowed traffic is going to create snags.

But we're used to it, as is everyone else. This part of Virginia has become a New Economy boomtown, with all the ills and advantages of a fast-growing, commercial hub. A recent *Fortune* magazine story claimed that the Tyson's area contained more office space than all of downtown Washington, that more people worked in information-technology companies than for the government, and that there were more software engineers in the area than lawyers.

The main highway of the area is Route 267, the Dulles Toll Road, a rolling superhighway that stretches from the Washington Beltway to Dulles International Airport and slices through canyons of towering glass and chrome. This has become the main artery of our nation's capital for the telecommunications, networking, and Internet industries. The neon logos on top of the buildings announce only some of the companies: Nextel, Teligent, PSINet, Ciena. And nearby, there's AOL, WorldCom, and Network Solutions, to name a few of the biggest players. This nest of information-services companies may not yet have acquired a name like California's Silicon Valley or New York's Silicon Alley, but it's still got plenty of character and color.

The traffic jam that comes with growth is a mixed blessing for our group, being a sign of prosperity but making it a lot harder to get quality meeting time. We've told our presenting entrepreneurs that it's important that they arrive early so they can mix and meet with our members during pre-dinner drinks. And we know they probably want to get a sense of the room and its layout before making what could be a life-altering pitch. They've been coached and given directions, and appear ready. We enter the room reassured—one of the presenters is already hooking up his slide show; another is chatting with several members at the bar.

One of our key associates, Anne Lord, is handing out name tags at the registration tables and offering members copies of executive summaries from tonight's presenting companies. She's also distributing reprints of a recent feature article in *Forbes ASAP* magazine about angel investing in America. The article profiles several angel groups around the country and includes an in-depth interview with us about the Dinner Club. The article also describes the different types of angels that make up the typical angel investing group (see Exhibit 1–1).

We're especially pleased about the *Forbes* article for a variety of reasons, starting with the mention of our club as one of the leading angel

---

Exhibit 1–1:
Exalt in Your Diversity: Angel Groups Benefit from a Wide Range of Participants
by Scott Lajoie

The right mix of personalities is crucial to the success of an angel organization, and members must be willing to take on specific roles to best benefit the group. "The group has not matured until the members know every strength, weakness, and bias of each other," explains the Dinner Club's Steve Walker.

Archangel: This charismatic figure serves as the group's chief. In Santa Fe, it is Tarby Bryant; Austin, David Gerhardt; northern Virginia, John May; Boston, David Solomont; Sausalito, Mike Pogue. The leader is responsible for motivating the group and being the voice of reason. "Nobody in Santa Fe—or all of New Mexico—has the energy Tarby has," says Robert Allio, one of the Gathering of Angels' investors. Often a cofounder of the group is just as influential in the group's decision making, but this more magnetic individual is still seen as the leader.

Prophet: This person is the most knowledgeable and savvy investor, and quite often the most active. Marc Seriff fills that role in Austin; Allio in Santa Fe; John Dunning in Sausalito. Older and usually retired, they serve as mentors to many of the young entrepreneurs whose companies they fund. During last December's Santa Fe meeting, Allio skipped a company presentation to meet with an entrepreneur whose startup he had invested in earlier that year.

Cherub: Most groups have a younger investor who also plays a key role. These individuals have often risen to prominence due to the sale of a company, previous investments, or independent wealth. Ken Lang, a former CTO at Lycos, fills that bill in Boston; Michael Grantham and Jeff Weiss are the cherubs of Santa Fe and northern Virginia, respectively.

Disciples: Each group also is littered with a handful of investors who have little or no technology background but are curious about the sector and have a desire to invest. They benefit most from other members' wisdom. In Boston, one such disciple is Ira Stepanian, former CEO of BankBoston; in Santa Fe, it is Stephen Coleman, an optometrist who bluntly admitted his ignorance of streaming video at one meeting. The downside: "I have seen groups that stack their membership with doctors and lawyers—anything to get their membership up—and they're less savvy as a result," says Robin Hood's Rob Weber.

Mortals: These folks attend the meetings not to invest but to sell their services to entrepreneurial companies. The Texas Angels allow reps from law firms and various consulting companies to mingle with the investors, offering their services to start-ups whose founders are very inexperienced in these areas. They claim that the added networking benefits their group as a whole. Some groups let these folks in; others see them as a distraction.

(Reprinted by permission of *Forbes* magazine © 2001 Forbes Inc.)

groups in the country! It confirms what we've been suspecting: Angel groups are popping up everywhere. The article reports at least fifty such organizations. It emphasizes that angels prefer companies close to home, and that this is more a grassroots, local movement than a national network. The details it offers about angel groups adding affiliates in areas like western Connecticut; Hilton Head, South Carolina; and Tucson, Arizona, attests to the vibrancy of angel investing as a new segment in the country's private equity markets.

As the room fills up, members seem a little more alert, a little more eager than usual. Loud voices and bursts of laughter punctuate the constant chatter. At one table, several members talk about the success that one of our portfolio companies is having attracting interest from a major venture capitalist to lead its next round of funding. Although all of us are seasoned investors, there's still great comfort when the professionals, like a mainstream VC, validate our judgment and back a company that we like. The VC lead could also mean that the value of our investment will shoot up.

Another hot topic among members is an upcoming vote on a company that presented to us last month. The due-diligence committee of club members has finished its report, and the club is ready to vote. We've also received proxy votes from members who aren't here. Although most members know that the committee report is positive, there are no sure things in our club. Members have lingering questions about the prospective investment, and those answers could turn the decision either way.

And of course, the subject of the stock market's gyrations pops up here and there. Members are especially shaking their heads in amazement at the recent plummet of a local company, MicroStrategy, and the falling fortunes of its CEO, Michael Saylor, whom many of us know. The news that the company had to restate earnings for the past year chopped Saylor's net worth from $12 billion to $2 billion in less than a week. The room is also bubbling with gossip and news surrounding a local merger—AOL and Time Warner. And one of our members, Jonathan Legg, a broker with Morgan Stanley Dean Witter, is encircled by members wanting his take on upcoming IPOs. About forty-five members have now arrived, joined by six or eight presenting executives, who usually bring along two or three people from each company, such as the CEO, finance officer, and technology expert.

THE MEET-AND-GREET: ENTREPRENEURS MINGLE WITH POTENTIAL INVESTORS

A little after six o'clock, waiters enter the room, their shoulders stooped with large trays covered with salads and bread baskets. Scattered around the room are eight round tables, each seating seven or eight people.

People sit anywhere; everyone has a clear view of the screen in the front of the room. No pre-assigned seating arrangements are made. However, we ask employees of the presenting companies to spread out so they will talk to members, not just each other. We want to keep the atmosphere as informal and friendly as possible. Sure, there are a couple of business suits in the room, but they're a minority. Sports shirts and khakis appear to reign. Presenters, however, are loaded for bear and have coats and ties on. (Chapter 3 provides details on how to make successful presentations, with tips and guidelines.)

Our members are an eclectic group, their business and investing expertise stemming from an assortment of industries and experiences. There's very little homogeneity. Art Marks, a member who's also a general partner of New Enterprises Associates (NEA), is seated next to Brandy Thomas, co-founder of a young company, Cyveillance. NEA is one of the leading venture funds, with interests in California's info-hub as well as northern Virginia's. Marks came out of General Electric Information Services, where he was president of the Software Products Operation, and hooked up with NEA in 1984. NEA has had a number of home runs, including UUNet. Like many seasoned businesspeople who earned their spurs in the early days of tech investing, Marks joined the Dinner Club to stay in the loop. "I like to keep my ear to the ground and stay in touch with companies at the earliest stages," he says.

Marks liked the young Thomas and referred his deal to the club. He ultimately decided to persuade NEA to lead the second-round financing for it. The company raised $6 million in its first round, with the Dinner Club putting in about $200,000. Thomas is here tonight to update the club on his company's progress, as well as ask for another round of financing, and Marks is here to give support to the chief executive, who has become his friend.

A table over are two active members, Rhea Schwartz and Rick Leavy. Although Schwartz is a decided minority at this dinner, there's no awkwardness. While the Dinner Club has few female investors, it would like more and goes out of its way to welcome prospective distaff angels. However, competition, so to speak, has recently cropped up with the creation of WomenAngels.net, an investment club based in downtown D.C., whose membership is all female. This is a great first for our region—women angel investors coinvesting with VCs and other clubs on hot deals. Schwartz's background is in law and real estate. Formerly an attorney with the banking industry, she cut her business teeth in real-estate development.

Rick Leavy is a cashed-out real estate and high-tech entrepreneur who seems to relish the networking and interaction of club meetings. He exudes enthusiasm for bright ideas and eager entrepreneurs, and is often one of the first members to volunteer to help a funded CEO make a contact or develop a marketing strategy. While Schwartz keeps her ears open for articulate, thoughtful presenters, Leavy likes to hear entrepreneurs who are persuasive at selling their concept. "If someone can't sell, I have a real problem with that," he declares. Like Schwartz and many of the other club members, Leavy is turned off by presenters who seem too full of themselves or a little too hyped. (Again, chapter 3 offers guidance to entrepreneurs on how to present themselves in the best possible light.)

For the next thirty minutes, the group eats and chats, and dinner-table conversation is as likely to cover the Washington Redskins football team as it is the latest business bestseller on the *New York Times* bestseller book list. Only when people are well into their meals, so they can turn their attention to the podium as much as to whether they want chicken cacciatore or pasta primavera, do we start the meeting. We begin by asking any member who has brought guests to introduce them to the group.

Club member Steve Comiskey has brought his son, David, from Boston, and introduces him as the co-founder of his own start-up, a company called EInk. The proud dad declares, "This company is a rocket. My claim to fame is being the father of this fine young gentleman who is taking the business world by storm." While everyone in the group knows that Steve is motivated by family pride, we realize that angel investing is about networks and contacts. Who knows—in a couple years' time, young Comiskey and the Dinner Club may be investment partners.

A club member introduces the founder of European Business Angel Network, or EBAN, which is based in Switzerland. Angel investing is slowly catching on in Europe, though it's been going great guns for a while in England, and he is in the States visiting various angel groups and gathering information. We hope he'll give us an update on angel activity on the Continent.

Another outsider introduces himself. He is a producer from the A&E Network and is gathering background for an upcoming film on the routes start-up companies take to funding their enterprises. A couple of members have also brought friends, whom they introduce. Although we're given only these people's names and sometimes an affiliation, like a company name, we suspect they're looking us over, perhaps thinking about joining, or know of young companies that could use our financial backing. Again, it's all about networks and the unstated philosophy that we're all here to meet, greet, and learn about investment opportunities, regardless of where they come from. (Chapter 3 describes networking and getting referrals and recommendations that will lead you to angels who may invest in your business.)

REVIEWING THE GROWTH OF COMPANIES IN WHICH WE'VE INVESTED

While waiters remove the appetizers and set down platters of meat and pasta, we review the evening's agenda, telling members whom they are going to hear from tonight, the due-diligence reports we'll be getting, and the deals we'll be voting on. We then introduce Brandy Thomas to give us an update on our earlier investment in his company and discuss the progress made in the past few months.

"Cyveillance is growing rapidly as the marketplace embraces our services," he begins. The lights are dimmed, and he clicks on the projector, which displays several milestones on the screen.

"We've gone from twenty employees, when you made your investment, to now over fifty people. We've added marquee clients to our customer list—namely, Disney, Coca-Cola, and Sony. We've gone from having one product, essentially a search service to determine any brand abuses online, to a suite of products that can be licensed by our customers," he continues.

As Thomas clicks through his PowerPoint slides, a murmur ripples through the group. People like what they're hearing and seeing. Six months ago, Thomas stood in front of this same audience, almost begging for its endorsement. A young African-American fresh out of business school, he hooked our group with his predictions of abuses of trademarks on the Web and his proposed solution for protecting those assets. At the time, Cyveillance was a ragtag team of programmers and marketers housed in a rundown townhouse. Now it was starting to look like a real company that has clients, products, experienced executives, and a head start into a lucrative Internet niche.

The slides pause for a few seconds, then disappear. "I'm pleased to tell you tonight that not one but two major venture-capital firms have presented us with term sheets to lead our next round of financing—and at a serious increase in valuation from where you participated less than a year ago." People put their forks down at this point. "When you invested, our company had a pre-closing valuation of $13.5 million. In the next round," Thomas declares, "we expect to raise about $20 million, at a pre-money valuation of $75 million."

Thomas continues to outline coming attractions. "According to the terms of the series A round of financing you participated in, the Dinner Club will be able to purchase their pro-rata share in this next round on the same terms as those being proposed to the lead VC firm."

The group is all smiles, and the food is tasting even better than usual. Thomas wraps up his talk by asking for questions. More than one member wants to know whether the club can purchase additional shares. We explain how the sequence of events will happen: "Once a final agreement has been negotiated, we'll propose a specific amount for investing and call for a vote. In our first purchase of shares, we invested $200,000. We thought at that time that we'd earmark another $200,000 to add to the investment if we got the chance and the company still looked good. That's the level we're thinking of for the next round."

Everyone knows that the prospects for Cyveillance at this point are quite rosy. The addition of a major VC firm leading the next round means, among other things, that the company has cleared its painstaking due diligence and still comes up aces. ("Due diligence" is the investigation conducted before an investor finalizes a deal.) The investment is still risky and illiquid, but the company sure seems to be on the right track. (Chapter 6 discusses in detail the fine points of negotiating investment terms.)

REVIEWING DUE DILIGENCE ON POTENTIAL INVESTMENTS

The next items on the agenda are committee reports from two groups doing due diligence on companies that presented at a previous meeting and were approved for investigation. Club member David Steinberg approaches the podium to talk about Sesla Inc. (Ship Everything, Sea Land or Air). A new member of the club, Steinberg came to us in an unusual way. He's the chief marketing officer of BioNetrix, a company the Dinner Club invested in at one of its first meetings. Steinberg became intrigued with the angel-club idea and later joined us. From our perspective, he is a perfect member for the due-diligence committee, combining the experiences of an entrepreneur with the sensibilities of an investor. (Chapter 5 discusses due diligence in depth, including details on Sesla.)

David was looking at Sesla even before the Dinner Club heard of the company. As sometimes happens, members of the club get wind of a promising venture before the club does and refer entrepreneurs to our group. Referrals from members like Steinberg help ensure that the club has a steady, busy deal flow. But before we asked Sesla to make a presentation, we managers met with the company's founders to see what stage they were at in their business and financing. We decided they were definitely worth a look from the entire club.

Sesla is a budding software company that proposes to solve shipping problems for companies ordering products online that need to be shipped from around the world. The Sesla software would be designed as a plug-in component to any e-commerce site, enabling consumers to order products and get immediate price quotes for shipping, documentation, customs, and delivery. It's a nifty idea—much of the time, getting complete, timely quotes for shipping is like pulling teeth, requiring days or even weeks, and they're not always accurate.

The management team also has appeal. One of the three founders is a repeat e-commerce entrepreneur. Only three months earlier, Frank Wood sold his first company, an image-based search engine called To Fish!, to AOL. Flush with his success, he jumped right back into the start-up world with the launch of Sesla. Though only twenty-four, Wood is considered an experienced Internet entrepreneur, regarded by his peers as something of an old hand at building and selling a company.

Unlike many other young programmers with a nifty idea, Wood has raised money before and knows the ropes. His experience showed in his presentation, which had been persuasive. His answers were honest and forthright, always a plus with us. However, a member of the club had pressed him on the issue of valuation: His formula seemed a tad inflated. Wood was seeking $1 million in return for 20 percent of his company, which would have given it a $5 million value. Some of us had considered that figure lofty for such an unformed venture. Wood also had revealed that he was talking to other investment groups and that he expected this financing round to close soon. If we wanted in, we would have to move quickly.

Now it is a month later, and Steinberg is about to deliver his committee's findings. Even before Steinberg's committee launched into action, Steinberg and two individual investors had begun their own due diligence. As part of their effort, Steinberg and the individual investors hired a marketing consultant to survey prospective users of Sesla's service. The consultant was also to look into any companies that might compete with Sesla. Steinberg describes what the consultant found: "We hired an expert in international sales and marketing to review Sesla's basic strategy and to validate for us the market readiness for such a service. Mary Ann Donaghy developed a twenty-question survey that she conducted via phone interviews with marketing or CEOs of roughly two dozen e-commerce companies." (Again, we'll talk more about this process in chapter 5, which also includes the questions the consultant asked.)

Steinberg pauses to give us Donaghy's marketing background, which is extensive. The survey was in the hands of an expert, and she had access to senior people at major Web companies. "She spoke with either the president or the senior marketing official at companies such as Outpost.com,

Wine.com, eToys.com, Crate and Barrel, Pier 1 Imports, Costco, and Value America," David reports. The nodding heads among the members suggest people are impressed with her thoroughness.

Steinberg pauses, then presents what Donaghy found. "A total of forty-two companies were contacted, and she conducted twenty-three interviews. Of those, fourteen contacts were VPs, presidents, or owners. Fifteen of the companies are presently accepting orders from and shipping to international customers. Of the fifteen, twelve said they considered the concept 'very' or 'somewhat' interesting."

The members perk up, this time pausing over their desserts. The figures suggest a concept with promise. Steinberg concludes: "The solution that Sesla is trying to achieve was clearly well received by the majority of the potential consumers the consultant contacted." He goes on to detail the committee's thoughts about the Sesla concept. "This is an operations solution as much as a sales and marketing vehicle. It will be absolutely critical that all sales and marketing communication address the issues, processes, and requirements of the customers. The key to success here will be in the details and the execution."

Our new angel has barely finished speaking before hands shoot up.

"I run a business that requires a lot of shipping of products," declares Fred Schaufeld, founder and chairman of a service-contract provider that employs 600 people. "And I think each of the major potential customers will already have systems in place that will require substantial integration with any new technology. How is Sesla going to deal with that?"

Scanning the consultant's notes, Steinberg answers, "It appears that there are very few companies for whom Sesla can provide a cookie-cutter solution. Flexibility and some customization will likely be necessary."

Another hand. Jack Daggitt, a former AOL product-development executive, wants to know, "What about theft? International orders are more vulnerable to credit-card theft and merchandise theft. Is insurance included in Sesla's basic quotes?"

Steinberg shakes his head, indicating he doesn't know. He nods toward Bill Roberts, a partner with a large D.C. law firm, Wiley, Rein and Fielding, who asks, "What about its ability to quote total delivered cost? Even if they can estimate this correctly, what about all the paperwork involved and the manpower required for accepting and fulfilling international orders?"

Questions and answers, some complete and some partial, fly for about ten minutes. Then the room quiets down, members looking about to see if anyone else wants to weigh in. Steinberg ends his report by saying that while his committee is not yet ready to recommend a vote, it's leaning toward supporting an investment.

"We have a couple of loose ends to tie up before recommending an investment," he says. "We're currently negotiating a term sheet in which we are offering to make a deal based on a pre-money valuation considerably lower than what the company has been seeking. We also believe the present CEO may need to step aside if the company can find someone with more shipping-industry experience. Those are going to be two very difficult propositions for the company to accept. But if they agree, we'll recommend going forward."

As David sits down, we explain to the club the process for a mail ballot, which might be required in this situation. In some cases, a company needs an answer from our club before our next meeting, and our bylaws allow for mail ballots at such times. Along with the ballot, we would circulate conclusions from the due-diligence committee and our recommendations, and ask the ballot to be faxed back to us within three days. As with our show-of-hands vote, a simple majority is needed on a mail ballot for us to approve an investment.

It's hard to gauge the group's reaction to what David has said about Sesla. It is a good-news, bad-news report, revealing that e-commerce companies could use such software while unearthing problems with the founders' experience and installing the technology. A week later, the company makes the decision for us.

Before we could mail ballots asking for an investment decision, the company unraveled. Frank Wood and his team thought long and hard about what his would-be angels had discovered, and decided that the hurdles were too big. To their credit, the Sesla executives understood that conceiving of a great idea, even having experience with the proposed technology, was not enough to make the venture happen. As someone once said, "Good ideas are a dime a dozen—execution is everything." Wood withdrew the Sesla request for financing and folded the company. Many club members agreed, however, that he would probably be back in the not-too-distant future with a new idea and a new company. We've found that entrepreneurs are enormously resilient and persistent. The desire to create and build a company seems to be as innate in some people as a fondness for sweets. And these natural-born entrepreneurs are the people we frequently support and invest in.

THE MEMBERS VOTE

Next up on the agenda is another due-diligence report on a prior presenter, a Baltimore-based company called Versient. We explain to the members that this is primarily an opportunity to ask questions before the group votes, since we've already circulated the committee's report and recommendations before tonight. Members know there's going to be an up-and-down vote, and those who aren't here have sent in their proxy votes.

Club members are enthusiastic about Versient, an Internet publishing company that enables companies to more efficiently handle their printed materials. Not only is it a business-to-business Internet venture, one of the few e-commerce niches that is healthy these days, but this company has customers and revenues. Numbers in the black, especially before receiving any angel or VC money, get our members very excited. Versient's founder, Ken Wahler, did this with only a $10,000 line of credit from Bank of America.

Club member Eric Becker leads the discussion. Becker is a managing partner of Baltimore-based Sterling Venture Partners, and has already committed his company as the lead investor in this round of financing. He's here tonight not only as a member but also as an advocate for Versient and someone who knows the business better than most.

The direction of the discussion quickly reveals how members are thinking. There are almost no questions about the business model or the due-diligence findings. Most of the queries concern the investment syndicate—what firms and angel groups are in or out—and how much our club will be allowed to invest. They focus on the terms. Eric explains that as lead investor, he'll do all he can to give us as big a piece as possible, but he has to temper this promise. Other investment groups are eager to join the Versient financing, so the pie may have to be cut into smaller pieces so that everyone gets something.

Eric's in the uncomfortable position of having almost too good a deal. His fund has spent considerable time and effort looking into Versient and structuring an acceptable offer. Now, as news of his findings gets out and interest builds, he knows that some parties are going to be disappointed with the size of their allowed investment and that even his firm may get less than it wanted.

This is a classic catch-22 of venture and angel investing. Entrepreneurs devote enormous amounts of time and personal resources to persuading an investor to back his business. But once a lead investor is secured and has given the OK, many of the others who were sitting on the fence saying "Maybe . . . we'll think about it . . . come back later" jump in. So now the lead investor has to not only negotiate the deal with the start-up but also juggle all of the me-too investment groups. And the lead investor doesn't want to tell everyone else to go jump in a lake and grab the whole investment for himself, because there will come a time when he's not the lead and wants to participate in another company's financing. It's a nice position to be in, despite the discomfort of knowing some investors are going to be disappointed.

Of course, we jump on Versient's bandwagon, along with Sterling Venture Partners and two other funds. Together, everyone chips in $6.5 million, with the Dinner Club putting in $750,000, which the company plans to use to add staff and expand its e-commerce product line. The company has twenty-six employees and immediate openings for another fifteen, and projects revenues to quadruple within a year.

Eric Becker's is the last of the committee reports, and members finish their cannoli and cheesecake while the first of tonight's presenters adjusts his tie, then fires up his laptop and PowerPoint presentation. The lights dim, and the LCD projector whirs to life. The presentation is a stunner, one of the best ever given to the club—and, it turns out, one of the most controversial.

ENTREPRENEURS MAKE THEIR PITCHES

At the front of the room is Mike Betzer, CEO of Ineto, and he certainly has our attention. Ineto is a software company and service provider that offers businesses the ability to communicate faster with their customers through a variety of platforms, including voice, e-mail, voice mail, fax, and Web chat. The Ineto software would enable businesses to provide their customers with first-class service and so hang on to them for repeat sales. Better yet, the software does not have to be purchased and installed by companies. Instead, Ineto sets it up and services it. All a company has to do is subscribe to the Ineto service. For investors, Ineto looks too good to be true: Not only does it have proprietary technology that adds value to its customer's products and services, but its revenue model is based on a steady stream of fees, not a onetime purchase.

Adding to the club's excitement is that Betzer is not a stranger to us. He came highly recommended by three club members, whom we refer to as the "MCI Guys." Gerry Taylor, Michael Rowny, and John Gerdelman have all been senior executives with the pioneering long-distance communications company. Taylor was CEO of MCI before retiring recently, Rowny led the international mergers-and-acquisitions activities, and Gerdelman ran several divisions of the company, including a unit where the idea for Ineto was born. Our club members figure that these guys know the technology, know the idea, and know the founder. And they have already invested individually. What better endorsement is there?

Ineto has a somewhat checkered history. After its promising start as a product within MCI, it got derailed around the time WorldCom decided to merge with the parent company, so the three executives decided to help it along once Betzer spun it off from the newly formed MCI WorldCom. It was a humble start for Betzer, who went from being project manager at one of the world's largest telecommunications companies to president of an independent start-up with four employees. He ramped up quickly,

raised angel seed funding, and within a year had added fifty-five employees and developed a suite of software products.

Betzer offers a contrast to the other presenters, who are young, relatively inexperienced yet enthusiastic pitchmen. A consummate professional salesman and recognized expert in the field, he seems to have little
in common with most of the other entrepreneurs we have met. Early in
his talk this night, he distinguishes himself with an impressive nugget of
information—he doesn't need our money. This really makes our group sit
up straight. Here is an experienced manager introducing a unique product that consumers are already paying for, and he's already enlisted the
backing of Austin Ventures, Intel, Broadwing Capital, and a cadre of past
MCI executives for this round.

There are other features to Betzer's company that break our mold and
demand members' attention. His company isn't local. Though it started
in our region, it's now headquartered in Austin, Texas. And Betzer isn't
aiming to raise our usual sweet-spot amount of $500,000 to $5 million,
the range we can typically afford to be comfortable with. Nope, he wants
$40 million, at a pre-money valuation of about $150 million. But the
angels in this private dining room don't bat an eye as Betzer deftly sails
past our usual guidelines. By the end of this presentation, the members
are ready to jump into this deal. Everyone knows that the point of angel-
club rules is to give us an edge in making smart investments, so we don't
take on too much risk and a deal with too many odds against us. But the
Ineto investment glitters.

Betzer finishes his slide show, and one member mutters that he'd sure
hate to be the guy who has to follow that act. As managers of the club, we
are a little nervous at this point, because we've offered a presentation that
defies the members' guidelines. We hold our breath for a few beats, wondering how people are going to react.

Art Bushkin, a successful high-tech manager turned superangel philan-
thropist, waves his hand to be called on. "Let's vote right now," his voice
booms. "And I'm in for as much side-by-side personally as I can get."

The room erupts with applause and "me-too"s. Another member
chimes in over the din, "What's there to talk about? If they'll let us in,
let's do it." (If only the club could get in at the prior round's price!) The

two of us breathe a joint sigh of relief. The club's spirited approval of the Ineto presentation has justified our hunch that members will leap at any good deal, regardless of the size of fund-raising or locale of the company. More important, it has affirmed our belief that the angel-club concept can give individual investors a role in launching promising young companies. As individuals, few of us would have been asked to participate in the Ineto deal. But as a group, we are being admitted to a coveted inner sanctum. Furthermore, knowing that Ineto can lift off without our money means that Betzer and his executives are looking to us for more than money. The MCI Guys understand that our club members can add substantial value by referring customers, helping recruit employees, and keeping them abreast of similar technological developments in other new ventures.

The angels don't quite bring out their checkbooks this night, but they do vote unanimously to fast-track the due diligence. Thirty days later, when major due-diligence information has been confirmed and we know what other investors are in the financing round and what size an investment we're being allowed, the Dinner Club votes to invest $1 million in Ineto.

One other company presents after Betzer finishes his talk. We have found that the group has interest and time for at least two presentations, but never more than three. This evening has been pretty busy, so the second presenter really has to work to keep the crowd engaged. Our members come to see new businesses, but they also come to talk with one another and to learn from the questions asked by other members of the club. Structured angel groups are about community as much as they are about investment returns. Our members enjoy being part of the group, and we as managers need to balance the business process with the entertainment component. We adjourn the meeting early enough to allow members to linger and talk informally with one another and the entrepreneurs who have presented this evening.

We hope this chapter has given you a feel for a typical evening with a group of angel investors. By reading on, you'll discover much more about what makes them tick, and if you are an entrepreneur you will learn many of the secrets of *successfully* finding and presenting your ideas to this audience.

In the next chapter, we'll raise the question of *when an entrepreneur is ready for angel funding.* We'll also explore a bit of the evolution of angel investing and how the game has changed recently. We'll share some examples of companies at different stages and how they successfully attracted angel capital.

■ Angel investing is about networks and compatible businesspeople as much as anything else. Make every effort to develop a network, even attending events where you might not know anyone or going out of your way to introduce yourself to people who might be interested in your venture. Be pleasant and well-mannered, yet aggressive.

■ In preparing for your presentation, pay attention to details. Nothing's too small to think about, from how your suit looks under the artificial light of a projector to whether you have a long enough extension cord or enough copies of your executive summary.

■ Do all you can to enlist support or active interest, if not investors, from other investment sources. The most comforting thing an angel can hear from a presenter is that so-and-so venture fund or superangel is very interested.

■ The rules of an angel club aren't written in stone. They're guidelines for the investors' benefit, not meant to discourage exceptional entrepreneurs. If you've got a good story, talented management, and the skill to pull it off—regardless of whether you fit the normal investment mode—angels want to hear about it.

2

When to Dance with an Angel

Everyone's looking for money. It's a rare entrepreneur or business founder who isn't always scouting backers. Before you even go looking for angels, you should know whether you're really ready to dance . . . and you'd better have on the right shoes and know all the steps.

The question of when an entrepreneur should make a presentation for funding to an angel depends on the individual, the business, and the requirements of the angel or angel group. An ill-conceived or badly timed pitch can suck all the air from a start-up. (And we'll discuss how to make successful pitches in chapter 3.) Repeated turndowns can make a venture look shopworn and call into question the assumptions a founder has made. Virtually every company founder has as many rejections as a beginning novelist, but there's a point at which the message isn't *try harder* but *rethink the idea.* Your venture may not be ready for the angel circuit. On the other hand, hitting it just right, when all the pieces are in place and everyone's willing and eager, can launch a new company into the stratosphere.

In the business of angel investing, like all else, timing is everything. This chapter offers several stories of entrepreneurs who were well prepared for angel investing, as well as a few who were just too inexperienced or whose companies were just too young—and who therefore didn't get the money they needed. Sometimes it comes down to being in the right place at the right time, as you will see in the following example of the fruit-juice company Nantucket Nectars. But even with a little luck, an entrepreneur must still be able to recognize the opportunity and capitalize on it quickly.

THE "JUICE GUYS" FIND AN ANGEL—JUST IN TIME

Sunlight gleamed off the water as Tom Scott's floating harbor store pulled alongside an eighty-six-foot yacht anchored in Nantucket Sound, twenty miles south of Cape Cod, Massachusetts. Scott and his friend Tom First had been plying the waters of this exclusive corner of the Northeast for the previous six years, operating the equivalent of a floating corner market, selling everything from boat-cleaning services to their own bottled fruit juice, which they called Nantucket Nectars.

On this day in 1992, Scott was polishing the brass and varnished teak of Mike Egan's boat, the Dancing Bear. Egan was well-known among locals as the man who had made a big splash in the business world by turning Alamo Rent-a-Car from an insignificant player into a serious rival to market leaders Hertz and Avis. He lived in Florida but spent summers off the Massachusetts coast sailing with his wife and two kids.

As Scott scrubbed barnacles from the gleaming ship, he knew few details about Egan's career as a turnaround expert. But he did know that Nantucket Nectars needed about $250,000 to keep going and build on its modest success, and he wasn't going to make that dough swabbing decks. He and First had been plowing their personal savings and most of their meager incomes into their juice company, and had reached the limit of how far they could take their dream.

They believed Nantucket Nectars could be more than a grown-up lemonade stand for the locals. They came up with the idea for a distinctively sweet, fruity drink with a catchy name and appealing logo as the national taste for cola soft drinks was branching out into fortified juices, power drinks, and the Snapple craze. In recent months, they had expanded from this sliver of the coast into a few shops in Boston and even Washington, D.C., by peddling their blended creations store by store. But to ramp up production and go any further, they needed cash.

The two Toms had met in college at Brown University years before and were not typical businessmen with B-school degrees, starched shirts, or a head for numbers. They did have a head for creative ideas and the drive to pursue them. *Cash flow, business plans,* and *term sheets* were concepts they avoided like wingtip shoes. "At Brown, *business* was a bad word," Scott reflected. "Nobody wanted to be an entrepreneur."

As Scott cleaned Egan's yacht, he mused over the venture capitalists and bankers he had met with recently, along with all the official documents he and First had been told to ponder or produce. And numerous times, they never got as far as talking about documents—many of the professional investors they approached dismissed the two sport-shirt-clad men as flaky juice vendors. Scott knew that he needed to keep knocking on doors to find the money he needed and wasn't about to give up on Nantucket Nectars. The guys just needed a different kind of investor. "I didn't want those Gordon Gekko types taking over my business or my life," he thought. "But we've run out of money enough times over enough years so we can't go on this way. I'm tired of shoe-stringing this company."

Scott decided to approach Egan, whose down-to-earth disposition struck him as quite different from the stiff bankers he and First had been talking to. He took his idea to his partner. "Mike Egan is the richest man we know. Let's send him some juice and a business plan. What have we got to lose?" he said. Obviously Egan had money, but would he be willing to invest in a couple of untested entrepreneurs?

Scott could not have predicted the importance of that decision. Egan was about to change Scott's life by agreeing to become an angel investor and fund the nascent bottled-fruit-juice business. He responded immediately to the Toms' request for money. Within weeks of sampling Nantucket Nectars and reading their plan, Egan arranged for Scott and First to visit his office in Miami. The two young men were ecstatic, particularly because Egan was obviously treating them and their idea with serious respect and consideration. Most of their time in Miami was spent talking with Egan—long, far-ranging conversations not only about their business but also about them. Egan wanted to know what made them tick—what motivated and drove them? Where did they see themselves years from now? Were they capable of the hard work and persistence a new venture required? Did they know their strengths and weaknesses?

"He asked a lot of questions about who we are, not what we can do for him or how much money we will make for him," Scott recalled, noting how different Egan's approach was from that of the bankers.

Scott and First left Miami buoyed and hopeful. Egan sounded like he was going to help them, but they couldn't breathe easier until they had the money in hand. Two weeks later, Egan wrote a check for $500,000, twice what they were seeking. This bump-up in the amount was to be the first of many lessons they'd learn from Egan about gearing up a business. Clearly, the rental-car tycoon knew what Nantucket Nectars needed to step up manufacturing, engage sales reps, and move it to the next level. Now the juice company was on its way.

Yet what Egan contributed was more than money to the fledgling venture. The value he added in practical experience, advice, and direction was priceless. He also brought a broader vision, showing Scott and his partner that their company could be much more than a local operation. Scott remembers thinking, "This guy can bring us value far beyond money. He's dreaming bigger than we are."

Two weeks after receiving the check, the Juice Guys met with their new investor. This time, Egan did most of the talking, analyzing their market and potential and explaining where Nantucket Nectars could go from here. "You need to go south," Egan said. "That's where the drinkers are. You'll sell a million cases in Florida, Texas, and California in no time."

Scott marveled at Egan's vision, realizing that his backer was eager to do the very thing the professional venture capitalists warned could not be done—taking on industry giants Coke and Pepsi for a piece of the $6 billion national beverages market. "I'm thinking, 'Wouldn't it be great to get into the BankBoston cafeteria?' and he's talking about big-time production, distribution centers, and selling a million cases in Florida alone. Wow!" said Scott.

Apparently, renting cars isn't too different from selling juice drinks. Just a few years later, Egan's instincts about the two Toms and their company would prove to be dead-on. "I never thought that juice in a bottle was where the action was," Egan recalled. "But these two boys showed almost Michelangelo-like creativity designing these juices. Their story was so charming that on that alone, I was hooked."

Over the next few years, Egan guided the Juice Guys in making critical decisions about how to distinguish their product from competitors with household names. If there was one thing Egan knew especially well from his Alamo triumph, it was how to better a rival. They went into cane sugar instead of using sweeter corn syrup, because it gave their drinks a fresher taste. They packaged the drinks in bigger, more distinctive bottles. Along the way, there were missteps—most notably, in trying to distribute the drink themselves rather than use a national distributor. But with Egan's sage advice, they learned quickly and got back on course. This was another reason Egan became their angel: He knew from their early talks that Scott and First didn't spin their wheels on ideas that didn't work and would quickly apply newfound knowledge.

And learn they did. Scott and First not only built Nantucket Nectars into a national powerhouse but, eventually, sold the company to Ocean Spray for $90 million. Of course, Egan too joined in their success, having invested another $1.3 million in the company and owning a significant minority stake.

In thinking back on the Juice Guys and Nantucket Nectars, Egan offers some typical angel rationales: "I don't want to make it sound as if somebody could walk in the office with a box of crushed graham crackers and get me interested in the businesses because they have a good opportunity. I am attracted to youth, vigor, foresight, inspiration, work ethic, and already-proven success. They started with nothing and had already spent a couple of years building the business."

IS YOUR BUSINESS READY FOR ANGEL MONEY?

If you have a fledgling business, you probably know the various stages of funding, beginning with your own money and friends-and-family, then moving through the food chain of knowledgeable investors that might include well-heeled individuals, angel groups, venture capitalists, investment banks, retail banks, strategic partners, and ultimately, in exceptional circumstances, some kind of stock sale or private placement. Exhibit 2–1 lists the sources of money supporting entrepreneurial ventures.

Until recently, the usual route for funding a new venture followed a predictable path, with each stop along the way fairly well defined and predictable. Friends-and-family money has always been the backbone of American business. By this we mean investments and loans from close family members, neighbors, business associates, and those with long personal relationships. Personal credit cards are an honored tradition in bankrolling new enterprises. Many angel groups, ours included, almost insist that any venture first be funded by money from the founders. Our logic is simple: If you don't have enough faith in your venture, why should

---

EXHIBIT 2–1:
WHERE THE MONEY COMES FROM

According to a 1991 study of entrepreneurs, these are the sources of initial capital for small, high-growth companies:

Entrepreneur's personal savings	74 percent
Business angels	7 percent
Nonfinancial corporations	6 percent
Family and friends	5 percent
Venture capitalists	5 percent
Public stock issues	3 percent
Commercial banks	0 percent

(From E. B. Roberts. *Entrepreneurs in High Technology: Lessons from MIT and Beyond.* New York: Oxford University Press, 1991.)

---

we? Money from your own bank account, and those of relatives and friends, generally doesn't cost much to raise and comes with few strings. Granted, more than one person has observed that a better name for this money, given that it comes with few questions asked, is friends-family-and-fools. Nevertheless, this is the time in a company's history when a founder's efforts become sweat equity and, with friendly money, is transformed into an ownership that has value.

Friends-and-family money usually taps out early. We have found with most of the start-ups that a founder generally goes looking for his or her first outside money when needs exceed around $100,000. At this point, the founder and perhaps one or two other principals are working full-time on the venture, and others may be poised to join.

This is when an entrepreneur, especially if unaware of angels or angel groups in his region, begins to cast about for institutional financing and approaches an investment or commercial bank. It's often an unsettling experience. Not many bankers will consider lending to a start-up. Banks operate by rules and regulations. They insist that a company have demonstrable cash flow, sometimes even positive revenue, as well as hard assets or some type of bankable collateral. (More than one desperate founder has been known to take out a second mortgage as a way to secure bank financing.) Without a solid balance sheet and more than pro-forma projections, an entrepreneur won't get very far with a banker.

Angel financing has been around a long time, although it's only now being recognized as dependable, widespread, and substantial. Business historians report that Alexander Graham Bell's new device was launched with angel money and that five angels backed Henry Ford's contraption with a $40,000 investment. They also say that the Golden Gate Bridge was partially built with angel money. Even the modern technology era was led by angel-funded ventures, namely Apple Computer and Amazon.com.

Angel funding today generally represents the second round of financing or the first outside round in the early days of a company. It's where you turn after you've tapped out your credit card and devoured friends-and-family money but don't have enough progress to merit the attentions of venture capitalists. It fills the financial gap between $100,000 and what a company might expect to receive from a venture-capital firm, which begins somewhere around $5 million.

It hasn't always been this way. Fifteen years ago, venture capitalists were operating with less money and were eager for small, promising deals; a typical VC pot might contain $20 million, and the firm would be looking for $500,000 deals. But VCs have vastly expanded their pool of investment money, bringing together hundreds of millions rather than tens, and now it's not unusual for a VC firm to refuse to consider any venture seeking less than $5 million. A 1998 survey found that the size of the average VC fund was $183 million, with the average size transaction over $10 million per company. These numbers grew larger in 1999 and 2000.

The amount of money a company needs is the first but by no means the only yardstick that angels use to gauge a company's readiness for angel financing. Naturally, the size of investments is determined not only by the size of the pot but, equally important, by how much angels need to invest to play an active role in a company's growth and success. And none of these numbers can exceed angels' comfort level. For the Dinner Club, our investment range is between $250,000 and $1.2 million, although we've been known to get in for less in the first round or look at bigger prospects occasionally. But just because a company needs an amount of money that we can provide does not qualify them. It's all about whether they're ready to apply the money and how they intend to use it.

It is important to know the characteristics of today's average angel. Exhibit 2–2 provides the results of one study showing some statistics that would be valuable to you as you search for this elusive funding source.

There are few hard-and-fast rules about the right time to seek angel financing, so what we offer here are general guidelines. Entrepreneurs whom we've voted not to invest in because we felt they were too unformed or needed to find more friends-and-family money have turned around to land other angel groups or VC backing, and gone on to be start-up stars. And founders who came to us at the perfect time and forged ahead with our dough may yet sink under the weight of start-up snafus. So it's in this spirit that we sketch the general outlines of a well-timed approach while also telling you about founders who have ventured outside the lines and done very nicely.

Exhibit 2-2:
Angel Financing (Averages)

What the Matching Services Tell Us About U.S. Angels, Entrepreneurs, and Themselves

	On Average	Median	Range
Characteristics of the Angel:			
Amount a typical angel investor has reserved for potential angel investments	$311,875	$225,000	$40,000 to $1 million
Amount invested per deal per angel	$144,687	$75,000	$25,000–500,000
Equity investors typically receive in a deal	21%	20%	1–50%
Service's members who have invested in last three years	59%	75%	4–100%
Angels who are serial investors	48%	45%	5–100%
Subscribers who have never made an angel investment	32%	20%	0–95%
Average age of angel investors	49	50	40–55
Angels who prefer to co-invest	77%	80%	20–100%
Deals in which there is co-investment	72%	75%	20–100%
Number of investors in an average angel deal	6	4	2–25
Amount invested per deal by an angel syndicate	$601,315	$300,000	$50,000 to $3 million
Equity a co-investment syndicate typically receives per deal	32%	25%	10–100%

(Sources: *Angel Investing*, Osnabrugge and Robinson; *Angel Financing*, Benjamin and Margulis)

WHEN YOU'RE NOT READY: GREEN MANAGEMENT

New companies frequently approach angels before they warrant the consideration of serious outside investors. *Financial need itself, even when it's backed by pages of spreadsheets and endless columns of numbers, is not enough to persuade others that your company needs half a million dollars.* Our angel clubs receive hundreds of inquiries a month from entrepreneurs looking for funding, and a common reason they go away empty-handed is that some facet of the venture is still too young.

The makeup of a company called UWapIT was typical of a firm unready for angel financing. (Pronounced "You Wap It," the name was derived from the concept of enabling data to be accessed over wireless appliances, or "WAP" devices, such as cell phones or personal digital assistants.) UWapIT was a wireless-technology company that enabled a user to access his server database from almost anywhere using a cell phone or personal data accessory. An executive at lunch with a client who needed figures on the spot could dial up his company's database without leaving the table. It was a good idea, and certainly one that fit a growing segment of the networking of computer databases. The founder, Roy Kime, was asking for between $1 million and $1.5 million and gave a lively presentation that piqued many members' interest. We decided to take the next step and look more closely at the company. As we scratched the surface of UWapIT, we learned that the company had only three employees, all partners in its founding and none a hired expert from outside. To say the venture was "pre-revenue" would be almost a compliment—it had not even the whiff of coming revenue or customers. It had no money to cover even the barest overhead, and the founders were working from a private home.

While this alone might not have disqualified them from the running, another element in their business model made it impossible for us to invest. Their idea happened to be so potentially commercial that they faced major competition. If they ever launched their program, they would go head-to-head against AT&T, Nokia, and Motorola. It was hard to imagine that this start-up would still be standing after a slugfest with those giants.

We told the founder that the venture was too early for us. A million dollars was a huge bet on a company so unformed that its corporate identity was spread across the founder's dining-room table. Kime and his partners were too green. While the company had vision, the prototype of a promising product, and perhaps the beginnings of a David-and-Goliath story, it needed experienced, seasoned management. Until the founders hired a professional CEO, at the very least, they weren't ready for the next stage. *In short, it takes more than an idea and some well-written programming to get funded. Investors need to see a team in place to execute the vision.* (More on this company in chapter 7.)

THERE ARE MANY PATHS TO YOUR GOAL

Just as we promised about experience often defying generalizations, our dealings with Ben Lilienthal and Nascent Technologies present an exception to our rule of thumb about avoiding companies with green management. Nascent was a software company that had developed a system for the management of multiple e-mail and voice-mail accounts. Their customers would be Internet service providers and possibly local telephone companies.

We first met Lilienthal as a referral from our accountant, Ned Scherer, who was doing the books for Nascent and said that the company was looking for ways to raise money. Ned is a savvy guy with good judgment, so on his recommendation alone, we called Ben. This often happens with angel investing—word of mouth can push a deal forward as persuasively as a PowerPoint presentation. Ben offered to send us an executive summary and confessed that he had yet to write a complete business plan.

"That's not important," we told him. "Ned said you were a good guy, so we want to know more about your company."

Because of schedule conflicts, a couple of weeks passed before we could meet Ben for a cup of coffee.

Once we managed to get together, suffice it to say that we were very impressed with the twenty-three-year-old entrepreneur. We found him to be articulate and obviously bright, and he really conveyed the sense of excitement for what they were doing at his fledgling firm. Even though the company was still only about six months old, they'd already landed a couple of key *Fortune* 1,000 clients, including software distributor Software.com. We could see this wasn't a guy just talking about a company. He already had a company. In fact, Nascent was on schedule to do just under a million dollars in revenue in its first year.

Up to that point, the company's funding had been basically just friends-and-family, the traditional situation. Ben's father was a lawyer, and he'd put some money in, as had a few of his friends, for a total investment of around $300,000 to $400,000, which was sufficient seed capital. Their offices were in a townhouse in Reston, Virginia, where Ben's father had once had a law firm.

Intrigued by our first meeting with Ben, and anxious to learn more, we went to the Nascent office. We wanted to check out their priorities. Were they ensconced in fancy digs and drawing fat salaries, or were they paying attention to the bottom line? Much to our satisfaction, we encountered eight guys in jeans and T-shirts crammed into a two-office suite writing code. Just what an entrepreneur should be doing at that stage of the game! (We later learned that Ben had a special distinction, as far as we were concerned: He was the only entrepreneur we'd met who still lived at home with his parents.)

After a couple more brief meetings with Ben—mainly just to get the names of some more clients and early investors to talk to—we decided to take the plunge and invest in Nascent personally. In addition, we told Ben we would be recommending the company to several other investors, who, along with us, became the first outsiders to look at the deal on its merits and say, "Yes, we'll take a flier on this." Eventually, Ben raised approximately $500,000, which bought about a third of the company.

Six months later, it was time to raise more money. At that point in the life of a young company, the entrepreneur has several options from which to choose. First, he can always go back to his original angels and ask for their vote of confidence by putting additional capital into the company. He could hire an investment banker or other professional, such as a lawyer or an accounting firm, to help raise money for a fee. If the idea is hot enough and the company is moving fast enough, he could attempt to raise the money himself, thus saving the fees. And his final choice would be to talk to a potential strategic investor (such as a current customer or partner) in order to facilitate a quick transaction. In this fast-paced world, the smart entrepreneur is one who will investigate all four options at the same time, thus operating on parallel tracks and saving time as well as money.

During the process, Ben met with an investment-banking firm, which listened to his story, checked him out a bit, and then announced that it would be only too happy to serve as an intermediary and raise money for Nascent—for a fee. But Ben felt he didn't need that service, that his company was sufficiently well established and its future relatively solid that he could raise the necessary money himself, and we agreed with him. (It's a lesson that other entrepreneurs, especially those with fledgling Internet firms, should keep in mind. While you may need the money, you may not need to pay that high a price for it.)

While it might look as if the time Ben spent with the investment bankers was wasted, that was not the case. Even though things happen very quickly in the start-up world, it is still necessary to go through the paces, even though, as Ben soon learned, many of the meetings turned out to be unnecessary. "Next time," he said later, "there'll be a lot of phone calls I won't make and meetings I won't attend. When I was getting started, everybody was a potential prospect or a potential customer—including people on my co-ed soccer team—and I would talk to anyone about our business. Now, with a little experience, I know what a qualified prospect—customer, investor, or partner—looks like. . . . They're not the people just being polite and asking standard questions. They are the ones who actually understand the product and see a need for it. They're the ones who *get it.*"

Without skipping a beat, Ben had also been approaching various venture-capital firms. The Dinner Club, as always, was searching for investment opportunities and selected Ben to present at one of its first meetings in 1999. To our astonishment, the club members turned him down. It wasn't that Ben made a bad presentation; in fact, he made a very good one. Here was an articulate young guy with a dot-com opportunity that was right in the sweet spot of our club's interest. Nor could it have been that he wasn't far enough along as a company, because just the opposite was true. He had real clients already signed up and paying him for his product: Qualcomm had already paid Nascent half a million dollars in service fees to buy the software, and Software.com was distributing the product. So he had excellent credentials.

Why was he turned down? According to the feedback we got from some of the members, the club just wasn't sure how effectively the current management of Nascent could grow the company. Another concern was that the members weren't sure how big the "space" in which he wanted to compete was—would he have to go up against some really big competitors? What if AT&T and MCI got into the picture? As for Ben, he didn't suffer any great trauma over our rejection: "It was just another in a long line of no's."

In any event, the Dinner Club members turned him down. Then something happened which caused us to go around shaking our heads. Just thirty days later, Ben received from CMGI (one of the bluest of the blue-chip companies doing Internet acquisitions) an offer he couldn't refuse, and sold the company for approximately $6 million. (Figuring out what the Dinner Club lost doesn't require higher math: If we had invested half a million to three-quarters of a million dollars, less than a month later that investment would have doubled.)

The story gets even better. CMGI bought Nascent with CMGI stock. (As is fairly typical in acquisitions, Nascent had to hold on to the stock for a "lock-up" period of one year.) This happened in March 1999. By year's end, CMGI stock had doubled in market value, which means that Nascent was bought not for $6 million but for $12 million.

"The original strategy from the start," Ben told us later, "was to found and build a dynamic, Internet-based company, and then sell it and have somebody else take it to the next level. I figured, I guess due to my naiveté more than anything else, we'd get up and running and be acquired in six to twelve months. But I had no real conception of product life-cycles, sales cycles, or just simple customer acceptance. So I was more relieved than surprised when the acquisition was completed."

We asked Ben if he thought his age was a plus or a minus. He said, "I think it was actually a plus—1996–98 was a time when the Internet was new, and there were in fact Internet 'whiz kids.' Think Marc Andreessen. Being young and knowledgeable about the technology but also able to speak the business language helped. Most of the people we were dealing with had not integrated the Internet into their businesses, and we were helping them do that. So, they looked to us as the Internet whiz kids."

How sweet was this deal for those who got in at the right time? One early investor who put in $100,000 saw that investment balloon at sale date to $400,000—a figure that then doubled within only six months by holding the CMGI stock. Not a bad gain. By pursuing multiple funding options, Ben put himself in a position to win. Ultimately, he accepted the offer to purchase the entire company, instead of just accepting second-round financing. Thus he won, his angels won, and CMGI won.

Ben did the right thing. He started his company with friends-and-family financing. Next he went out and got an angel round of financing, and then he was in the process of making his pitch to structured angel groups (like the Dinner Club) and other venture funds. On a parallel track, he was talking to strategic investors (CMGI). Our point is that *it's very appropriate to be running on parallel tracks, because you don't know who the right partner might be at any given moment in the company's history.* Not only is it all right for an entrepreneur to do this, it is advisable.

And what did Ben Lilienthal do after all his serendipity? He went surfing—the kind you do on the beach, not in cyberspace—and had a celebratory dinner: "Not a big blowout. Just dinner with some friends." Now he's beginning to look for new opportunities—this time as an investor.

Ben said, "It feels great to be an angel, although I'm not all that active yet. I feel my greatest add-on will not be money but, rather, the experience I have and the ability to help people in the earliest stages get a little farther along the path. It's really connecting the dots—but the hard part is knowing which dots to connect, and where to go from here to get there. As for preferring one over the other, I like the stability of not being in the middle of a start-up, where every day you're worried about staying in business, improving your product, not running out of money, and new competitors. Every day at Nascent was more stressful, with more ups and down, than in a typical week now."

The last time we talked to Ben (via e-mail) he was in Asuncion, Paraguay (not the most stressful place on the globe), still on his extended vacation that had begun in Baja California. He told us he'll be back . . . when he feels like it.

AT THE TAIL END OF YOUTH

In some instances, approaching an angel at the right time can not only put a company on firm financial footing but propel it to the next level. More than once, we have funded a new venture whose management was incomplete but beginning to take shape. And the founder's recognition that he needed to recruit talent, perhaps to the point of having already identified a candidate, helped seal an angel commitment.

Sometimes angels provide help other than writing checks. Often experienced businessmen take equity stakes in early-stage companies in exchange for coming on board as an employee or making introductions to funding sources and then representing those groups on the company's board.

The story of Washington, D.C., angel James Kimsey is a classic case of perfect angel timing filling a key management hole. Kimsey was the right angel in the right place at the right time, and the result was fabulous success for the venture, and for him.

Like many angels, Kimsey is a self-made man. A Washington, D.C., native, he graduated from West Point and set out for a career in the military. He became an airborne ranger, rose to the rank of major, did two tours in Vietnam and one in the Dominican Republic, and received awards for valor and service as a combat leader. At the end of his military career, he applied his leadership skills to lucrative efforts in real estate, restaurant management, and financial services. By the mid-1980s, Kimsey was well established as a successful entrepreneur.

A Dinner Club member, Phil Gross, related to us the background on how Kimsey came to lead one of the technology world's great success stories, America Online. Phil, one of the company's first Chief Financial Officers, was present for much of the creation.

An old Army buddy of Kimsey's, Frank Caufield, now a very successful venture capitalist at the firm of Kleiner Perkins Caufield and Beyer, was involved in a Washington area start up called Control Video. The founder, Bill Von Meister was a pioneering techie who had developed a way to link multiple computers using standard telephone lines. While he had made some interesting progress with his company, it just wasn't attracting customers and his venture capitalists were searching for ways to get it on track. One of the earliest backers, a San Francisco banker named Dan Case, was helping the tech wizard put together a management team. In casting about for managerial expertise, Case convinced his brother Steve, who was then an executive in the food-products industry, to lead Control Video's marketing.

But the company still needed a CEO. Enter Jim Kimsey, referred by his old friend at Kleiner Perkins. Kimsey was a natural for Control Video and the renamed and re-launched company, Quantum Computer Services. The former Army ranger moved quickly to expand the software venture into bigger markets. Working with Steve Case and Marc Seriff, together as a team they developed the next stage in Quantum's growth, a relationship with the then largest personal computer maker, Commodore. With the insight of someone who had built companies before, Kimsey, working with Case, did not simply sell this online service to Commodore—they forged a strategic partnership so that the two companies could broaden and enhance the service. It was their initiative, doing the face-to-face negotiations and making time to make the follow-up calls, that added a weight of substance that convinced Commodore that Quantum was a serious vendor to deal with. "It got off the ground, started to get traction, and we could see there was a market for it," Kimsey remembers. "Then, when IBM selected us to go on their new PC, we realized we might be able to win the whole shebang."

Win it they did. A few years later, angel Kimsey stepped aside for the marketing director, Steve Case, who became CEO of the renamed company, America Online (AOL).

Seeing what AOL has become today it's hard to realize that only a few years ago, their officers were attending venture capital conferences seeking early-stage capital. In Appendix E we have reproduced the company's summary which introduced Phil Gross as a speaker at the Mid-Atlantic Venture Fair in 1988. Phil (as CFO) was seeking to raise 5 million dollars. Imagine what that investment is worth today!

It can be a tricky dance, knowing the right time in a venture's managerial life to seek out an angel. For UWapIT, the company executives were too early in their development. With Kimsey and the venture that would become AOL, it was at a key transition stage.

THE INGREDIENTS OF PERFECT TIMING

Perfect timing for an entrepreneur and angels coming together is rarer than you might think. In these instances, an exceptional individual emerges when the financial, technological, and commercial stars are aligned just right. At these times, success seems fated. All the pieces fall in place: A charismatic founder comes up with an innovative idea whose time is ripe and attracts the attention of farsighted investors. This happened with Phillip Merrick and his northern Virginia company, webMethods, which vaulted from conception to an IPO and an opening-day gain of 600 percent, all in eighteen months.

A thirtysomething Australian, Merrick was working as a software engineer at Open Software Associates when he quit to start a company based on an obscure technology, a computer language known as XML, that enabled corporate computers to exchange information and conduct transactions quickly and efficiently. At the time, 1996, most business computers depended on the industry standard HTML, and so getting in the business of developing and promoting a new common language must have made Merrick feel like an Esperanto instructor.

But Merrick stubbornly believed he could find a better way for corporate computers to communicate, and his hunch was right. His new venture, webMethods, was touting business-to-business solutions months before B2B became the buzzword du jour. He also had a strong stomach for risk. Calling on friends, family, and an angel investor, he pulled together $400,000. But as technology developers know, that amount of money doesn't travel very far. Within months, Merrick had gone through the seed money, maxed out his credit cards, and was looking at a checking account containing $31.

But he had all the pieces of a star-quality enterprise. He was a knowledgeable, driven entrepreneur with a *Little Engine That Could* story ("I think I can, I think I can") in trying to convince computer giants to ditch HTML and try XML. He was aiming at a potentially lucrative niche, B2B, that companies were only beginning to recognize as worthy of a return phone call. And he had the backing of an angel who would later become a partner in a Silicon Valley venture fund.

Merrick himself acknowledges that his timing was terrific. He stuck to his belief that XML would be the next big thing . . . and he was right. For months, he struggled to find backing. "But once the word got out about both XML and B2B, we started getting a lot of VC attention," he says. Relief arrived soon after the seed money disappeared—Merrick's company turned more heads than those of angels. Within months, he had secured financing for just under $1 million from a technology venture fund that paired its investment with angels. But like the first infusion, the money drained quickly, and Merrick was almost out of options when he received a $3.6 million shot of venture capital. His success was basically due to the fact that he kept at it. Sometimes it just takes a lot of calls until you stumble on the right investor.

Merrick's efforts paid off. He signed up large customers like the delivery service DHL and Dell Computer, along with a personal investment from its founder, Michael Dell. Given the speed at which Web technologies evolve and mature—under six months is considered normal—it's not surprising that webMethods found an underwriter eager to take it public. Even with the convergence of perfect timing and a sizzling market for IPOs, it's still amazing that webMethods' first-day bump from offering price to closing price set a NASDAQ record of 600 percent. Dancing with angels (and VCs and investment bankers) really paid off! Merrick stuck to his guns. Not only did he develop great new software—he wisely used his venture capital to build a management team and to sign up great customers. He got all the pieces right, not just part of it.

GET READY FOR MANY PARTNERS

The timing question is often complicated by the reality that angels prefer not to dance alone. You could say we're partial to line dancing. Once a founder has decided to cast outside the pool of friends and family and talk to angels, he or she needs to be prepared for the way angels think. Angels very much like having other investors show interest in, and provide backing to, the companies they invest in. So when you're ready to talk to a single angel, you should be ready for scrutiny from a band of angels, as well as gangs of venture capitalists.

Angels are always on the lookout for other angels, other groups, other sources of funding to piggyback on, or even lead, our investments. Other investors are brought in for a couple of reasons. The most obvious is to spread the risk for all investors. More pockets mean deeper pockets, which improves the likelihood that a company secures the financing it needs not only to launch itself but to grow. In early-stage financing, risk is foremost in our minds.

Another reason is psychological. Finding investors who view an entrepreneur and venture the same way we do reassures us that our positive reaction is based on objective facts. It confirms our judgment. We are very uncomfortable, indeed, when we like a company and want to invest in its future—and find no one else shares our view. A group of angels, as opposed to an individual angel, spreads the risk and increases the comfort level, but our group, like many others, likes to toss an even wider net.

Structured angel groups, like the eMedia Club and the Dinner Club, usually prefer not to lead deals. We believe our clubs can be great co-investors, with professional VCs at the head of the pack to orchestrate the due diligence, structure the term sheet, and establish valuation (topics that are covered in detail in chapter 5). While individual angels are great sources for seed capital, groups of angels are shifting away from the Lone Ranger approach to assuming the role of co-investing sidekick.

When entrepreneurs are ready to make a presentation to us, especially when they show promise—coming in with numerous references and perhaps a fabulous business plan—we strongly encourage them to try to enlist others. We suggest they make presentations at venture fairs, which are excellent forums for attracting investors, and point them to other investor groups operating in our region. This may sound like we deliberately encourage competition among first-stage outside investors, but in our experience, more is always better in early financing.

If a company is unprepared for attention and scrutiny, it risks turning off potential angels and losing the deal entirely. For example, Tom Klaff was deep into information technology, working on government and military contracts, when he and Ric Fleisher decided to make a better technological mousetrap. Klaff and Fleisher had flirted with two previous ventures, dot-com attempts, and were experienced entrepreneurs. "We've got six start-ups between the two of us, so we know where the potholes are," Klaff reflected.

In preparing their new company, Reliacast, for outside financing, they made some brilliant decisions. They had their technology firmly under control—multicast software that improves the way commercial websites handle customers—but were still tinkering with the business plan and management team. Bolstered by their earlier start-up experiences, and sensing the potential commercial value of the technology and pace of new developments in Internet technology, they plunged ahead and began talking to angels five months after incorporating. The timing for launching Reliacast into the world of outside investors, like most other Internet technology companies, was set more by the marketplace than by its business plan.

Our members still talk about the Reliacast presentation at the Dinner Club. The lights dimmed in the dining room, the members stopped eating and focused on a PowerPoint screen. As Klaff introduced himself, a shapely young woman clad in only a short nightie appeared in full color. A few members chuckled as Klaff's voice flowed over the room.

"Remember the Victoria's Secret debacle?" he asked.

The chuckles burst into laughter. Club members were well aware of what happened when the popular lingerie company held a fashion show on the Web: So many viewers—or voyeurs—logged on that Internet servers crashed under the weight of the traffic. Klaff went on to explain how Reliacast multicasting technology could have saved Victoria's Secret from that economic and public-relations hit. Klaff got a round of applause and our hearty endorsement, and a month later he took his presentation on the road.

An early stop was the Early Stage East venture fair, in Wilmington, Delaware, a daylong event that brings together entrepreneurs making ten-minute presentations and all types of investors, including angels, angel syndicates, venture capitalists, and institutional money (banks, pension funds, etc). Klaff made an impression not only with his Victoria's Secret opening but in giving a multimedia demonstration of how Reliacast could help website marketers solve the big problem of expansion. While the ill-fated Victoria's Secret show was designed to accommodate only 300,000 visitors, he vividly illustrated, Reliacast technology would have enabled it to handle 4 million users.

Listening to Klaff's presentation a second time, and to the enthusiastic response from the investors listening to it, we knew that Reliacast was going to be a hot ticket. He dangled the prospect of innovative technology and a big market, music to investors' ears. Although we were already doing due diligence on the company, and preliminary reports suggested it would get a green light from our group, we suspected that this deal would not proceed at the usual pace.

Klaff, too, sensed that the venture fair would accelerate Reliacast's momentum. "The smartest thing we did was to present at the annual venture fair," he said. With 350 investors in attendance, the event is certainly worthwhile.

Klaff was asking for $2.5 million to develop and beta-test his technology, and so would need deeper pockets than ours. Our strategy was to become a co-investor and ensure a spot for ourselves in possible later rounds. Within two months of the venture-fair presentation, Reliacast was being courted by three investor groups—a syndicate composed of two angels and two venture funds, a large telecommunications venture fund, and a group of investors from North Carolina. The question of whether Reliacast was ready to seek outside funding had been answered loudly and clearly.

Our angel group decided to join the first investor faction, the two angels, and two VC funds. A partnership with these other angels meant that our stake in the investment would be less than what we normally contributed, but we felt that any investment was better than being shut out. Since our alliance had been tracking Reliacast the longest and had completed full due diligence, Klaff and Fleisher decided to negotiate a term sheet with it for a $1 million investment. A term sheet outlines the key elements of an investment such as price, shareholder rights, and conditions for closing the deal. Our portion of the investment was to be a modest $50,000, but we were glad to have a seat at the table. Then the two other suitors backed off.

Negotiations and more research dragged on for six weeks, not a good sign. Our investment partners were having second thoughts. "The technology is too complex," they said. "The management team needs strengthening." Worse yet, they felt, "Not everyone in the syndicate sees eye-to-eye on value." The deal was off, and, unable to assume the role of lead investor, we too stepped to the sidelines.

Klaff seemed to know that when a deal bogs down, trouble looms. While many elements of a deal's timing are out of an entrepreneur's hands, he can produce the papers and make the phone calls necessary to maintain some kind of momentum. Without momentum, a deal is nowhere. Klaff wisely had stayed in touch with Viridian Capital Partners, a North Carolina fund, and contacted them when our group bowed out.

We scrambled as well, still wanting to invest in his company, and managed to grab a position with the second, now-active investment group. The North Carolina investors offered a term sheet for a $1.25 million investment, with the Dinner Club offering to put in $150,000. This time, negotiations moved swiftly, with quick agreement on key issues like valuation, use of proceeds, board seats, and the composition of the entire investment syndicate. The collapse of the first investment group had increased our participation, though it was still below our investing sweet spot. We didn't complain because we knew that our investment secured a place for us in any follow-on investing, and we very much wanted to be part of Reliacast's growth.

This deal moved so quickly—faster than our usual pace and probably faster than Klaff and Fleisher expected—that another round in the near future was very possible. Our investment guaranteed that we'd be in the loop when the hat was passed around again. And so we were. Less than six months later, Reliacast received an $8 million infusion from Viridian's group of heavyweight investors, including KKR, Hicks Muse, and Thomas Weisel Partners, and increased the young company's valuation elevenfold.

We took away a number of lessons from the Reliacast deal. Entrepreneurs often wonder what they can do, if anything, to break loose a deal caught on a snag. Once they have made their pitch, is the progress of due diligence and negotiations completely out of their hands? Yes and no, we tell them. Most angels have their own pace at which they want to evaluate a deal, but it also depends on what stage the company is at. With an extremely young company, there's not much due diligence to be done, so the bulk of the evaluation focuses on the entrepreneur. More mature ventures have management, employees, products, markets, competition, and books that can be scrutinized.

Assessing the potential of a young company usually proceeds more quickly but, with all the intangibles, is more difficult than scrutinizing something that's up and running. *Founders of an older company who feel a deal has become bogged down need to make sure that the holdup isn't on their end and that all the due-diligence requests are being satisfied.* At the end of the day, however, *founders should know that angels can't be rushed and that an entrepreneur who's too pushy sends up red flags.*

Timing becomes unpredictable and momentum stalled when there's disagreement over the basic business concept or over a company's value, which determines the terms of the investment. In this case, it was a valuation division between Reliacast and the other angels. Reliacast took a huge gamble in rejecting the first group's terms and going back to the North Carolina group. Most angels and investment groups take only one look at a prospect. Returning to a rejected suitor raises legitimate questions about the founder's assumptions and thinking. If he's second-guessing himself, angels will surely think twice about the accuracy and truthfulness of the business plan.

Founders and angels alike have to combine firm, consistent guidelines with an eagerness to get a deal done. *The deals that work best for entrepreneurs and angels have momentum. Good deals don't get bogged down in complex negotiations, distracting outside issues, wrangling over old messes—like a tax problem—or layers of decision-makers.* Neither side digs in for the last few cents and jeopardizes the entire relationship. Angels can't be too demanding, and entrepreneurs have to recognize that ultimately the marketplace determines the value of their venture.

Beware, however, because a deal with momentum does not necessarily move at a steady pace. It can rush ahead, halt, go backward, then lurch forward again. But there is *always* movement. When a deal bogs down completely—people aren't talking, papers aren't being signed, phone calls aren't being returned—then it's in serious jeopardy.

A MATTER OF PERSPECTIVE

Sometimes timing is in the eye of the beholder. The perceptions of the angels we work with can be greatly at odds with those of other angels. Every entrepreneur gets used to hearing no, and should not mistakenly assume that if an angel group says no, then it's not ready for outside investors. One of the beauties of angels, as opposed to professional venture capitalists, is that there are many of us and we are by no means monolithic in our thinking. Being rejected by a VC firm often signals that a young company is not ready for that level of financing. Being rejected by an angel group only means you dust yourself off and prepare for the next pitch. Seth Goldman, who concocted a unique sweetened drink called Honest Tea, discovered this in spades.

Goldman had two excellent qualifications to start his bottled-drink company. He had always been an avid consumer of bottled drinks, although unsatisfied with sweet Snapple and bored by mineral water. And he possessed a solid business education, including an MBA from

Yale (and winning a business-plan writing competition) and experience working with a multinational company. After college, he wandered the globe; during his time in China, he developed a love for tea. Goldman's idea for Honest Tea brewed for years before he was ready to serve it. He frequently talked with his favorite marketing professor from Yale, Barry Nalebuff, another tea lover, about how hard it was to buy real, made-from-leaves tea.

Gradually their conversations turned into action as they devised a plan to mix a kind of tea totally different from what was currently on the market. Goldman quit his well-paying job as head of marketing and sales for a mutual-fund company and set up shop in his kitchen experimenting with tea formulas. The brews he produced were not just original but tasty. Using leaves from around the world, with a light hand on the sweeteners, he came up with three brews—Moroccan Mint, Black Forest Berry, and Kashmiri Chai.

Barry Nalebuff and Seth's family provided Honest Tea with its first family-and-friends investment, $200,000, so Goldman could incorporate and develop a design prototype and marketing materials. Goldman was encouraged by early success. He traveled through the Washington, D.C., metro area offering samples to supermarket managers, who loved the brew and the artful Honest Tea label on each bottle. Helping his positioning was the fact that each Honest Tea bottle was slightly larger and sold for twenty to forty cents more than Snapple and other teas, boosting everyone's margin.

Goldman clearly believed Honest Tea was ready for prime time when he made his presentation to our angel group. He brought along samples and delivered a thoughtful presentation. Although he did not yet have any sales outside a few health-food outlets, the business plan was well conceived. And we loved the samples—for a while Honest Tea was more popular than the table wine. He was asking for $800,000 and knew exactly what he would do with the money: arrange for product design and bottling, hire employees, and develop a marketing and distribution plan. But for all his confidence, he also knew that his creation was largely on paper. "The whole idea of creating this company required a leap of faith—from the buyer, the customer, and us. Our first investor was really investing in two guys and an idea," he said later.

Despite thinking he had a great drink, our angel group decided not to invest in Honest Tea. We could not agree on the valuation, with Goldman and Nalebuff having a richer idea of its worth than us. Undeterred, he went looking for other angels. Nalebuff provided him with names of businesspeople, and Goldman put out feelers to classmates, business associates around D.C., family friends, and industry contacts. His encounters with our angels changed his mind not about the valuation but about the money-raising process. "A lot of people think it's enough to have a great product. It's not. Our backgrounds have been useful to us not just because of what we know about running a business, but also because of our connections," he noted. Goldman was learning that finding the right investor frequently boils down to who you know.

He was a quick student. Goldman sent out numerous copies of the Honest Tea business plan to virtually anyone who asked and, within ninety days, had found angels willing to invest more money than he was looking for at his original valuation. Angels descended from everywhere—a family of third-generation grocery distributors from Boston, a nationally known New York City money manager, a woman in Cleveland who invested in companies that made products for the diet-conscious. Investors wanted to put in $100,000 more than he wanted; so as not to dilute his ownership, he accepted only $800,000 and began the makings of a national brand.

Honest Tea is still going, although not expanding as quickly as Seth Goldman would like. It's become a trendy tea and can be found in specialty stores, health-food stores, exclusive chains like Whole Foods Market, and a few mainstream grocers. He's got stiff competition, especially from Lipton, owned by PepsiCo, and Nestea, owned jointly by Coca-Cola and Nestlé. Nevertheless, reports are that his revenues are picking up—*Fortune* magazine predicted they would hit $3 million in 1999 sales.

Of course, a story like Seth Goldman's makes us pause and wonder whether we should have invested. On reflection, for our group we made the right decision. Although the time was right for Honest Tea, it wasn't for our angels. We needed less risk to be comfortable. There were no other institutional investors yet, no outside board of directors. This company was ideal for active angel support but not for structured angel groups yet. Fortunately for Goldman, the world is full of angels, and he managed to locate some for whom the time was perfect.

What we've seen in this chapter is that funding for seed-stage businesses comes only after arduous travels down many paths. The goal is to find the right value-added individual investors to support founders and their families. You learn that it's time to dance with an angel after you've clarified your vision, have a plan, and are ready for some "adult supervision." As you will see in the next chapter, the expansion of financing opportunities from lone-ranger individuals to groups, clubs, and angel-backed funds gives entrepreneurs more avenues than ever to find the right match.

- Angels are part of a larger investment food chain, in the niche between friends-and-family and superangels or venture-capital money. Be sure your needs and stage of growth match the kinds and size of ventures that angels back. UWapIT, for instance, was just too young for angel investing.

- Angels prefer seasoned management, but inexperience alone does not eliminate a company from consideration. An inexperienced founder who shows that he or she learns quickly in applying on-the-job business lessons and avoids repeated missteps gets our full attention. We invested in Nascent Technologies for this very reason.

- Perfect timing may seem like a matter of luck, but luck can be found if an entrepreneur assembles all the right pieces: the right management, market, product or service, and competitive space. And it doesn't hurt to toss in great contacts. This was certainly true of AOL in its early days.

- Be prepared for a spirited line dance with lots of partners, not an intimate slow dance for two. You're ready to talk to angels if you're prepared for scrutiny from numerous investors. Angels don't like to invest alone. They like to spread the risk and know that other experienced investors share their opinion of a start-up. Reliacast, which makes software for handling website customer transactions, obtained financing from many angels.

- The right timing includes eagerness to get a deal done. This eagerness is what fuels momentum, which is essential for a deal to happen. There's give-and-take on both sides, and while founders can't be too pushy, they can make sure that all requests for information are met quickly. The founder of Reliacast kept in touch with all interested potential investors, which stood him in good stead when one group's deal bogged down and eventually died.

- The right time for one group of angels may not be the right time for another. Timing is often in the eye of the investor, and founders with hides toughened from repeated no's should keep looking. Although we passed on Honest Tea, the company's founder kept looking and finally found more money than he even needed.

3

Finding Angels and Making Your Pitch

Within a year, we predict, despite a slowing economy, more than a million business angels will be investing in hundreds of thousands of companies. There will be an organized angel group in almost every major community in America. This represents a sea change for American business. Not so long ago, angels flew alone. They were solitary investors, writing checks on personal bank accounts and handing them over to entrepreneurs who had sold them on a new restaurant concept, a way to enhance computer graphics, or a miracle chemical that purifies wastewater. The investing habits of one of us, Cal, was typical for the time: Entrepreneurs found him through word of mouth, and he did the same for locating promising start-ups. There were no directories or websites on new businesses or likely angels. Finding angels was made more difficult because they not only flew solo but liked to keep under the radar and not draw attention to themselves. They guarded their privacy, in part because of fear of being besieged by requests for money from the wrong people.

This chapter is about locating angel investors and preparing your presentation to them. We'll show you how times have changed and the search for funding has become much more formalized and businesslike. We'll take you through the steps of the process, from locating a potential investor to presenting a well-crafted business proposal to closing the sale.

And we'll introduce you to several groups of angels around the country and discuss the various approaches they take to screening and then evaluating businesses. Although raising money is still a tough proposition for most entrepreneurs, it should be comforting to note that there are more organized sources of investment capital out there than ever before. This chapter will help prepare you to be successful in both finding those sources and winning them over.

SEARCHING FOR AN ANGEL: SOMETIMES THEY'RE RIGHT DOWN THE STREET

Angel investing used to be a small world, confined largely to who knew whom and informal connections. For example, in the 1980s Robert Giaimo owned a string of successful Washington-area restaurants called the American Café. After selling that operation, he decided to take what he had learned and create a new kind of eatery, an old-fashioned, '50s-style diner. He and Cal knew each other from the Young Presidents' Organization, an international business network, where they struck up a friendship. Shortly after opening his first Silver Diner, Giaimo was out looking for investors to expand his new concept. With that in mind, he asked Cal to visit his operation. The Silver Diner headquarters was in Bethesda, Maryland, and when Cal arrived, he expected that he and Bob would talk business over coffee at the lunch counter. But Bob had instructed him to walk to the back and down a level. Here, beneath the pad holding the bullet-shaped diner, Cal discovered an elaborate office complex. He was impressed: The arrangement showed that Giaimo was thinking like a businessman and combining back-office operations with a flair for showmanship.

After a tour of the office, they went upstairs for lunch. Giaimo insisted on ordering for Cal and proceeded to request four entrées, and a tabletop covered with appetizers and desserts. The restaurateur wanted the possible angel to taste the fare and know exactly what he was backing. Along with other angels, Cal bought stock at $2 a share in the Silver Diner.

It turned out to be a fun investment, with lots of good eats and an exciting ride on the IPO train. Silver Diner went public at $4 a share, then steadily moved to $6, yet many angel investors did not sell at this point, believing that Giaimo's passion would propel the company to greater heights. The restaurateur had opened eleven restaurants and was aiming to build an empire of hundreds of diners, and few wanted to bail too soon. But the concept never quite caught on, and the restaurant industry hit a bad patch. (See chapter 8 for tips on "When to Exit.") Today Silver Diner stock hovers around $1 per share. Nevertheless, Cal optimistically still keeps the stock and believes the investment will ultimately become a home run.

This is what angel investing is all about. Entrepreneurs develop a business plan that they then need help funding. They share their passion with anyone who will listen—often acquaintances or friends of friends. Individuals invest because they believe in the entrepreneurs' vision and their commitment to realizing the dream. And the investors are hoping for a home run. Angels rarely invest because they think the business will grow a little bit. They want to be part of *big* things. What convinced Cal to invest in Silver Diner was Bob Giaimo's grand plan, and the detailed game plan he had for executing the business. Cal invested because Bob was an experienced entrepreneur who had already proven himself capable of building a business. But he also invested because of the strength of Bob's *presentation.* You see, angels can be wooed by an exciting plan, but they ultimately invest in carefully planned, well-constructed businesses. So, how do you find these angels, and what do you need to show them to persuade them to write a check?

THE SHIFT FROM INFORMAL TO STRUCTURED PRESENTATIONS

In the early days of business angel investing, somewhere in the late 1970s and early 1980s, business founders learned about angels by asking work associates, their lawyer, accountant, or a business-school professor. It was a word-of-mouth network, and who you knew and how well you could sell your idea were the keys to motivating someone to write a check. Some regions of the country went professional earlier than others—San Francisco and Boston evolved first.

Whether the investment produced any results or the company went anywhere was catch-as-catch-can even in those pioneering regions. "I was just plain lucky as an angel," says C. Richard Kramlich, who gave a couple of Bay Area geeks $22,500, which Steven Jobs and Steve Wozniak parlayed into Apple Computer.

The pioneer days of angel investing were rugged for investor and entrepreneur alike. Angels making decisions on their own had a limited scope and limited opportunities. They were generally small-business ideas or opportunities, unlike today's high-growth companies. The deals that came to them usually happened by chance, so there was no regular stream of start-ups to evaluate, or depend on. The due-diligence process, especially when an angel wasn't in the same business as the entrepreneur, tended to be spotty and cursory. An angel might make a couple of phone calls to check out references or ask family members what they thought of the prospect. But more often than not, the decision was truly on a wing and a prayer.

Adding to the gamble was the time and legal cost involved in crafting an agreement. For each deal, the terms were negotiated from scratch because so few deals were done. This led many entrepreneurs to "wing it," to fail to give a comprehensive plan and presentation.

The entrepreneur was equally adrift, not knowing how to find someone who had sufficient investment funds and was willing to take a chance with it. Occasionally bankers or stockbrokers kept lists of wealthy clients interested in private placement investments. These opportunities were primarily real-estate-oriented—the decades of the '70s and '80s were tax-driven more than investment-growth-driven. After the tax act of 1986, which took away most real-estate tax havens, investor attention shifted to public equity markets, and then private equity or venture capital. And even when a guy with a great idea for a new company snagged a live angel, the likelihood that this person could also contribute business know-how was slim. Economic-development groups, chambers of commerce, universities, and state commerce agencies tried to spur on seed financing and angel investing, but with limited success. The nonprofit groups lacked the motivation and resources of later angels.

A burgeoning opportunity for entrepreneurs to meet key players in their community and to network with overseas counterparts is the organization First Tuesday. Begun in London in 1998 by four Internet entrepreneurs, this loose-knit group of city-centric monthly meetings has grown to over 30,000 participants in 110 cities in 46 countries. City organizing committees (totaling over 400, including John May in the Washington, D.C., chapter) and sponsors (like the Sonnenschein law firm, Internet service provider UUNet, and consulting firm Accenture) host evening meetings on the first Tuesday of each month—hence the name!—where New Economy entrepreneurs, professional service providers, and investors—mainly angels—mingle and exchange business cards.

THE GREATEST CREATION OF WEALTH

The landscape for angel investing changed dramatically in the 1990s. The bulldozer that did it was a phenomenal surge in personal wealth in this country. John Doerr, the Big Kahuna of venture capitalists, has called this occurrence "the single greatest legal creation of wealth in the history of the planet." Billions of dollars poured into people's pockets from the confluence of widely held stock that became highly valuable and new issues that rocketed from almost worthless to better than gold. Companies like Microsoft, Apple, Intel, and Hewlett-Packard handed out stock options as part of employee compensation, and then millions of people hopped on this country's longest and strongest market boom. The explosion in public stock investing in the 1990s led to diversification of this new wealth into the illiquid private markets as well.

And the IPO frenzy, led by Netscape's launch—which took it from a market value of nothing to $6 billion within 18 months—made everyone drool. The boom fueled itself with a dizzying increase in the number of new companies going public. Netscape was only the beginning—market-crazed

Americans closely followed the surging IPOs of Yahoo!, Amazon.com, and AOL. And hotbeds of technological wizardry like Stanford University virtually guaranteed a steady torrent of bright, shiny enterprises. Furthermore, the newly minted millionaires weren't buying villas on private islands and clipping coupons, as the wealthy of prior generations had done. They were plowing their winnings back into younger, faster versions of their ventures.

Of course, the public fascination with business and corporate personalities—the supposed sniping between Steve Jobs and Bill Gates, the extravagant spending habits of Oracle's Larry Ellison—and stories of instant gazillionaires were like lighter fuel to last week's *Barron's*. After reading how one New York financier and angel, Kevin Kimberlin, put $100,000 into Ciena Corp. in 1994 and three years later, when it went public, had an investment worth $285 million, who wouldn't be transfixed? This country had become fascinated with wealth and what it could do. In such a climate, more and more angels weren't going to stay anonymous, or disorganized for long.

ANGELS BEGIN TO BAND TOGETHER

One of the first organized groups of angels was the highly publicized Band of Angels, which continues to meet at the Los Altos Golf & Country Club, the epicenter of the Silicon Valley high-tech boom. In 1995, a handful of cashed-out engineers, scientists, and computer pioneers joined forces to invest in new technology through a fun and entertaining vehicle. The man who pulled this group together, Hans Severiens, had been writing small checks on his own to struggling tech companies for thirty years. And he knew other such angels, in particular an executive at Intel and a higher-up at Apple. They decided to join forces. "We thought, wouldn't it be nice to have a club . . . where you could look at private deals and experts can tell you whether these deals are worth investing in or not," Severiens remembers.

The Band of Angels adopted rituals that would be duplicated by angel groups across the land, although the structures of the groups would vary.

Membership is limited and selective. A hundred or so investors, mostly men, gather once a month for dinner. Outsiders may be invited to the dinner and to hear the presentation but are not allowed to stick around for the members' discussion. The pitch can't be longer than ten minutes, and members are free to quiz the presenter. Individual members are expected to be able to invest at least $50,000 into a deal, and some get into more deals than others. Over its first three years, the Band of Angels funneled $27 million into aspiring enterprises.

Naturally, just getting the privilege to watch the group eat salmon filets and sip pinot noir while you deliver the most important ten-minute talk of your life doesn't come easily. Severiens, the gatekeeper, receives hundreds of business plans and requests annually and from the pile extracts just three a month. Further raising the bar is that a company must have two sponsors from among the club membership—people who already know the entrepreneur and are prepared to invest in him or her, if they haven't yet.

Around the same time the Band of Angels began pooling resources and sharing the demands of complex due diligence, the notion occurred to others. Organized groups of angels popped up wherever there was a supercharged industry and people with the bucks to bankroll its offspring. Next door to Band of Angels, the Angel Breakfast Club formed in Palo Alto. Technology Capital Network popped up in the shadow of Massachusetts Institute of Technology in Cambridge; the Capital Network in Austin, Texas; Gathering of Angels in Santa Fe; Private Investors Group in Philadelphia; and Capital Network in Boston. Each serviced its own region in its own distinctive way, with no one approach dominating the landscape. (Appendix C provides a list of many of these angel groups, with contact information.)

Since the organized-angel idea has blossomed, and the economy has continued to chug along and rain prosperity on many, dozens—maybe hundreds—of angels groups are meeting in hotels or clubs to hear a Steve Jobs or Jeff Bezos wannabe. While the Northern Virginia–Washington, D.C., area has more than its share of hot technology companies, the region's explosion of angel organizations surely isn't unique. It's the rapidity and structure of our approach that makes the region a leader among angel groups. Since the formation of the high-profile Capital Investors Group (aka the Billionaires Club), the Dinner Club and eMedia Club have swung into action, followed by WomenAngels.net and the Washington Dinner Club, all started within a two-year period. If every metropolitan area is like ours, angel groups have to be multiplying faster than websites. And that's not counting the angel groups coming together in smaller economically vibrant niches like Boise, Colorado Springs, and Jacksonville. Though no one's counting, business experts estimate that there are 300,000 to 500,000 active angels in the country, investing around $30 billion annually in young hopefuls.

STRUCTURED ANGEL CLUBS

The term "structured angel group," in contrast to a group of angels who hear presentations together but make individual decisions and write separate checks, is credited to Doug Greenwood, a former executive with Deutsche Banc Alex. Brown. In his travels around the country to attend venture fairs and meet with angels, he noticed that the organized groups of angels lowered two hurdles confronting individual angels. By pooling funds before they found deals, structured angel groups had more financial firepower and were more efficient.

By arranging the logistics and therefore easing the hassles of meeting planning, a knowledgeable manager helps the deal flow. He can prescreen entrepreneurs wanting to make presentations, weeding out the unsuitable or unready, or identify new ventures that the group might want to invest in. The manager also enforces the group's policy on admission to their ranks—turning away unwanted joiners, suggesting new members if they're wanted, and ensuring that members are accredited investors. Most angel groups insist that their members meet the SEC requirements for an accredited investor—namely, liquid net worth of at least $1 million and annual income, for at least two years running, of $200,000 ($300,000 if married). This standard works to the entrepreneur's advantage by ensuring that he doesn't waste his time romancing people without real investment money, and it assures later institutional investors that preceding investors won't react like novices during the inevitable ups and downs ahead.

It also falls to the manager to discover co-investors and, very probably, follow-on investors. This requires staying active in the investment community, wooing VC firms and investment banks, and selling others on the angels' latest comer. Individual angels don't have to get involved in the messy work of screening hundreds of candidates, preparing the paperwork for deals, or worrying about whether to serve beef or chicken at investor sessions. One VC has quipped, "Angels worked hard making their money, and they don't want to work that hard again."

Most structured angel groups today are limited liability companies or limited partnerships, so the individual angels are usually called members; the manager is the general partner. As a result, angel groups write one check and have one tax ID number and one set of books, making life easier for angel as well as entrepreneur.

Investors join angel groups not only for the financial rewards. There's a lot of camaraderie and schmoozing, too. The charter of the fifteen-member Walnut Venture Associates in Boston states that members should be "fun to hang around with." This may be why organized angels have found that groups that meet over a meal are more successful than those serving bagels and muffins, which sets an eat-and-run tone.

Another trend in the angel world is nationwide networks. Investment groups are coalescing around causes or targeted investing, instead of geography. For instance, Investors' Circle, based in Boston, has 150 accredited investors from around the country who invest in "socially responsible" companies. John May helped to cofound it in 1991 and has seen it grow to nationwide scope. It meets once or twice a year around venture fairs. Environmental Capital Network in Ann Arbor has a similar agenda, aiming its money at socially responsible companies involved in health, energy efficiency, the environment, community development, and similar businesses.

Given all this wing-flapping, it's no wonder that some regions now boast organizations or firms whose purpose is managing the traffic. Mainly, they put people together—matching entrepreneurs with angel groups, individual angels with structured angel clubs—and sometimes offer educational programs. The Mid-Atlantic Venture Association brings together accredited investors and sponsors venture fairs and conferences. Other such groups are the Michiana Investment Network in South Bend, Indiana, and International Capital Resources, which has affiliates across the country and is connected to the Web-based Nvst.com in Bellevue, Washington.

Being managers of structured angel clubs, we are, of course, partial to this type of organization. We believe it's the direction investors are headed in—it provides an efficient marketplace for entrepreneurs looking for seed money and for investors to get the best returns on their venture capital. The clubs formalize what has been a chaotic, loosely connected network of businesspeople, investors, and entrepreneurs. With published requirements and standards for investors and entrepreneurs alike, they level the economic playing field. These groups enable angels to participate in ventures they never could have gotten into as individuals and provide access to start-up capital for entrepreneurs who couldn't find a champion. In chapter 6, you'll read about other types of angel organizations, like matching services that put together entrepreneurs and angels. Another variety of organization are angel forums, groups that meet regularly to hear presentations but perform due diligence, make decisions, and write checks—individually.

These are the structured angel groups we are familiar with, although new ones are popping up daily. This movement has paralleled the advent of increasing venture-capital activity throughout the country and the need for more efficient ways for companies and money sources to meet. Both angels and venture capitalists support the growing number of regional venture fairs, entrepreneur forums, and investor showcases—all similar functions for allowing entrepreneurs to pitch would-be investors.

DANCING AT THE VENTURE FAIR

Imagine streams of Dockers-clad men and women armed with cell phones and expensive leather binders, their eyes raking the crowd for someone to invest in. Imagine the midway at a carnival lined with booths containing entrepreneurs handing out pens, coffee mugs, and slick company brochures. Imagine expansive ballrooms, lights dimmed except for the spot on the stage, and a fast-talking CEO sharing his plans for taking over the world.

If you can envision all this, you know what a venture fair is like. Venture fairs are to money-hungry entrepreneurs and deal-hungry investors as church socials were to prairie pioneers. If you're looking for an angel partner to add money and muscle to your company, this is a great place to start. In fact, the Dinner Club strongly recommends that the companies it has invested in *continue* to make presentations at venture fairs, because entrepreneurs are almost always preparing for their next round of financing.

Whether dubbed a fair, conference, or forum, the venture fair is based on a cattle-show model, with entrepreneurs strutting their stuff and cattle owners—or, in this case, investors—listening to lots of spiels, shaking lots of hands, collecting lots of literature, and taking notes about worthwhile deals. A venture fair usually lasts for one or two days, and during this time, entrepreneurs make formal presentations every ten or twenty minutes. In the course of a single fair, sixty or so start-ups may be talking about their companies.

The presentations tend to be similar in format, although the ease, humor, and clarity of the CEOs and founders differ widely. Some wear coats and ties and some wear khakis and sport shirts, but almost all use a large screen to present a series of colorful explanations of who they are and what they do. Fast, clipped descriptions, often loaded with strings of tech jargon, can be mind-numbing, so well-timed humor goes over well. And listeners seem to pay the most attention to founders who tell a story about their company: where it's headed, the dragons it's going to slay, the pots of gold it's going to unearth.

Simultaneously buzzing with action is an exposition hall where the presenting companies go one-on-one with passersby, clicking on monitors to demonstrate products, services, or technology, handing out bios of key management people, and generally schmoozing. Lots of business cards get exchanged and logo-splattered pens, coffee mugs, and T-shirts handed out. Yet another area of the fair, typically held in a large hotel, has hospitality suites usually sponsored by corporations and investment firms.

Venture fairs are organized and presented by associations, like the Mid-Atlantic Venture Association (MAVA), and regional consortiums of universities, venture-capital funds, or service providers. To participate and make a presentation, companies pay from $250 to $500. Attendees pay a fee, usually between $300 to $1,200. The fees don't appear to deter anyone—the turnout at these fairs is normally very good. At a recent Mid-Atlantic Venture Fair, we had 350 companies vying to make one of sixty presentations. The "winners" were chosen by a joint committee of venture investors and service providers according to their stage of development, location, and prior rounds of finance. Once selected, the companies received coaching on how to present to an audience of more than 1,000 attendees.

Mary Naylor, founder of the Web-based concierge service VIPdesk, swears by them. "I would absolutely advise any entrepreneur to present to a venture fair. It's a matter of time and efficiency. You, as an entrepreneur, are doing two things, both of which turn into full-time jobs: raising money and, at the same time, building and running your company. So the faster and more efficiently you can do it, the better. But you'd better have a well-honed presentation, because you have to be selected to even get into these group presentations. This is all about packaging and storytelling. How well you tell your story makes a huge difference."

Not only are venture fairs hosted by region-wide venture industry groups like MAVA or economic development supporters like Fairfax County Economic Development Authority, but targeted events like Springboard 2000 have "sprung up." In early 2000, the National Women's Business Council and a few key women executives created a women-entrepreneur-only venture fair series. After a very well received inaugural fair in Silicon Valley in the spring of 2000, co-hosted by Oracle Corporation, McKinsey and Company, and others, a national roll-out of these well-attended events has begun. Preceded by an exhaustive and professional selection process (oftentimes hundreds of women-led businesses applied), 23 to 30 companies are selected to present and exhibit to a regional audience of hundreds of angel investors and venture capitalists.

Fairs have been held in Boston, northern Virginia, Chicago, New York City, and Austin. These events have been universally praised for the quality of the coaching skills given to participants and the quality of business concepts presented. Hundreds of millions of dollars have been raised from angel and VC investors. Women entrepreneurs have historically received little venture financing from the established institutional VC community (oftentimes referred to as an old boys' club) so these fairs represent a large step forward in access to capital for this underserved market segment.

APPROACHING AN ANGEL CLUB

Before you can present, you need to wangle an invitation. There are a number of dos and don'ts useful to remember when you approach an angel club or the manager of a venture fair. We'll focus here on presenting to a structured angel club, but the guidelines are the same for getting in front of any organized group of investors. Of course, you've got to nail down the basics: name of contact person or club manager, names and backgrounds of key members, the club's investment guidelines and history, and what kind of package the club wants from applicants. Websites or brochures of these now-public vehicles should suffice as door openers.

The perfect way to make a first approach is to be referred by a member of the group and then to send a brief executive summary either via e-mail or fax to the club manager. Ask around to learn members' names. Look for company press releases for quotes; call the club manager or staff for names of officers or leading members.

Never send a large package in this first go-around, and absolutely never send a large package cold. The soup-to-nuts business plan should go out only when someone has asked for it. And send it by messenger or overnight delivery, not snail mail—and definitely not as an e-mail attachment. In all your dealings with the group, keep two goals in mind: brevity and setting the hook. Angel groups get pelted with business plans and entreaties from entrepreneurs just as VCs do, so sorting through the slush piles and phone messages tends to be a quick and dirty process. Brief, concise, easy-to-understand summaries will be read and remembered much more than windy ramblings.

To set the hook, lead with your best bait. Start your summary with the special feature of your venture that's going to make it a winner—you've got fabulous growth prospects, you've already landed a big customer, you have a new invention that everyone is going to want. Maybe your best lure is the experience of the founder—he or she has done other start-ups, knows the business better than anyone else, is a fantastic motivator and salesperson. *Find something about your company that makes it shine, and push that feature out in front.* You need a good hook because everyone is chasing the same few funding fish.

MAKING THE CUT

Suppose your executive summary, and later your business plan, has landed on the desk of the lead angel or the angel-club manager. It's there along with a couple dozen others, and the manager is going to ask only two or three of the entrepreneurs to make a presentation in front of the club at the next meeting. So how do you make the cut? For starters, *don't lose points out of sloppiness or carelessness.* Typos, misspellings, small and dense type, badly organized plans, a writing style laden with technical jargon, sentences that go on and on, and generally amateurish work annoy people, especially busy people. Use short sentences. You don't want a manager's first impression to be of someone who can't string together two coherent ideas without tripping. Give the manager a chance to evaluate your company on substance, not style.

Applying a little creativity to your campaign to stand out is not a bad idea. For example, the founders of a business-to-business Internet company in New York City learned the flight times of two key angel investors so they could make a ten-minute impromptu pitch with a PowerPoint presentation on a table at the airport's Legal Seafood restaurant. GirlGeeks, a website for high-tech women in California (even a company name can be a hook), e-mailed angels invitations to become part of the beta test for a Web-hosted talk show even before sending out a business plan or asking anyone for money. Inviting angels to a special reception or sponsored event, like a skybox at a baseball game, puts your name out there. Attending events where angels might cluster, for example, industry trade fairs, charity fundraisers, or celebrity golf or tennis events, can be an entree to chance introductions. You've got to explore many paths.

When an angel-group organizer or manager looks at a business plan for the first time, numerous questions float through his or her mind. How the company answers these determines how enthusiastic he or she is about a venture. Here are the questions:

- How experienced and able are the entrepreneur and management team?
- What's the size of the potential market and the profit margins?
- Is the product or service developed? Any patents or proprietary technology?
- Who's already invested in the company? Any other angels? Any VCs indicated interest in being lead investor?
- Is the entrepreneur realistic in terms of revenue projections, exit strategy, valuation, and financial need?
- How much "skin in the game" does the founding group have?

The answers to the questions raised above should be embedded in the executive summary you prepared as well as in the full business plan (see chapter 5), which you need to be able to provide upon request. Condensing this plan into a PowerPoint presentation and well-rehearsed oral pitch is essential.

SHOW TIME

Angels are swayed by a good story—a founder who surmounts incredible obstacles, comes up with a brilliant idea, solves a problem everyone has thought insoluble, defies the odds, or persists until success is in view. A compelling story can follow any number of possible plotlines, but angels know when they are hooked.

In May 1999, the Dinner Club heard a presentation by Stephen Mefferd, the president of a medical-supply company called BioFX. BioFX was the sort of company that would have had a hard time finding investors in a bygone era when angels weren't as active and taking risks wasn't considered a standard feature in promising investments. The company was headed by a soft-spoken president and M.D., a newly hired CEO, and a creative-genius type—a self-proclaimed mad scientist whose research lab in Columbia, Maryland, was as disorganized as a teenager's bedroom. He worked surrounded by towers of storage boxes filled with ancient papers that he would never need again. The scientist was a pack rat, refusing to throw anything away that might someday, regardless of how far in the future, be asked about. This quirky scientist was the key to BioFX's future.

A few years earlier, the scientist had made a startling discovery—a unique compound that could revolutionize home-testing kits for pregnancy as well as lab tests for serious illnesses, including AIDS. Assisted by his equally gifted daughter, scientist Tom Woerner developed a simple process by which a positive response turned a testing substance red, for easy reading by the customer.

The active substance in most testing kits—like the one that produces a red square if you're pregnant and a blue one if you're not—is highly unreliable. The batches of testing fluid in each kit can be made only in relatively small quantities, so quality control is a problem, and production is expensive because it can't be produced in bulk. Furthermore, the substance used in most testing kits has to be refrigerated, which makes distribution expensive.

But with BioFX's magic compound, quality was easy to maintain, and rates of false-positives were lower than the industry norm. The positive response was clearer, too, which meant that customers wouldn't go crazy wondering whether the pink they saw was red enough to be considered positive, a problem with many home-pregnancy kits. Best of all, the substance didn't need to be kept cold, so trucking it from the plant to the customer was a lot less costly. President Stephen Mefferd was convinced its product would be widely adopted, if only it could get a facility big enough to make more of the stuff.

Before the bespectacled president made his presentation to the Dinner Club, he put a small vial of whitish liquid on each round dinner table where angels sat. As he gave his pitch, individual angels fiddled with the vials. Some of the angels were underwhelmed by Mefferd's initial pitch, finding him low-key and methodical, unlike the high-energy entrepreneurs who had preceded him. The vials were something else. Filled with red liquid, the liquid in the vials turned milky white when shaken, then to red again when the substance settled. Cool, some thought.

Mefferd's story had intriguing elements as well as a fun show-and-tell. Sigma, a large producer of home-testing kits, was keen to buy large quantities of the compound. However, it would not commit until it was sure that BioFX could fill its needs. And BioFX needed a patent, which would cost more money than the company had. It had already tried to raise money from venture capitalists, but the mad scientist and his daughter did not make the best of impressions, especially when they mentioned that they stumbled on this scientific breakthrough by accident. Even though some of the world's greatest discoveries—Alexander Fleming's penicillin, for instance—were made by accident, bankers don't like to invest in a product based on a lab experiment gone awry.

And then there was the little detail about only four people in the world knowing the secret to the compound: the president, the CEO, the mad scientist, and his daughter. Mefferd's quip, "We don't fly on the same plane," could not have endeared him to the established money men.

The Dinner Club members, however, were perfectly willing to stretch their imaginations beyond the happenstance beginnings and envision a huge market potential for the product. Despite the low-key presentation, the members were impressed with an entrepreneur who could explain and sell them on the business potential of a complicated chemical compound, and the show-and-tell helped, too. Hooked on the story, club members voted to pursue due diligence on BioFX.

Due diligence revealed not only a disorganized lab but other small areas of concern. Mike Hertzberg, a Dinner Club angel who worked on the committee, told his fellow members, "The CEO's biggest job will be to rein in the scientist. This is a guy who, when you are sitting in his office talking to him about his marketing strategy for the testing product, suddenly starts pulling out boxes of stuff to show you his latest discovery in molecular biology. Keeping him focused on the product at hand is a full-time job in itself."

The committee also came up with lots of positive features. The company had already received funding from the state of Maryland, which offers early grants to start-ups and has created "incubators" to help small companies grow and work with the two largest industries in the area, the National Institutes of Health in Bethesda and the telecommunications firms along the I-270 corridor. Angels like third-party references and endorsements. Early funding through an incubator program, research grants, an individual angel, or a tight relationship with a top-tier corporate partner help reduce uncertainty and risk.

About two months after members first shook the small vials, the Dinner Club voted to invest in BioFX more than it had ever put into a new enterprise. The club itself put up $400,000, and individual members, enamored with a founder and product that promised to change medical testing, wrote checks for an additional $400,000. The Dinner Club received a 12 percent stake in BioFX, and the company received enough cash to build a bigger production facility and take its product big-time. A subset of the club—six investors—agreed to provide as-needed help in the coming months.

The angels were hooked on the story and pleased with their investment. "I got into this club to take part in the Internet revolution by investing in start-ups," a member said. "I never thought I'd be shaking lab vials of red firewater. But this stuff is great. And if what they say about the market is true, what a huge possibility."

Mefferd did what all magnetic entrepreneurs seem to do so well—get a "hook" into the audience through technique and delivery. The club was convinced that he knew his stuff, that he was sincere and believable, and his body language matched his pitch. In the next sections, we offer specific advice on what you can do to make your own presentation as believable and successful.

Make sure your presentation is smooth. Many entrepreneurs get professional public-speaking coaching for help in learning how to deliver a can't-miss presentation. We mention this not to necessarily recommend spending money on a coach but to impress upon entrepreneurs the importance of thoughtful preparation. Winging it will not work. *This is a high-stakes show, and you must consider every element of your presentation, and rehearse.* Like it or not, at this point it's a beauty contest, so you've got to put your best stuff forward.

Make sure your CEO or founder makes the presentation. Usually the CEO or founder does the presentation, and not because he or she is the company's best speaker. The reason for this person to take the stage is that the angels are judging the person propelling the company as much as the business itself. They back *people.* They want to see and hear the founder, get a sense of the person's style and people skills. If a founder feels totally inept at public speaking, he or she can share the duties with someone else in the company, doing something of a duet. But founders can't do a no-show. While the founder's under the spotlight, it's fine to bring along and introduce other key people.

Grab your listeners with a strong opening. Before you start practicing your pitch, assemble the pieces, namely the lead, or first couple of sentences. Grab your listeners with this. For example, we recently heard a great opening from VIPdesk CEO Mary Naylor. She started with a quick anecdote about her company, saying it was changing directions, even after a long profitable history, because the market potential of the new target was so huge. She was leaving a secure past and enticing investors to join her next adventure. Her delivery had energy and punch, and got people's heads nodding. Sometimes an entrepreneur begins with, "You should invest in my company because . . ." and that can work.

Summarize your company's mission in an easy-to-understand way, right off the bat. Many entrepreneurs practice what's known as the "elevator pitch." You know the scene: You've just bumped into someone who just might be an angel, and you have one minute to explain why he or she should invest in your company. Public-speaking experts say that the most critical part of your presentation is the first sentence, which should grab and captivate. Rehearse it. Say it to friends and family; see how they react. Practice in front of the mirror to check your facial expression and body language.

Consider doing something visually dramatic. For example, Dinner Club members still remember the president of a company called Firewater, which sells community-building tools to Internet sites—things like news feeds, chat rooms, and personalized messaging. Weeks after the meeting, none of us could remember the explanation for the name Firewater, but no one in the room that night will ever forget the imagery created by the presenter.

To make his pitch before an intimidating group of money men, he came in wearing a fireman's jacket. He did the entire presentation with this heavy rubberized coat on, its clanging belts, hooks, and clasps providing a light background melody. When he finished, he got a big round of applause. More important, the angels remembered him and Firewater. He got to first base, a major stretch. We're not necessarily advocating that every entrepreneur needs a gimmick to be remembered by, but your goal should be *to be remembered,* however best you can achieve that.

Prepare slides or a PowerPoint presentation. Livening up a pitch with a PowerPoint presentation, or at least projected slides, has become standard for these talks, as they are in venture-fair presentations. Sure, you can show up without one, just as you can also show up not wearing socks or with spinach between your teeth, but you probably don't want to. (Dress-code advisory: Although your angels will probably be in biz casual, you shouldn't. Coats, ties, suits or dresses are still generally the uniform of the day.) If you don't have a visual display, your listeners will have to work harder to understand your company (most people are visual, not aural, learners), and angels don't like to strain, at least at such an early stage in the game. The slides should be in color, and each frame should have simple sentences or lists or easy-to-follow diagrams—nothing crowded, crammed, or complicated. Don't get too jazzy or artsy. You get no points for creativity here. The words should be readable thirty feet from the screen.

Prepare handouts, which have become another essential ingredient in your pitch. It can be a company brochure, an executive summary of your plan, a one-page flier. You can reproduce printouts of your slides or a flier on a distinctive product. It can be on slick paper and typeset or produced by the office computer. But no bulky binders or fat sheaves of paper stapled together. Angels fly light.

Practice your pitch repeatedly, and use a watch to make sure it's within the allotted time. Be sure to get the exact starting time and preferred length of the presentation from your host. You'll get the hook before an angel group lets you rattle on, which hardly makes a good impression.

Carefully think through how much to say about your technology. Even though your listeners have already made it in business, maybe in a tech-heavy business, that doesn't mean everyone speaks the same language. Someone simultaneously listening to you talk and looking at a complex diagram on a screen absorbs very little. People remember impressions more than facts, so if every other word from your mouth is a string of initials, your listeners may well remember you as the guy who had a hard time communicating, not the guy with great technology or a terrific company. "Pretend you're explaining your business to an eleven-year-old," advises a venture capitalist.

Be prepared for something to go wrong. It always does. Malfunctioning equipment. Loud noises from the next room. Bored, sleepy, or rude listeners. Poor lighting. Laryngitis. A bad case of nerves. During a presentation in a hotel dining room, one company founder had to contend with an A/C system that produced a loud, rasping sound that made it hard for people in the back of the room to hear him. So he casually moved the podium to the middle of the room while speaking, and slowly rotated in a circle during his talk so everyone could hear him. And he continued even as maintenance men with ladders removed ceiling tiles and repaired the offending unit.

Getting comfortable under any circumstances through practice ensures that you won't be thrown off your stride. One presenter at a venture fair was prepared for a sleepy, inattentive audience. Midway through the PowerPoint show, as eyes began to droop, her associate cracked a loud bullwhip. Woke even the waiters up! And people left that presentation remembering her name.

When Jamey Harvey, CEO of a young company called Digital Addiction, came to an angel breakfast, his practicing paid off in spades. Bright-eyed and bushy-tailed, he stepped to the podium to discover that the overhead projector was on the fritz. He could have wasted half his allotted time fiddling with cords, bulbs, and slide trays, and making excuses, but he didn't. As smooth as silk, he slid into his talk. "To heck with it," he smiled. "Let me tell you about my company." No charts, no notes, no colorful diagrams. With just his voice and his hands, he sold his company. Three angels signed up on the spot.

Make sure you provide all the necessary information about your company. We've found that angels expect to hear certain basics about your company. Don't wander into the infield when you should be touching all the bases. Be ready for any and all questions from your audience. Smart angels know all the tough questions, because they've been in your shoes.

This is what a company seeking angel financing needs to have to make a presentation before an angel club or venture fair:

- Company name
- Entrepreneur/founder's name
- Officers/key management names
- Names of auditor, legal counsel, advisory board members
- Contact person
- Phone, fax, e-mail address
- Type of business
- Description of business—your mission or vision
- Product or service—its industry, niche, model

- Any patents or proprietary technology
- Years in business
- Last year's revenues
- Projected revenues for next three years
- Statement of income and expenses for current year
- Financing to date
- Financing requirements
- Intended use of financing
- Management background—who you are and your team's background
- Business plan
- Nature and size of your competitors
- Why your audience should invest

Rehearse your answers to possible questions. Part of practice should include rehearsing answers for the post-talk questions the angels will lob at you. Your answers must be concise and to the point. No long-winded explanations, no let-me-tell-you-a-little-story, no "I don't know, I'll get back to you." So *conjure up dozens of possible questions, and have a snappy answer for each.* Practice in front of different kinds of audiences, so you're ready for

---

"How Much Can You Say in Eight Minutes?"

Here's what the *Entrepreneur's Guide to the Mid-Atlantic Venture Association Fair* recommends:

- The gong really does sound at eight minutes. Rehearse for seven minutes, and keep a steady tempo.
- Don't dwell on your fabulous technology. Focus on the business opportunity, market strategy, customer impact, and competitive edge.
- Stay away from detailed product descriptions. Do provide a sufficient overview of your product or service.
- Slides should be brief and to the point.
- Ensure readability by using the slide-format guidelines provided.
- Don't minimize the importance of good presentation skills. Get all the help you can on the basics.

anything—a questioner with a lisp, speaking heavily accented English, mumbling, whatever. Many entrepreneurs believe the common wisdom that the more questions, the better, and if the angels don't pepper him with them, they're not interested. Untrue. We've heard many pitches that elicited only one or two questions but that got the green light.

THUMBS UP, THUMBS DOWN

At Dinner Club meetings, a presenter is asked to leave the room after the members' questions and answers, so we can raise pros and cons and vote whether to take the next step into due diligence. The comments are sometimes questions, sometimes opinions. "She didn't say anything about the competition," remarked one angel during such a discussion. "I don't understand the technology," said an angel about another company, and then added, "but I think they're in a space we need to look at." It helps supplicants enormously if they have a champion within the group, an angel who knows them and the company and can amplify and explain. One such supporter declared, "These guys are going to be winners." Whether the investors are an ad hoc group of friends or a formal structured angel fund, decisions are often determined by a vote. The Dinner Club votes with a show of hands. A simple majority moves the group into due diligence. When angels are considering how to vote, they examine factors like the ones in the following checklist.

A SIMPLE CHECKLIST

Factors angels consider when deciding whether to invest in an entrepreneur:

PERSONAL ISSUES

Do I know enough about this product/service category to add value?
Do I like and trust the entrepreneur? Is there good chemistry between us?
Is the company a "right fit" for my portfolio? (i.e., Am I looking for diversification or making multiple bets in the same space?)

MANAGEMENT ISSUES

Is the management sufficiently experienced—not just in the product space but in prior start-ups? Is there a leader people will follow?

What gaps are there in the management team? Can the holes be filled with the time and money available?

How does management stack up against the competition?

MARKET ISSUES

Is there a need for the program product or service? Is the solution a "must have" or a "would like to have"?

What is the size of the market? Is it growing or shrinking? Can the company be a leader in the market?

FINANCIAL ISSUES

How soon can the company break even? Are they raising enough money in this round to carry them to profitability—or if not, how much more will be needed?

If the company has been operating a while, are the financial accounts in good order? (If not, run away, don't walk.)

THE GREEN LIGHT

Sometimes even with the best planning, it is something intangible that makes the difference, as you will see in the following story. In mid-2000, a company named JuniorJobs.com made a presentation before the Dinner Club. The company, led by a sixteen-year-old high school junior and advised by his mother, who had driven him to the club meeting, proposed to create a website service that would hook up large employers with part-time teenage employees. It was an intriguing idea, and members saw immediately that it could be very popular both with employers and kids looking for summer or holiday jobs. He not only brought a well-presented PowerPoint slide show, but used heavy metal music as a back-drop—to show how the company would relate to its young consumers. After the presentation and a couple of questions, the young founder left the room. We opened up the discussion, and it was soon clear that most of the members felt that the company was still too unformed, too early in its development for our participation. No angels or other backers were on board yet; the business was still in the planning stage. We voted not to pursue due diligence, and went on to the next business. But that's not the end of the story.

We were deep into discussing a second company, with most members inclined to go further, when a member raised his hand to question the JuniorJobs vote. The member was Art Marks, managing partner of NEA, a large, highly successful venture-capital fund. Art didn't understand why the group wasn't interested in JuniorJobs. He *liked* its concept and didn't get why the members were more impressed with the second presentation. Marks is an investor famous for his savvy selections. As he talked about why he liked JuniorJobs, we could feel the temperature in the room changing. Other voices began to murmur agreement. Someone raised her hand and asked if the group could vote again on JuniorJobs, and so we did.

The vote passed, and we decided to pursue JuniorJobs. The moral of this story is that the idea, the presentation, and the dynamics of the individuals within angel groups can make a huge difference in their response. Angels are no different from other people—they'll defer to experts and vote with the people whose judgment they know and respect. In almost all our votes, we can see angels glancing about, taking note of who's voting for and who's voting against. Hands go up slowly as people read the sentiments of de facto leaders. In the same way, a positive or negative word from an influential member can determine a vote. *You never know what is going to happen during or after your presentation!*

Our group doesn't like to keep people waiting, so we let the entrepreneurs know right after the vote whether we're going ahead. Part of the vote, a postscript, is a request for club members to volunteer for due diligence (a topic that's covered in detail in chapter 5). Although it's usually hard to get businesspeople to join a committee, we rarely have difficulty fielding a strong team. The members most knowledgeable, or most curious, about the new venture readily raise their hands. Due diligence is one of the streamlined features of a structured angel group. With all the experience, education, and talent among our angels, due diligence is done by business pros. And then they share their insights with the rest of the group.

In chapter 5, we'll talk about the need for solid answers to tough questions in due diligence, but suffice it to say that succeeding at the first hurdle of gaining potential investors' interest is only the beginning of the entire process. In this chapter, we have tried to emphasize the importance of preparation and good communication in convincing angels to consider investing in your idea. Whether taking part in a one-on-one discussion or delivering a formal presentation to a venture-fair audience, the winning entrepreneur will be the one who makes an impression and can back it up with a good solid plan. In the following chapter, we will talk about a seldom-discussed aspect of financing your business—the right money instead of *any* money. Finding the right angel is key; heartache can occur if you naively assume that all money is the same.

■ Know your angel group before you approach it. Study the companies it has already invested in and look for what features might have sold them. Talk to prior presenters or investees of the group.

■ Probably the best way to find a structured angel group is through a venture fair. These are announced in the business press, online through websites and e-mail notices, and in event-calendar listings. If these sources don't work, call the largest VC firm in your area and ask about upcoming venture fairs. They usually occur once or twice a year. (See list in Appendix B.)

■ No matter how young and financially strapped your company, hire a professional to design your logo and corporate identity. This is going to be your calling card, literally and figuratively, for years. It should look corporate and established.

■ Angels need to hear about friends-and-family money. It's important to them to know that entrepreneurs have put their own savings into a company, and that people close to them also believe in the venture. Disclose all amounts and terms of any such financing.

■ When talking about your company, include negative information, whether it's the absence of revenues, a patent-infringement lawsuit, or a nasty split with an early founder. Bringing it up first shows candor and honesty. Professional investors will find out eventually, so early disclosure enhances your credibility.

■ Anticipate investor doubts. Address how your company will deal with market risk, technology risk, and execution risk.

■ Even if your company isn't ready to present at a venture fair, or you don't make the cut, pay the fee and attend. You'll acquire reams of practical knowledge about ways to present your company when asking for financing.

4

A Match Made in Heaven:
Finding the Right Partner

Angel investing, despite all the dollar signs and high-tech hype, is about people: listening to people, assessing and judging people, and forming partnerships with people. Entrepreneurs and founders approach angels often believing that they're looking only for money. And sometimes they make the mistake of accepting a deal with an angel or larger investor largely because of the depth of the pockets. *The best deal, every time, is a partnership cemented not only by money but by people who understand, like, and trust each other.* It's a match, not a random pairing. It's not unlike dating—you've got to be wild about your partner, or the relationship isn't going to last. This chapter offers several examples that show what it takes to be a "good partner" (on both sides of the partnership) and what added value a good investor can bring to the relationship. The chapter also offers insight into how to find such partners.

THE IMPORTANCE OF A GOOD REFERRAL

"Morning, Cal. What do you say to a brewski?"

I had to laugh. It was not ten in the morning, but Jerry Bailey, the balding, middle-aged man sitting in front of me, wasn't kidding. In fact, he was all business. Plopping an Igloo cooler in the middle of the desk, he pulled out two ice-cold frosty ones.

"What do you think?" he asked, handing a bottle to me.

I inspected the label. A classy-looking script spelled out Old Dominion Beer, and at the bottom was Jerry's signature. The kicker was in between: It was a pledge of freshness. This was several years before Budweiser began to put brewing dates on its cans and bottle. I laughed, again.

"You mean, 'We serve no beer before its time'?"

"Yeah," said Jerry, "something like that. Serious beer drinkers care about when it was made—whether it's fresh or so old it tastes stale."

I was not a serious beer drinker, but I knew a serious entrepreneur when I saw one and was favorably impressed with Jerry. Also, I put great value on the opinion of the friend who'd sent him to me, as he had a lot of experience with start-ups. I asked Jerry to tell me more about his product.

"With pleasure," he said, "but first things first." He reached into the cooler and extracted two chilled beer mugs. Uncapping one of the bottles, he poured each of us about a third of a glass. "Cheers," he said, smiling. The beer, an amber brew that was neither too light nor too heavy, was excellent, even at ten in the morning.

As Jerry talked, schooling me on the importance of freshness for his product, how much care and attention to detail it required, and why he was so sure that there was a market for this beer, I listened carefully. And through it all, I remembered how good it tasted.

When he stopped to take a breath, I slipped in a question. "What's the downside?"

"Well," he said, still smiling, "I've never run a business before. I spent twenty years in the government as a career civil servant. But I'm so sure this is a good idea that I quit to pursue this dream full time." He went on to tell me how he had been peddling the beer almost door-to-door.

It was my turn to smile, but I did so mentally. Of the several investment criteria angels like before considering an investment, he'd already met most of them. The only thing he lacked was relevant business experience. But the more Jerry talked, the less I worried about that.

As soon as he left, I was on the phone. By noon, I had found enough investor friends to round out the $250,000 needed to back Old Dominion Brewing Co. in its first outside round of financing. It has turned out to be one of the best, and soberest, decisions I ever made.

Jerry Bailey first came to me because he was referred by a good friend of mine. I knew next to nothing of the investment I was going to hear about. All I knew was the character of the person who had started the ball rolling, and that was enough to give the process a good push. The friend, a lawyer named Bill Mutryn, had credibility, having been involved in numerous successful start-ups. When Bill told me that he was investing in the deal not money, but his own time and energy, providing legal services in return for equity, that gave Jerry Bailey the ultimate personal seal of approval.

Of course, there were other features of Jerry's business that were attractive. He had already satisfied one of the first requirements of angel investing by rounding up $500,000 from family and friends. He had found close to thirty investors, not only family but neighbors and high-income professionals. Many others clearly believed in Jerry. This is an unusually large number of people for a founder to enlist and maintain—investors can be very high-maintenance, wanting constant updates about developments and company progress, and regular hand-holding.

Most entrepreneurs prefer to be in bed with fewer people. By nature strong-willed and individualistic, founders often have a hard time answering to more than a few backers. Like Tom First and Tom Scott of Nantucket Nectars, many are most comfortable with a single angel like Mike Egan and would chafe under the yoke of a multi-angel partnership like Bailey had forged. But his numerous investors had a big upside, especially for him as the novice entrepreneur: They were a constant and diverse source of crucial advice. He intuitively knew that the less experience he had, the more angels he needed to guide his way.

Another element of his business that reflected his character was what he was doing to sell the beer. He had an innate understanding of what works in sales—face-to-face persuasion. He had been driving around the metro area going from restaurants to bars, asking bartenders and managers to try his beer, and making sales on the spot. He was a natural salesman, backed by a great product.

Probably what clinched the deal for me—when I stopped thinking, "Is this a good investment?" and turned my thoughts to "Where can I find the money?"—was yet another personal quality of Jerry Bailey's. The man was candid and honest. He didn't try to recast his years in government as really a business experience and reinvent himself as a guy well versed in the for-profit world. He was upfront about his lack of familiarity with many elements of entrepreneurship. He didn't know much about marketing, distribution, strategic partnerships, or finance, but he knew not to try to bluff.

THE COST OF CHOOSING THE WRONG PARTNER

Bailey's investor-partners gave him the financial, professional, and psychic support that enabled him to build his business. On the other hand, the wrong partners can have just the opposite effect. Founders sometimes learn this the hard way. A businessman who launched a microbrewery similar to Old Dominion Brewing made a number of alliances that soured his venture quicker than rumors of urine in the brew would have. The forty-four-year-old had grown tired of his nine-to-five job and came up with a bright idea for a new beer called Good Times Brew (we've changed the name here). He plowed enormous amounts of time and friends-and-family money into his company, and with a pleasant-tasting product and clever marketing campaign, he shipped close to 400,000 cases of Good Times Brew in the first six months of operation.

He was growing so fast that national distributors were begging him to let them handle the product. However, they insisted that he launch a national marketing campaign in conjunction with their efforts, and the entrepreneur didn't have the money. So he turned to the first angel who could give him the money he needed and traded 15 percent of his company for the investment. As the businessman would discover, this angel's first priority was a hefty piece of the action, not the company's long-term well-being.

The company blossomed for a few years until the founder decided to explore going public. He needed the capital an IPO would provide and was sure his company would be a big hit in the open market. It never happened. The SEC informed him that his company could not go public if a large portion of it, like the 15 percent held by the angel, was owned by a single individual. The whole matter went into litigation, where it remains today, and Good Times Brew went flat. *Remember that all three factors need to combine to ensure a good relationship—understanding, liking each other, and trusting each other.*

GOOD PARTNERSHIPS DON'T JUST HAPPEN

Jerry Bailey was smarter about his angels. He didn't pay too high a price for their money, and he found people whose expectations and interests were in line with his. Old Dominion Beer was a huge commercial success, and the brewery won awards for the quality of its beer. Sales increased every year, Bailey added new varieties of his drink, large companies like Host Marriott Services wanted partnerships, and Old Dominion became the dominant microbrewery in the Washington, D.C., area.

Bailey has been equally attentive to the needs of his investors. Once a year, Old Dominion holds a shareholders' meeting at the brewery. Seated in folding chairs assembled on the cement warehouse floor next to the bottling line, investors hear about their company's progress and its managers' plans for the future. When the meeting is over, everyone adjourns to picnic tables for a meal of bratwurst, beans, and beer.

Bailey also writes to his investors three or four times a year, giving them a summary of financial activity and, even more vital, his thoughts on how the business is going and a candid assessment of his decisions. As he did in that first meeting, he doesn't sugarcoat problems, and it's not unusual for investors to read about Bailey's mistakes. A letter might confess, "My naiveté really cost us on this one. The new bottling line I had allowed for in projections to be completed in three months took twice that long and was 50 percent more expensive than I had thought it would be."

Jerry Bailey's partnership with his investors has been solidified and nurtured. The strength of this relationship helped the company survive a potentially disastrous omission in his initial negotiation of terms with his angels.

A very early discussion between founders and business angels needs to explore each person's expectations for the investment, and "expectations" mean more than unbridled optimism over the company's future. Of course, everyone hopes that the start-up will hit a home run, and there will probably be lots of bantering about a skyrocketing IPO or a fat acquisition. Expectations of a home run, big payday, or sensational return should be talked about in detail, with numbers attached. Typically, venture-capital firms look for an annual return of 30 to 50 percent compounded, or three to five times their invested dollars in three to five years (lofty expectations are the main reason VC firms concentrate in the mercurial high-tech sector). While angels tend to be less demanding of their entrepreneurial partners, since financial gain usually isn't the sole reason they invest, they nevertheless have firm ideas of how they want their money to perform. And founders and angels should continue to talk about expectations even after everyone's arrived on the same page, because people's ideas of success can change over time.

Expectations can't be talked about without getting into possible and probable exit strategies, which is what Jerry Bailey neglected. He assumed that everyone wanted to be partners for the long haul, which I discovered meant many years. Some of his angels were in for the long term and felt that Old Dominion had hit one out of the park, while others felt that doubling, tripling, or even quadrupling their money was great but not sending them to the Ferrari dealership. Enticed by other investments, these angels told Bailey that they wanted a way to sell their privately held shares. They felt that the company had gone through its most rapid growth phase and did not want to continue investing in what was looking like a mature company.

Fortunately, Bailey and his angel investors had a good understanding of each other, despite this obvious hole in their talks. Bailey could have stuck to the original terms of their investment, which didn't specify an exit strategy and left the investors to their own devices in finding a way to unload their Old Dominion holdings. But he didn't. Although he loved being in the brewery business, he opened negotiations for selling his company to a major beer manufacturer. When that deal was voted down by Bailey's board of directors, he devised another solution. Knowing that some of his angels believed the company still had plenty of upside potential, he offered to arrange for the private sale of shares from investors who wanted out to existing angels who wanted to increase their holdings, as well as to new angels. In essence, he became a market maker.

Old Dominion's belated exit strategy worked for everyone because Bailey and his angels were well matched. Even with key elements of their relationship undefined, each side understood and trusted the other enough to smooth over a very sticky situation. *Picking the right angel partner requires sharing views on a wide range of personal and business issues.*

Again, the give-and-take is like *The Dating Game*—people contemplating marriage explore their would-be partners' views on children, money, religion, family, and lifestyle. The equivalent checklist for an entrepreneur-angel partnership would cover not only exit strategies but follow-on investments, rates of return, and a time frame for certain investment or company benchmarks, like profitability, and hiring plan for key staff. Angels don't want to handcuff entrepreneurs with rigid performance criteria, but they do expect these issues to be raised and explored, not only at the beginning of the relationship but throughout.

ANGELS LIKE PEOPLE LIKE THEMSELVES

Angels come in all shapes and sizes. Friends, neighbors, business associates, lawyers, accountants, tennis partners—they're all potential angels, but each is different. While venture capitalists are motivated almost exclusively by financial returns, angels look for more in a start-up than a big payday. As we've talked about, the passive angel is a rare bird—most angels want to be involved in their ventures. How much involvement is usually a matter of personal experience, temperament, and time, and can change over the life of an investment. While the personal elements of the angel-founder relationship may be difficult to set down on paper, they have to be raised. There needs to be a meeting of the minds.

Business-school consultants who track private investment activity say that angels are looking for entrepreneurs who are enthusiastic and trustworthy, who possess expertise, and whom they like. *Likeability and personal chemistry are fundamental to a good partnership.* For some angels, what makes a founder likable is a readiness to listen. "I only invest in entrepreneurs who know how to listen," says the manager of an angel group. A quality that can turn off investors and angels is pushiness.

Pushiness is not the same as persistence, a positive characteristic. Pushiness has a tinge of inappropriate aggressiveness. Being pushy is buttonholing people in a public restroom; being persistent is hanging around the lobby maneuvering for an opportune time to "by chance" bump into someone you want to talk to. Those who insist on always being right and dominating a relationship will find themselves alone at the altar. Entrepreneurs are often told, "Don't take no for an answer," but this doesn't mean bombarding angels with phone calls or forcing issues that need time to develop. It's just like dating—jumping your date on your first outing will get the door slammed in your face.

Founders and start-up artists can get a good sense of the kind of people that angels gravitate toward by looking at an angel's background. For example, angel Steve Walker looks for company founders on whom he can be an early and active influence. The last thing he wants is to be an anonymous, one-of-the-pack investor. He looks for a hands-on relationship and a founder who can benefit from his extensive experience.

Walker is the kind of man who likes to build things, companies as well as relationships. He left a career with the National Security Agency as soon as he clocked twenty years, even though he was only thirty-nine, so he could create his own company. He formed Trusted Information Systems (TIS), which offered advice on safeguarding computer systems, and set up shop in his home. Toiling at his new venture for two years, adding clients and carving out partnerships with government agencies, he soon outgrew the home office. His building efforts gathered speed.

"In 1985, there were five of us, then there were eighteen of us, then there were thirty-five of us. We were consulting in network security and computer security for IBM, DEC, Cray, all the computer manufacturers. Then we started doing research for DARPA [Defense Advanced Research Project Agency, the direct antecedent of the Internet] and NSA. We had a great business going," he said.

Thirteen years later, Walker's dedication to building a company peaked, and he sold TIS for $350 million, with his share coming to $70 million. Rather than tuck it away, he decided to build again. He hung out a shingle for Steve Walker & Associates, yet another incursion into the consulting business, this time advising new companies on how to structure their ventures as well as providing angel financing. Besides a penchant for building things, another theme in Walker's thinking is intense involvement.

There's nothing dilettantish about his efforts—he threw himself into the culture and business of entrepreneurship. He ticks off all the angel groups and venture-capital firms he hooked up with. "When I started this, I joined the Dinner Club and Capital Investors. I also joined Draper, NextGen, and Novak Biddle because I really wanted to find out how these people work. I became a limited partner in all of them. The idea was that I was going to learn about how to do this because I've been *running* a company," he says, pointing out that until this time, his knowledge of new businesses had been one-sided.

He quickly honed his skills as an insightful angel investor and applied his newfound education to a host of investments. Closely studying BioNetrix, which was developing advanced techniques for computer security systems, Walker detected a number of holes in its management. The company badly needed an older, wiser executive who had the kind of experience and contacts that it would take the company's young founder years to acquire—someone with gray in his hair and gold in his Palm Pilot. Walker helped match BioNetrix with one of the titans of the northern Virginia technology world, Bill Melton, the founder and onetime CEO of

CyberCash, VeriFone, and Transaction Network Systems, and a board member of AOL. Walker knew what BioNetrix needed and that, with a net worth of many millions, Melton wasn't looking for a job.

Melton joined the BioNetrix board and became instrumental in the company's growth. He provided contact names and introductions to people at companies that BioNetrix needed to partner with and helped it negotiate these partnerships. And he showed the young company how superangels and venture capitalists think, and helped the founder structure the terms for the next round of financing. (We will give you further insights about the BioNetrix story in chapter 7.)

If you ask Steve Walker why he invests in a company, he's likely to reply, "I love being there—I love being there first." It's a good bet that that desire to be ahead of the parade, to break new ground, is what he looks for in an entrepreneur, too. The picture of Walker that emerges is of an angel who looks for people like himself—a quick learner with enormous energy and vision who can readily turn an idea into a going concern.

TALKING THE SAME LANGUAGE

The perfect angel match involves not only simpatico personalities and outlook but an investor and founder with similar backgrounds and experience—two people who talk the same language. Although an identical matchup may be hard to find, entrepreneurs should be looking for and listening to angels whose technologies or markets overlap theirs. Sometimes, the common ground may be the simple fact that an angel has direct experience with a competitor that a start-up may be facing.

For example, there was much about Mark Merrick, founder of Step 9, for the dinner club angels to like. His résumé was packed with years of solving business problems with Arthur Andersen, and his company offered a high-tech solution and low-tech service to a potentially lucrative telecommunications niche. The breakup of AT&T and the Bell system in the 1980s spawned the creation of CLECs, community local exchange carriers, which basically were local phone companies. Merrick and his partners, who were consultants, lawyers, and engineers, were intimately familiar with the inner workings of CLECs and recognized a glaring problem in their day-to-day operations: a need for back-office support, from sales to tech support. Thus Step 9 developed a software package to handle a CLEC's accounting, billing and statement flow, and record-keeping. It could integrate a carrier's front office, back office, and trading partners—all the pieces a phone company needed for a smooth operation. It was a solution-in-a-box.

Merrick's presentation hooked us, and we voted to go into due diligence (a subject covered in detail in chapter 5). A big question we had was the nature of the market the company was aiming for and whether Step 9 could be a leader in serving it. Various club members volunteered to serve on the due-diligence committee, including Michael Rowny, who had once been senior vice president in charge of MCI's international acquisitions. Rowny was an ideal person to poke inside Step 9. He knew the industry, and he knew what was needed in an enterprise aiming to serve it. And he was acutely aware of the gap in CLEC operations that begged for a company like Step 9 to fill.

Rowny and Merrick have very different personalities, but they clicked. The former MCI exec is quiet, thoughtful, and given to concise answers, while the entrepreneur is intense and articulate. Early in their meetings, Rowny went out of his way to get to know Merrick. They had dinner together, just the two of them, so Rowny could learn about the man he was thinking about making a large investment with. What were Merrick's values? Where did family life fit in with his work? How did he make hard decisions? What was important to him—what got him out of bed in the morning?

Rowny emerged from the due-diligence meetings with an insider's perspective. He was sold on Merrick the entrepreneur and the person. He saw that the company's opportunity to seize its niche was bigger than originally thought, and that Step 9 would need more than it was asking for. Rather than being discouraged by a start-up that would require more than this group of angels could provide, Rowny proposed a solution.

"We need a VC to lead this deal," he told club members, saying that the new company needed $3 million to $4 million to get launched. He also explained that he managed a fund called Rowny Capital that had the wherewithal to step in. "We would be willing to lead and put $1 million into Step 9."

Rowny believed that he could contribute more to Step 9 than money. Young entrepreneurs usually begin a company with close friends, and as the venture grows, they have a difficult time separating their friendship from tough business decisions. Rowny had seen founders encounter this obstacle before, and he thought he could provide Merrick with mentor-like advice to help him address it.

Rowny was the perfect angel for Step 9, bringing to the fledgling company not only financial support but market expertise, industry knowledge, and managerial wisdom. One of our dinner clubs offered the new venture a package with Rowny Capital as lead VC, the club as co-investor at $500,000, individual members for $180,000, and Mike Rowny as a board member. We expected Step 9 to accept our offer but didn't expect such an enthusiastic response. Mike Rowny was not only known to them but the kind of consultant they had been looking to hire. Now he was coming to them gratis, along with all his wisdom.

A perfect match like Rowny adds value to everyone involved in a deal. Merrick and his partners got the services of a sophisticated board member who had spent ten years working in the space they were going after and who could help them recruit additional talent. And the dinner club got in on the ground floor of an investment that soon showed progress—in the next round, its value was pegged at more than four times our valuation.

THE BEST FIT COMES FROM YOUR OWN INDUSTRY BACKYARD

One way entrepreneurs and founders can narrow their search for the perfect angel is by looking at individuals or groups that specialize in their industry. Angels may concentrate their investments on not just technology companies but an even smaller slice of the industry, like Internet-related or software firms. Angels may limit their investments to companies mainly in low-tech industries, in foreign markets, owned by women, in life sciences or medical technology, or that address social or environmental needs.

The chances of a successful partnership between entrepreneur and angel multiply when everyone at the table is well versed in the same business, its tools or technology, and its market. A peek inside one of the country's premier high-tech angel clubs, our neighbor Capital Investors, shows how specializing can generate phenomenal synergy between an entrepreneur and angel.

Capital Investors, considered a group of superangels, is composed of business leaders whose technology companies have brought them extreme wealth. There's Steve Case of AOL fame, Alex Mandl of Teligent, Michael Saylor with MicroStrategy, John Sidgmore of MCI WorldCom, Mario Morino, former vice chairman of Legent, Mark Warner, a co-founder of Nextel, Netscape creator Marc Andreessen, and Alan Spoon, president of the Washington Post Co. As with most angel groups, members each put in an initial $100,000, with more money coming later depending on the deals.

Like the Dinner Club, Capital Investors was the net result of a couple of friends and successful tech guys sitting around talking about all the new ventures cropping up in the Washington, D.C., area and how hard it is to get a great idea off the ground. Knowing from firsthand experience that the hardest money to find is seed capital, the seasoned investors decided to band together to funnel some of their handsome profits into like-minded start-ups. They decided to invest between $100,000 and $750,000, and occasionally more, to companies working on Internet and Internet content technology, software, telecommunications, new-generation media, or tech services. The group also pledged to try to stick to investments in which they are among the first backers—they want enterprises that have been making progress on friends-and-family money and are now looking beyond Mom, Dad, and the neighbors.

The tale of Greg Keogh and his brothers Jonathan and Timothy, who founded a company called Zona Financiera, illustrates how a highly specialized angel group like Capital Investors fashions successful partnerships. Capital Investors first heard about Zona through a member who had met Greg Keogh months earlier. The referral came with enthusiasm for the energy of Keogh and his brothers—and a little confusion about what exactly the company did. "I'm not sure what Zona's all about, but Greg sounds so good at what he's doing and creating something that nobody has done before, let's throw some money at them," he told the Capital Investors angels. As the group learned when Keogh made his presentation, Zona Financiera is an online services company providing financial information to Web users in Latin America. The company's name is Spanish for "zone of finance," and it was aiming to launch a website that offered interactive information on bank loan rates for mortgages and cars, credit-card interest rates, insurance policies, financial futures, and stock quotes, to Spanish- and Portuguese-speaking people.

However, the attractiveness of the idea—to grab "virgin" Internet real estate in Latin America and become a southern-hemisphere Amazon.com in the financial-services field—was at first overshadowed by the questions surrounding the Keoghs. Who were these guys, what did they know about Latin America, and did they have the stuff to really create such a website? The answers turned out to be almost more intriguing than the business concept.

Greg Keogh, who spoke Spanish like a native, had lived and worked in South America as an officer of the Central Intelligence Agency. Though he offered few details about his work there, his résumé stated that he "acted as contact between the U.S. and rebel forces and extreme right-wing political factions." His brothers were no less qualified for their positions in Zona. Timothy was the software guru, having managed Intuit's Web and interactive insurance systems. Jonathan was another webhead, having garnered experience as a webmaster for AOL in Canada. Adding to the trifecta of the Keogh brothers' history was an earlier experience with developing a loan-quoting engine for people shopping for mortgages online. The business failed but gave them up-close-and-personal experience with the financial-services market.

The Keogh brothers turned the basement of their parents' home into their office and set about to create "the one source for online personal finance in Latin America." Their bank account held about $200,000 from their savings, and then was infused with $400,000, proceeds from the sale of the licensing technology from the loan-quoting business.

Greg Keogh made a flawless twenty-minute pitch to Capital Investors, his smooth delivery evidence of an entrepreneur accustomed to reaching out to investors. In some ways, he was preaching to the choir. His audience probably knew as much about the Web technology Zona was developing as did Keogh's brothers, and especially where he might trip over land mines or find easy going. The questions from this Net-savvy group came fast. One person wanted to know the status of Internet service providers (ISPs) operating in the region. Another angel asked about competition from a Venezuelan media company. Keogh completed his presentation and waited to hear the verdict from this group of tech angels.

Capital Investors' decision rang loud and clear with the voice of experience. The angels opted to put money into Zona but with a proposed valuation of $2 million, less than half of what Greg Keogh believed his company was worth. "You have three brothers in a basement with a T-1 line who'd made some progress in making contacts—how do you value that?" reflected Capital Investors manager Jeff Tonkel.

Negotiations for the deal didn't sail smoothly, even with everyone understanding the business model. Capital Investors altered the terms from an equity investment to a convertible note with an option to convert at a discount in the next round of financing. Valuation figures, conversion terms, and equity percentages went back and forth between Zona and Capital Investors, and it required six weeks of negotiating to strike a deal. Capital Investors sealed the deal with a valuation of $3.5 million—almost twice the initial assessment—and $300,000 for notes convertible at 50 percent of the price of the next financing, making their stake in the Keogh's venture 18.5 percent.

The valuation doubled because the business idea was very sound. The Keoghs were targeting a specialized underserved market and were the first to do so with this service. They captured the business opportunity well in their plan, and they were convincing to angels that they could pull it off quickly. The tough negotiating was about the pieces of the deal and, once they shook hands, didn't spill over to the angels' commitment to Zona. The marriage between Zona and Capital Investors was surely made in heaven. Instead of chasing after several individual angels and consultants to help them, they got a concentrated, interested group of investors with expertise in the business markets vital to their plan. Within this structured angel group were several well-connected business executives. Capital Investors member Marc Andreessen contacted some of his techie buddies to research competition in the Latin space. Teligent founder Alex Mandl checked out technology with former AT&T associates. Club manager Jeff Tonkel used his position at the investment banking firm of Friedman Billings Ramsey to sift through valuation comparisons from analysts covering telecommunications and ISP markets.

Zona's angels rallied around the brothers, filling marketing and knowledge holes as the company gathered speed. Other angel groups undoubtedly would have been as supportive as Capital Investors, but it's hard to imagine a comparable group of technological and entrepreneurial wizards stepping forward to partner with three-guys-in-a-basement-with-a-T-1-line.

STICKING CLOSE TO HOME: FINDING LOCAL INVESTORS

Angel investors are notoriously small-minded—geographically, that is. The Dinner Club and eMedia, as well as high-profile clubs like Capital Investors, Tri-State Venture Group, and Band of Angels in Silicon Valley draw a line around their areas and insist that companies they look at be headquartered locally. Venture-capital firms, in contrast, roam the map for promising start-ups. The reasons angels prefer to stick close to home are tied to the unique nature of this kind of investing. Angels like to be involved in their companies beyond sitting on an advisory board or board of directors; sometimes angels take paid positions as consultants—or in some cases may even become full-time executives of the company. Forming a relationship with a founder so that decisions and quandaries can be talked about comfortably is difficult without regular face-to-face contact. Angels, like anyone else, don't want to fly thousands of miles for a lunch meeting at which important business may or may not come up.

One trend appears to be with angel groups becoming even more concentrated on local business, not expanding their wings. The Dinner Club has been cloning its concept and now has affiliated Dinner Clubs in major metropolitan areas around the country.

While angels may have a firm idea of their boundaries, entrepreneurs and founders may be uncertain. "A hands-on angel partner is great," they may reason, "but my budding enterprise needs to find money wherever it can." Any venture with legs arrives at this point: When is a business sufficiently launched and funded that it has to look outside its neighborhood for financing? Mary Naylor, the ambitious CEO of VIPdesk, faced this dilemma. Her company had a long history and profitable track record even before she sought out angels, and she was looking toward distant horizons to expand the business.

Naylor was a hustling start-up artist with a novel idea years before the Golden Age of Entrepreneurs. In the early 1980s, she had been working as a corporate trainer in Los Angeles and encountered a company offering concierge services to its employees. Thinking she'd like to create such a company in the Washington, D.C., area, she talked to the founder and summoned the nerve to start her own business. In 1986, barely in her twenties, Naylor began Capitol Concierge, a personal-services firm that did errands, arranged for concert tickets, sent flowers, and did almost anything else her corporate clients requested. It was a bricks-and-mortar company that placed its concierges in an office building to provide employees with personal services. Corporations signed up because providing for daily time-consuming tasks like picking up dry cleaning or walking a dog freed up employee time for work, and the company could offer it as a valuable perk to retain and recruit people.

The number of contracts and clients for Capitol Concierge multiplied, and in 1997, Naylor extended her enterprise to concierge service by telephone, which she called the Concierge Club. Two years later, she added yet another outlet for her personal-services firm, a click-and-order website offering a virtual personal assistant day or night. With this latest incarnation came the name, VIPdesk. Naylor's business was growing by leaps and bounds. She had representatives serving eighty local corporate clients and was booking $6 million in revenues.

Naylor had angel backing when she first started Capitol Concierge, including an investor who became a member of the Dinner Club, but when she decided to spread out and go after clients in other regions, she looked farther afield. This time she figured that money from anywhere, especially the deep pockets of West Coast venture capitalists and angels, would do the job. Her company was developed and aged enough that she felt it needed bucks more than board members. In the hunt for $3 million to $6 million, she sought out Silicon Valley's Sand Hill Road glamour VCs, who at first greeted her with open arms and enthusiastic questions. With dollar signs dancing in her eyes, Naylor returned their flirtations and for months traveled back and forth between the coasts to romance them. In the end, she went home empty-handed. They told her they don't do early-stage, East Coast investing.

She reflected about the experience: "I learned in the process that because the deal flow is so great right now—there are so many phenomenal opportunities to look at, purely from a bandwidth or resource point of view—that VCs in California typically don't have the time to travel for a day to the East Coast for a board meeting. And they want a co-lead that's on the East Coast. The real point is that the entrepreneur needs to do his or her research on the VCs, because they all do certain deals."

So Naylor put away her roll-on suitcase and went calling on local angels and investor groups and made a presentation at the Mid-Atlantic Venture Fair, which was holding its annual gathering in Washington. Venture fairs are a show-and-tell for young companies looking for financing. Companies, usually its founder or CEO, give ten-minute Power-Point presentations to audiences that easily run into the hundreds, made up of angels, superangels, venture capitalists, investment bankers, and others involved in the start-up field, like M&A lawyers and accountants. Applying the same kind of insight she used to build a business to her appearance at the fair, Naylor decided she needed to stand out from the sixty other eager presenters. So she set up a shoeshine stand in the lobby and hired someone to provide a free buff-and-polish to anyone. And as the attendees' shoes acquired a high gloss, Naylor was there talking about VIPdesk and handing out company literature.

She succeeded. Within a month of her presentation at the fair, she had offers of financing from two major regional investment firms. People with both of the funds, Pennsylvania Early Stage Partners and Scripps Ventures, remembered the friendly blonde woman at the shoeshine stand who talked about her Web-based personal-services company and stuck a business plan under their noses.

Naylor also managed to secure local angel financing, including a $460,000 commitment from the Dinner Club as well as an infusion from the Washington-based Women's Growth Capital Fund, and two superangels. At the end of her travels, this time by car rather than plane, Naylor had managed to find $3.75 million, all from regional sources. And though she wasn't looking for a partnership relationship, she found that too.

Mary Naylor learned that you're never too old for a well-connected partner. "We were looking for financing alone, but some obvious strategic partners emerged. We got funding from people who could provide us with more than money in terms of resources, connections, and opening doors. We like portfolio companies where there are synergies. We welcome help. From the standpoint of accessibility—say you want one of your board members to interview a key hire or you need a quick meeting—time and pure access are vital. But the most important thing is that it be the best fit, from the standpoint of what you're trying to do," she concluded. Naylor had learned a valuable lesson about investors bringing more than money to the game. Later, her original investors helped arrange a larger round of funding and provided valuable introductions to strategic customers. Both the original "seed" angel investors and those angels who were part of the Dinner Club contributed customer contacts, future financial sources, and management candidates to the entrepreneur because it was mutually beneficial. All part of finding partners who are "the right fit."

We can't emphasize enough the need for finding and wooing the right angel—not just one with a big checkbook. The right angel brings industry knowledge and deal knowledge as well as a vision about the future resource needs of the enterprise. A growing source for warm money—and enough of it—is angel clubs and funds, which are featured in the next chapter, on structured angel groups.

■ Perhaps the single most important quality that determines the success of an angel-entrepreneur partnership is personal trust. If you have any doubts about an individual's honesty and candor, don't do the deal. This applies to both sides of the deal—it must feel right to both entrepreneur and investor. Just consider the two very different outcomes of the microbreweries mentioned in this chapter. One went on to great success with a team of supportive investors; the other ended up floundering in litigation.

■ Educate yourself about the experiences and expertise of individual angels you'll be meeting. Information about their investments and professional history can often be found through websites, industry newsletters, and regional business publications. Also note the criteria they use in making investments, and strictly adhere to them. Otherwise, it's like getting a résumé from a graphic designer when you've advertised for a marketing person—highly annoying and quick to label the sender as clueless, desperate, or both.

■ Rather than look for angels with expertise in your corner of an industry, identify the leaders in your business and see if they have any angel affiliations. For example, Michael Rowny at Step 9 is possibly an illustration of serendipity, but the entrepreneurs could easily have sought him out. Maybe that is the point: They were lucky, but they could have *made* it happen.

Remember:

■ The entrepreneur benefits from good connections to angels.

■ The angel should understand, like, and trust the entrepreneur . . . and charisma can outweigh a failed business (as in the Keogh brothers' case).

■ The ideal angel has technical or market background in the same area as the entrepreneur.

- **The angel is geographically close to the entrepreneur.** There are great benefits of having local contacts, easy access for meetings, and familiarity with the regional business-community infrastructure.

- **Candor is admired by angels,** who have been there, done that themselves—either in their own businesses or their investment careers. As illustrated by Jerry Bailey's success finding money for his Old Dominion Brewing, honesty is certainly the best policy.

5

Passing Inspection:
The Due-Diligence Process

Finding an angel investor is a series of competitions, with each round getting more demanding and more difficult. The entrepreneur first must gain access to an angel and request an opportunity to make a presentation. The second round is the presentation itself, and if you're still standing after that, it's on to due diligence. Due diligence might consist of a few phone calls and a visit or two, or weeks of meetings, documents flying back and forth, and questions, questions, questions. If angel investing were *The Dating Game,* due diligence would be the snoop through your date's closet and meeting the parents, and negotiations would be deciding prenuptials and how much to spend on the engagement ring.

This chapter describes how the due-diligence process that follows a handshake either makes or breaks the marriage between entrepreneur and funding partner.

WHO CONDUCTS THE DUE-DILIGENCE PROCESS— AND WHAT THEY'RE LOOKING FOR

Angel due diligence, compared with that of VCs, tends to rely less on financial or market data, since with a start-up there's usually very little of it, and more on insight and experience. Also, most of these people have day jobs, and so their due-diligence tasks have to be squeezed into a few calls during the day, then nights and weekends.

At our angel-club dinners, we decide which members will work with the managers to conduct the due diligence for a company as soon as we vote, and the people who volunteer are usually experts in a related field and know something about the business they'll be probing. They may or may not have formal training but have years of practical experience as accountants, lawyers, or management consultants. And their familiarity with the business may encompass a broad industry, rather than the specific sector. Sometimes an angel group hires experts to help examine a target company. Rare but not unheard of is bringing in a private investigator to check out a founder and his company. A PI can verify academic degrees and report on an individual's personal financial history.

An especially tricky area of due diligence is checking out new technology or proprietary processes, and determining if they're as wonderful and workable as the founder claims. This task can sound like listening to Urdu, given the sophistication of the software and Internet technology that newcomers are developing. In these situations, when the technology is way over their heads, angels often mimic their bigger VC siblings. They do what the international financier George Soros has done—go directly to the top programmer, scientist, or developer and have him or her explain it—or they bring in an outside technical expert to talk with the inventor.

Another murky area for due diligence is assessing whether an entrepreneur's projections for growth are realistic. We all believe we can win the lottery—why else would we buy a ticket? But the odds are something else, and this is where an angel has to probe. *Be prepared to share your thinking and sources of information on all your assumptions* (and it better be more than a dartboard!).

Due diligence will probably be carried out by two or three angels, each with a slightly different perspective. What exactly will they be poking into? The answer is "As much as there is," which may not be a lot. Due diligence for angels looking at a brand-new company is art more than science. The usual yardsticks for judging performance—customers, suppliers, financial history, employees and employee contracts, manufacturing, and distribution—may not exist, yet.

The essence of productive due diligence is the quality of the questions. Anyone performing a due-diligence examination can't assume that everything an entrepreneur says is true or accurate. In the same vein, a skilled due-diligence examiner doesn't assume that what other examiners have looked at, like plans, references, and contracts, have actually been examined. The best information for due diligence is firsthand information, and this is what investors should be after.

A due-diligence committee will ask to review numerous documents and for answers to all sorts of questions. Exhibit 5–1 offers a shopping list of the information an angel wants, whether up front or sometime during the process.

Exhibit 5–1:
Information Potential Investors
Want During Due Diligence

- Bios and work history of the founder and other key executives. The names of business references.
- Bios and background of directors and members of any advisory board.
- Amount of officer compensation and company ownership of management (a capitalization table).
- Any past or pending legal action (lawsuits, tax liability, criminal or civil convictions) involving any company executive or the firm.
- Employees: who, how many, plans for future hiring. Background of marquee names or anyone in the company who is well known in an industry. Give résumés.
- Industry details: size, geography, growth rate, barriers to entry, success rate of newcomers, regulations.
- Technology, products, and services: time and cost of development, unique features, flaws or shortcomings, demand, profit margin, production timetable, status of patents, market share of competitors.
- Intellectual property protection—pending or approved? Patents, pending or approved? If not approved, expert opinion as to a patent's value.

- Competitors: Five or ten largest and their market share, financial health, strengths and weaknesses, features that distinguish each, expectations for growth or changes, your company's relationship with them. (Never say there are none.)
- Suppliers, off-site manufacturers, contractors: Size, financial health, union status, how selected, problems to date or anticipated, alternative or secondary sources.
- Marketing and sales: Strategy, contracts or letters of intent from customers, method of sales, financing terms for customers, warranties or guarantees made, joint venture agreements.
- Financials: Income and expenses, fluctuations in cash burn rate, retained earnings or paid-in capital, liabilities, assets, access to credit or working capital, type, class, and distribution of stock, bank and accounting references, in-house accounting procedures.
- Basis for current valuation and projected financial needs and growth.
- Business plans given to prior investors.

Daunting as the list in Exhibit 5–1 is, it isn't complete or exhaustive. Angel investors are also going to want references from an entrepreneur. In using references as a source of information, we apply the "Rule of 21." We ask for three references—names of customers, business clients, personal references, industry professionals—and call each one. During those calls, we ask each person for the names of one or two other people who know the entrepreneur, then ask for one or two names from each of those people. It's like a telephone tree, and pretty soon we've talked to at least twenty-one people who have some knowledge of the entrepreneur. This gives us a pretty good picture of who we're dealing with.

If the angels are doing a thorough job, they spend a lot of time on the phone talking to references and people on the periphery of your business. They may call your landlord to verify your lease; your clients, customers, and suppliers; your banker to ask about your account history; your former employer; or your insurance broker. They may ask touchy questions about your character flaws or work habits. Don't despair—it's a good sign. And an angel isn't going to spend that kind of effort on a start-up that isn't intriguing. Lots of tough questions also show thoroughness. Neither party, you or your angel, wants surprises after the deal is done. *That's* when things can get ugly.

Another less formal but no less vital part of due diligence is getting to know a founder personally. This may sound like sensitive, New Age stuff, but don't dismiss it. Angels are acutely aware that, ultimately, their assessment of a brand-new business may come down to instincts about the character and competence of the founder. And the best way to discover this is in face-to-face meetings, formal and informal. We know an angel who claims he never invests in a company until he's had the founder drive him somewhere. At some point during the negotiations, he arranges for the founder to pick him up and do the driving. His theory is that you can tell how someone manages the world by the way he or she drives. We also know angels who go to quirky lengths to play golf or tennis with someone, again in the belief that how people conduct themselves in a competitive situation reveals volumes about their values and attitudes.

One of the more extreme instances of getting-to-know-you is the Washington-area angel who always hosts a small cocktail or dinner party for a target company's founder or entrepreneur. The guest list usually includes businesspeople in the same industry, associates of the investor, spouses—and, unknown to the group, a professional psychologist. After the affair, everyone departs except for the investor and psychologist, who delivers a full report on the entrepreneur's behavior and personality. Clearly, this investor does not like surprises from the entrepreneurs he invests in.

Angels whose due diligence has rested largely on phone conversations with an entrepreneur have come to regret it. *So be prepared for lots of up-close-and-personal*—family talk, bull sessions, blue-sky musings, and questions about what keeps you awake at night.

We've witnessed successful due diligence that sails through in a week, and we've seen due diligence that's dragged on for several months. But if there's any generalization that rings true most often, it's that good deals get done quickly. After two or three meetings, we have a sense of whether the deal will happen smoothly and quickly. But if meetings drag on, with agendas and papers going back and forth, the investment probably won't happen. Angels don't have much tolerance for extra meetings, and if entrepreneurs don't have their ducks all lined up, the deal will probably die.

NON-DISCLOSURE AGREEMENTS: PROTECTING CONFIDENTIALITY DURING DUE DILIGENCE

How due diligence unfolds depends on the angels and the business. Before due diligence begins, an entrepreneur may ask angels to sign a nondisclosure agreement. Most individual angels have little hesitation in agreeing not to reveal anything that is learned during the due-diligence process. However, many angel organizations, like ours, do not sign NDAs because of the liability complication. We have no way of ensuring or enforcing an agreement for sixty-plus individuals. Of course, we tell the entrepreneur we'll make our very best effort to keep all information confidential, but we can't legally bind everyone in the group.

Occasionally we encounter a young company that won't talk to angel groups that cannot sign an NDA. We had such a case with a company whose business plan was to develop an online warranty service for consumer products. It was an intriguing idea: a single website where people could centralize all their warranty service agreements, and get access to manufacturers when warranty service was needed. We liked the company and the founder, but when we told him we couldn't sign an NDA, he hesitated and asked to see our membership list. On the list, he saw the name of a direct competitor—someone who could do something with the founder's idea if he knew about it. The founder chose not to make a presentation to us, which probably was the right decision.

PUT OUT THE WELCOME MAT

Undergoing due diligence is like having relatives visit. You change the sheets, put out fresh towels, and plan special meals, but you also think of them as family. For your business, this means you buff and polish, but you don't make any big changes and don't alter your core operations. And you treat them well. These are people who want to like you and invest in you. *Show them what they want to see, and answer all their questions.* Of course, they will want to see your dirty laundry and how you're dealing with it. Under no circumstances try to shove it under the bed. Perfection is found only in nature, so don't even strive for it. Anyhow, dirty laundry's much more interesting when you demonstrate how well you clean it. And it's going to be discovered eventually.

In truth, a big reason for due diligence is the dirty laundry—to see how bad it is. Interested investors dig into a company not because they want to know how wonderful it is or how much money they can make. That's easy to figure out: bundles. No, their real mission is to determine how risky an investment in your company would be. They want to know the likelihood of certain events and can learn this only by studying potential problem areas. They didn't expect a perfect story, just an honest and fully disclosed one.

For example, angels at one of our clubs, the eMedia Club, loved the presentation made by Brian Alperstein and Frank Wood, founders of a newcomer called Sesla, Inc., an acronym for Ship Everything, Sea Land or Air, an online price-quote and shipping service for Internet merchants. (You may recall that we described this company's pitch to the Dinner Club in chapter 1.) This was the second start-up for Wood, who had sold his first business, another Internet venture dubbed To Fish!, to AOL. Alperstein also had great credentials for this enterprise, having been a partner with an international law firm. The two founders had designed a unique algorithm for software that would enable Sesla to provide immediate, accurate quotes for shipping, documentation, and delivering anything from anywhere. And the company would arrange and oversee the actual shipping.

The eMedia angels eagerly voted to pursue due diligence on Sesla. Three members had been looking at the company and were already committed to helping it raise $750,000 in this first hunt for outside money. With the blessing of the eMedia due-diligence committee members, the earlier backers hired an independent consultant to check out the company's claims about producing a Web application that would stream-line global transactions. The consultant, Mary Ann Donaghy, was a mar-keting expert with years of experience working with *Fortune* 100 companies and knew how to find information. She interviewed numer-ous dot-com firms about whether they needed and would use a service like Sesla's.

The consultant produced a thorough, warts-and-all report. She pin-pointed the positive elements of the business model and the potentially large demand, and included quotes from executives about how useful such a program would be. And the report revealed a critical underlying flaw: Many people were uncertain about whether the concept could be executed. Was this a great idea too good to be realized? they wondered. The report also included unanswerable questions about software devel-opment, marketing, and international trade complications.

The eMedia committee showed the report to Alperstein and Wood. They were chagrined and a little defensive, suggesting that maybe the consultant had gotten it wrong. They felt that the uncertainties had received undue attention. It was all doable, and they would prove it. The Sesla team retreated and regrouped. The eMedia angels, on the other hand, were impressed by the depth and exhaustiveness of the report. They felt it represented exactly what due diligence is supposed to smoke out. (The accompanying box shows the questions that the consultant asked of potential customers of Sesla.)

An Example of Due Diligence in Top Form

These are the questions asked by the marketing consultant for the due-diligence exami-nation in the Sesla deal. They illustrate the extent and amount of detail that is needed about a company's concept in order to complete a thorough due diligence. And remember, this survey was only one part of due diligence. After introducing herself, explaining that she was doing a study on international trade, and asking the person's position in the company, she asked about its business needs.

1. Can you tell me approximately how many orders per day your com-pany processes?

---

2. Are you presently selling products outside the United States?

IF ANSWER IS NO:

A. What are the reasons?
B. Is there a market for your products outside the United States?
C. Does your company have a desire to sell outside the United States?
D. What are your plans to develop international sales and distribution capabilities?
E. What companies or services are you planning to use to develop your capabilities, or will you do so internally?
F. What are your impressions of UPS and Federal Express—their services and ability to meet your needs?

IF ANSWER IS YES:

A. What percentage of your sales are outside the United States?
B. In which countries and/or regions of the world do you do the majority of your business?
C. How many international orders do you fill each month?
D. Do you have online ordering capabilities?
E. What percentage of your total orders are received online?
F. What percentage of your international orders are received online?
G. Are there countries that do a higher percentage of their ordering online?
H. What are your present offline issues for selling and shipping overseas?
I. What are your present online issues for selling and shipping overseas?
J. What products or services are you presently using to address those issues?
K. What are your impressions of UPS and Federal Express—their services and ability to meet your needs?
L. What products or services are you investigating to address those issues?
M. If there were a service that would allow you to (Sesla service description), would this have an impact on your ability and likelihood to increase your international sales and distribution capabilities? Why/Why not?

3. Are online sales and shipments part of your international development plans?

IF ANSWER IS NO:

A. Why not? What are the specific issues you're facing?
B. What types of solutions would you need?
C. If there were a service that would allow you to (Sesla service description), would this have an impact on your ability and likelihood to develop international sales and distribution capabilities? Why/Why not?
D. So how interesting would you say that service would be to your company? (Not very, somewhat, very)

IF ANSWER IS YES:

A. How soon will you be developing those capabilities?
B. What services are you planning to use to facilitate the development of those capabilities?
C. What are your impressions of UPS and FedEx—their services and their ability to meet your needs?
D. What are your biggest issues?
E. In what countries and/or areas of the world do you believe you will be doing the most business?

A week or so later, Brian Alperstein was back in touch with eMedia. He had reviewed the consultant's report and examined his business model, and had arrived at the same painful conclusion: The concept was not workable, and Sesla was ceasing operations.

The Sesla story is less about due diligence turning up dirty laundry than it being a useful learning process for companies. Entrepreneurs shouldn't be afraid of due diligence. Although what Sesla did with the due-diligence information is extreme, the process can and often does turn up information about a company and its market that is useful. Due diligence can be akin more to free consulting than a trip to the woodshed.

As with visiting relatives, due diligence has no formal rules. It can be quick, easy, and painless or drag on for months, involve meetings, and stir up rancor. Richard Sears, a business angel interested in investing in a little start-up called Grandma Pfeiffer's Cakes-in-a-Jar, conducted his own version of due diligence by spending three months selling Pfeiffer's cakes at trade fairs and talking to customers before offering $150,000. On the other hand, an angel may need just one crucial piece of information. A former director of an angel matching service in Massachusetts describes an unusual due diligence: "We had a candy-bar manufacturer, Paris Chocolates. The angel tried the candy, said it was the best damn candy he had ever had, and cut a check on the spot."

SEVERAL HEADS ARE BETTER THAN ONE

Consumer Info (we've changed the name) was one company that didn't survive the due-diligence process. CI is a business-in-formation and a typical struggling start-up. Its owner, Janice Smith, is a striking, articulate African-American with dark hair and lean stature. She was calm and poised as she eyed the crowd of forty angels, but minutes before she could be found in the ladies' room nervously rehearsing every sentence of her presentation. She asked the Dinner Club for $2 million to build a national sales force in order to take her product—a marketing tool that helps online retailers track customer behavior—to the national arena.

Smith glided through the standard pitch: who she is, what her company does, why it's unique. She then got to what angels consider the creative part of presenting a business—revenue projections. Most small companies have an unrealistic idea of what kind of revenue they will generate. Their figures for anticipated revenue reflect more hope than hard numbers. It isn't unusual for a company seeking angel money to be "pre-revenue," that is, not making a cent. Dinner Club members know that often the most they can expect are sophisticated guesses. Yet some figures require larger leaps of faith than others. Smith stated that in her current year she expected to make $100,000, then for CI revenues to explode.

Jeanette Lee White was one of the potential angels listening to this pitch. She was impressed by the young woman's polished delivery and her confident request for financial backing. When we first approached White about joining the Dinner Club, we knew her high-tech background would make her a valuable presence on our investment team. Although we don't actively recruit members, we are always on the lookout for successful businesspeople who will contribute more than money to our projects. We first met White through another organization, the Young Presidents' Organization, a national group limited to people who, by age forty, have become president of a company with significant revenues. White frequently helped organize local YPO education events, so we knew that she dove into every activity she committed to and would be willing to match her hard-earned $80,000 investment with entrepreneurial elbow grease.

White joined the Dinner Club to make money and garner experience. Like most of the members of the club, she hoped that her investment would triple in three years. She also hoped to learn all she could about how other small companies operate and to pick the brains of promising entrepreneurs. "I want to learn more about how other people do it," she told us. She was also on the hunt for acquisitions that might add value to her own enterprise. As founders made pitches before the Dinner Club, White listened intently and later volunteered to become involved in almost every phase of our due diligence in the first year of operations. She sat on three due-diligence committees, sorting through freshly inked business plans, pro forma financial statements, and optimistic marketing strategies. There was nothing passive about White's investment. "For me, $80,000 is not money to throw around," she said with a laugh.

Halfway through Smith's presentation, White decided she liked what she saw: an energetic, thoughtful, determined young executive. Not unlike herself when she first opened the doors of Sytel Inc. twelve years ago in her basement with a couple of phone lines. Smith's presentation was well received, and White wasn't the only person impressed. After Smith left the dining room, the Dinner Club members finished their coffee and cheesecake and decided to take the next bite of Consumer Info. They voted unanimously to proceed to the next stage—due diligence.

Smith had cleared a big hurdle. Of the hundreds of business plans and executive summaries it has received over the years, the Dinner Club has winnowed the group to a few dozen and gone ahead with due diligence for two-thirds of its presenting companies.

White signed up for the due-diligence committee and, three days later, was scrutinizing CI's business plan. In her office, reviewing the company's financial statement, she saw something worrisome: The revenue projections were way too high. She knew from her own experience that they couldn't reach the stratospheric levels Smith predicted. Although her business experience was limited to her solitary venture, Smith was an expert numbers cruncher; she had produced numerous proposals and evaluated many budgets. CI's plan showed revenues rising from almost nothing to $100 million in two years, from a company that had yet to finish developing its main product. Smith's prediction was tantamount to claiming that her new car would go from zero to sixty mph in six seconds, even before she had dropped in the engine or put on tires.

The business plan revealed more flawed thinking. The basic idea of CI—providing customer surveys for online retailers—sounded fantastic. What company wouldn't want to know what its customers think about its website, its products, and its online service? However, White detected problems with the proprietary nature of the shopping data CI would gather. Why would Lands' End, for instance, pay CI to conduct customer surveys if the information that came from it—such as women preferring a shopping Web page featuring two, not ten, items—wasn't confidential? Part of CI's strength was that its database would contain information from many different customer surveys. What was to prevent CI from selling the information from the Lands' End survey to rival Eddie Bauer?

White thought that companies would not let CI contact their customers unless they were assured that the information would not be shared with a competitor, and given that kind of restriction, the CI database could be quite small. It was a catch-22 with real revenue implications—just the kind of issue due diligence was intended to smoke out.

During the initial pitch to the Dinner Club, Smith had glossed over the complicated marketing strategy for building her database, in part because she didn't have time to get into the details. In the fifteen minutes allotted for her presentation, her job was to sell the angels enough on the concept that they would want to dig deeper.

Digging deeper was the job of the due-diligence committee, and White was an ideal member of that group. "You want to get into a company understanding fully what the potential problems are to minimize surprises down the line," she explains. "That's why I question *everything*."

She was also concerned that CI had not yet worked out all the kinks in the software that would track customer buying habits and would be integral to the service CI would sell its prospective *Fortune* 500 clients. CI already had a few impressive clients, including L.L. Bean, but the contracts were small, and Smith didn't have the capability yet to scale up enough to handle more. Her creation was still in the body shop and not yet ready for the race track.

"They needed the money more for product development than marketing," White noted, "and that is very, very risky. With product development, you can easily spend double your budget with your eyes closed."

An entrepreneur's business plan, in a use of funds section or budget expenses, usually indicates how he or she intends to use investment money. Sometimes the new funds are to be spread out for an array of functions, like recruitment and salaries, product development, marketing campaigns, or customer acquisition. When a deal between an entrepreneur and angel group gets to the point of negotiating the particulars of a funding agreement (what investors call a term sheet), the angels may specify how their investment is to be used. For instance, product development isn't always a bad thing, but usually angels prefer to back a company after a product or service is fully operational.

Occasionally angels will make an investment in stages. A $1 million investment may be doled out in thirds, with the first third up front, the second third when a product is out of beta testing, and the final third when the product is shipped, a customer is signed, or a key employee hired. Angels like to "kick the tires," taste the product, see the service in action. While angels don't want to go into too much detail and handcuff the entrepreneur, they know from experience what kinds of activity burn money. And their expertise, as well as money, is best used when a business is up and running, when a ramp-up in production or expansion in marketing is the next step.

White and the other members of the due-diligence committee decided that the club should not invest in CI, at least until the company had completed work on its product. There was time for individuals to help, but a larger round with pros wasn't in the cards yet.

We know of deal after deal that fell apart as investor and entrepreneur approached the altar because of mistakes and miscommunication during the research, the due-diligence process. You must review all the key questions, historic data, personal records, and business-plan details that inevitably become part of the decision-making file used by funders. If you have ever been through a real-estate purchase transaction with loan paperwork, you are only part of the way there. In the real-estate deal, there are hard assets—the land or building—for the lender to go after in bad times. In the venture transaction, there may be nothing left for the angel investor but bad memories in a worst-case situation. That is why the money side is so careful, diligent, and slow sometimes in amassing information, reviewing it, checking it, and re-checking it. Once the money changes hands, there may be no recourse—only the good faith that the enterprise will succeed in bringing many times return of capital in the future.

In the next chapter, we will see how this investigation forms the basis of the next phase of the dance: the negotiation on exact terms and value for the investment in your company. If due diligence provides a secure, stable foundation, then the give-and-take on exact terms and conditions of the final transaction will go more smoothly.

- What an angel discovers during due diligence about a company's market and financial projections can dramatically influence valuation, so be very certain of the reliability of information you use for financial projections.

- Keep copies of everything you give to the funder.

- Peel the onion when giving sensitive data to funders, especially if you are dealing with more than one at a time—list everything they get each time, and let them ask for more detailed items.

- Try to give complicated items or financial records in a face-to-face meeting, so you can explain each document and any details.

- Call your key references to alert them that prospective investors may be contacting them, and about what issues—don't let them surprise your key customers or suppliers.

6

Let's Make a Deal:
Negotiating Investment Terms

If your company survives due diligence, it's on to negotiating the valuation and term sheet. This chapter describes how a term sheet—the contract between entrepreneur and funder—is negotiated. We describe how to understand angel investors' valuation approaches, and we describe various methods that you should consider using when doing your own valuation. The chapter also offers advice on how to negotiate effectively with your angels.

NEGOTIATING WITH AN ANGEL: SETTING THE TERMS OF THE FINANCING DEAL

An entrepreneur knows that due diligence has gone well when someone on the committee or in the angel organization asks to meet to talk terms. This is a buy signal that says that the angels want to invest in you and your company. Negotiating terms of a financing deal is like driving through a city you've never visited before. Even if you have a map and can see your destination in the distance, there are street closings, one-way avenues that have been switched, and many unknown hazards. You need to have an anticipated outcome. For example, when you are thinking about how much money you are looking to raise, have you considered carefully how much less you will accept?

Your potential investors are certainly going to focus much of the negotiations on the valuation you have set on the business. Have you prepared a strong defense justifying any numbers you are proposing? Can you assign values to intellectual property you won, or to lines of distribution you have established? Is there precedent in the marketplace for the range of value you are assigning to your enterprise? All of these questions help to prepare you for the negotiating phase. This chapter provides real-world tips for navigating the tricky path, from excitement about partnering to who gets what at the lawyers' closing table; you will be given tips on how angels differ from venture capitalists and how to deal with the most critical issue—valuation of the company, your baby.

Entrepreneurs shouldn't go into negotiations without having done their homework. You should learn as much as possible about the negotiating process before you commence. Through books or intermediaries, get samples of term sheets used by venture capitalists. Ask your lawyer to explain legal terms to you. Have your CPA show you financial terms. Research how other companies like yours are being valued, from sales data and financing data. A couple of hours on the Web or going through trade publications will unearth details about start-up financing for companies in your industry and about your size. In short, comparables. A word of caution about comparables: Exact matches are nonexistent. No company is exactly like yours, and you must make allowances for the differences. Generally, the companies and deals that get written about are established, sometimes public companies, so you have to discount your figures when making comparisons. And as everyone knows, early-stage, private companies are worth less than companies whose shares can be bought or sold anytime.

While you're at it, look for figures relating to company growth within your industry and specifics of valuations for financing beyond the seed-capital stage. Professional journals like *VentureOne* and *Private Equity Analyst* offer useful information. Another source of information about how companies similar to yours have been valued and financed is an expert. Investment bankers, venture capitalists, business consulting firms, and business brokers have entire divisions dedicated to helping small businesses price their companies. Of course, information from their handy databanks of other deals isn't free, and you'll have to decide whether using a professional is worth it, and that decision is discussed in the next section of this chapter. However, by and large, we've found that what an expert costs in fees is more than made up for in the value he or she can add to a deal.

THE STARTING GATE: YOUR BUSINESS PLAN

No successful high-growth business can obtain significant capital from professional money—VCs or angels—without a well-thought-out, well-written business plan. Negotiating the term sheet starts with your business plan, where you outline the status of the company, how much you hope to raise, and how you will deploy that money. Many books have been written on how to write a business plan, so we'll make just a few comments here, but the important point is to recognize that the plan initiates the negotiation.

Exhibit 6–1 shows the financing history and requirements from the business plan of DiamondBack Vision, an Internet video technology company that the eMedia Club co-invested in with venture capitalists. Although the company was looking for more money than most angel groups provide, its business plan offers an excellent illustration of the kinds of financing a start-up can find. You'll notice that, under the use-of-proceeds section, the bulk of the money will be applied to salaries, and while it's unusual to earmark such a large chunk of early-stage money for a payroll, the company explains it with its extensive plans for hiring.

■ When preparing your own request for financing, you could do well by emulating the straightforward approach taken by the DiamondBack founders. They offer a simple, honest history showing the range of sources for prior funding, including contributions by the founder and key employees as well as the use of credit-card

---

Exhibit 6-1:
Company Background and Prior Financing
Presentation for DiamondBack Vision

DiamondBack was incorporated on January 29, 1998, and has completed seed-stage financing through a variety of bootstrapping methods, including founder's sweat equity and real equity, barter-for-services, credit-card debt, and government grants and contracts. The company operated through 1998 and half of 1999 with labor of the founder and four technical consultants. In June of 1999, Dr. Douglass [the president] extended offers to six current full-time employees.

SOURCES OF EARLY-STAGE FINANCING:

Founder	$152,842	1/98–6/99
Revenues	$432,944	1/98–10/99
VP of technology	$ 35,000	8/99
Credit cards	$ 32,000	7–8/99
Founder	$ 25,000	8/99

---

debt and, importantly, some revenues from operations. They then, in a direct manner, discuss the use of proceeds, showing a thoughtful, well-considered plan designed to achieve their objectives. Here are a few other tips: Remember to answer questions before they are raised in the investigation process.

- Give full descriptions of your core management team and their prior successes in life and in business.
- Explain how you've funded yourself to date, and be clear on how you've valued the company's work up till now.
- Never ignore the competition section of a plan—be ruthlessly honest about current competitors' strengths and weaknesses—explaining how you'll overcome the strongest competitive threats.

You have a plan; you've prepared great valuation arguments. Is this enough? No, because you and your angel funders now have to go one-on-one to cut a deal. No one but you can negotiate a lasting, mutually beneficial partnering arrangement. Unlike a real-estate transaction that uses comparable historic sales prices for similar houses, your new business idea may have no easy comparables. You need to know as much as the angel you are dealing with about the optional approaches and the pros and cons of using them in your situation.

GET OUT YOUR CALCULATOR: VALUATION METHODS

Determining the value of a company hinges on two questions: How much does an entrepreneur need, and how much is he or she willing to give up? Negotiations often begin with the first question and an entrepreneur claiming that a certain amount is needed for certain activities. And in early financing involving angels, entrepreneurs usually follow up the detailed request by saying they're willing to give up, typically, 25 to 35 percent of the company to get that funding. This is the starting point for many valuation discussions. From here, negotiators examine each half of the equation—amount needed and percentage relinquished—to see if they're realistic. Does the company really need that much? Maybe more, maybe less. Then talk shifts to the simple equation: if an entrepreneur is willing to give up 25 percent of his company for, say, $1 million, is the company truly worth $4 million?

This equation is the nub of the valuation negotiations. *Entrepreneurs who try to inject other rationales for their valuation not only annoy angels but drive them away.* Arguments about what other businesses have received in financing and valuation totals, highly publicized deals with hefty valuations, or what entrepreneurs feel their efforts are worth raise bright red flags for angels. Any valuation discussion that isn't grounded on how much a company actually needs and will apply to activities that will help it grow is doomed to fail.

There are accounting formulas for valuation, and the guys with the calculators generally use one of three common methods: looking at multiples and ratios, asset value, or discounted future cash flow. However, the first two are seldom applied to start-ups, which you'll understand as we explain them. You'll see that they work mostly for established companies, not bright, shiny newcomers. (Bear in mind that this is a sketch of these methods—akin to *Valuation for Dummies*—and you'll need the help of an accountant to do thorough number-crunching.)

The multiples-and-ratios method. This method of valuation measures a company's financial performance by a number of yardsticks applied to companies similar to yours but with a known valuation. These yardsticks are multiples and ratios, which include price-to-earnings (PE), pre-tax price-to-earnings, after-tax cash flow, and individual industry ratios. So, once you have a figure for earnings, say, $500,000, and your company is similar to one with a PE of 6 to 8, then your value is between $3 million and $4 million. However, PE ratios can be all over the map. The ratios for some dot-com companies, those that did have earnings, have reached into the hundreds, while the ratios for companies with no earnings are frequently a humble three times revenues. As you might guess, multiple-and-ratio valuation methods depend on a company actually having earnings and cash flow, which are often elusive for the start-up. Furthermore, published ratios and multiples usually apply to publicly held companies, and their inherent liquidity adds value. The illiquidity of a small, private company is thus translated into a deep discount on industry ratios and multiples.

The asset-valuation method. This method is most often applied to rusty, old companies. Just like the name implies, the value of a company is the sum total of its tangible and intangible assets. This method is used mostly when breaking up or liquidating a company. Once negotiators have decided how to value the company's assets, whether to use book or market value and resolve the sticky subject of a company's goodwill—that is, its reputation—then liabilities are subtracted. The bottom line is your asset value. For companies that are breaking new ground, for instance in technology or bioscience, intellectual property can be counted as a valuable asset.

The discounted-cash-flow method. The method that many accountants who work with start-ups may use is the discounted cash flow (DCF) or variations of it. Although the term suggests it's a rigid, arcane formula, it's really a crapshoot, because of all the variables and unknowns. The premise makes sense: You project how much money your company will earn in a certain number of years, then discount that number to allow for all the risk, and voilà, you have a valuation. And if you believe that, we've got a bridge to sell you!

DCF is not quite that bad, but it does have a large number of unknowns, especially for a new company that has no cash flow, revenues, or earnings. Of course, looking at the growth trajectories of similar companies, if those numbers are available, can be enlightening. Nevertheless, you're going to have to contend with such mysteries as the future size and growth of your market and industry sector, the uniqueness of your technology, product, or service along with its demand, the cost of the marketing effort required to position your technology or product, and the size and health of the competition. These are the question marks that pop into an investor's head when computing the discount percentage.

Venture capitalists have a variation on DCF that likewise works backward and includes how much an investment at a certain level will boost cash flow or earnings. It's in essence a discounted future-value calculation. Naturally, this method, too, is loaded with subjective numbers, like an appropriate PE and the risks that are used to figure what kind of return investors anticipate. Furthermore, the question of follow-on financing—when you might need it and how much—raises the specter that the angel's initial investment will be diluted, so that has to be hashed out.

OTHER CONSIDERATIONS IN VALUING A BUSINESS

The truth about valuing a start-up is that it's often a guess. Even people armed with accounting degrees and decades of experience with new companies can't always fill in all the boxes and compute precise numbers. This doesn't mean that the deal isn't complete. It does mean that there's a lot of room for negotiation, and haggling over small percentage points is often counterproductive.

There's a lot of emotion involved in hammering out a company's valuation and the percentage of equity an investment represents. The most emotion, perhaps, swirls around the issue of sweat equity. You quit your $100,000-a-year job and have been working without pay for years, sacrificing your credit history, not to mention nights and weekends, to turn your dream into an enterprise, and believe all this has value. It does—but it's hard to put a finger on. What matters most about your sweat equity is not how many hours you've invested or how much you've given up, but the results of your efforts and how they will contribute to your company tomorrow. So if you raise the sweat-equity argument when tossing out valuation figures, frame it in terms of what it has produced for the years ahead.

Don't relax yet—valuation's not finished. Other issues need addressing, namely share-price value and class of stock and timing for both the investment and the return. Angels often invest in stages, promising a certain amount to be portioned out as a company meets performance landmarks, like landing a big client or finishing beta testing. Another variation is an investment divided into different kinds of contribution, such as cash, debt, and services. An angel in the Dinner Club, Steve Walker, crafted an arrangement with BioNetrix, the security company we introduced in chapter 4 whereby an investment of $750,000 included $250,000 in consulting services. The following example shows how structuring the terms of the investment can be the determining factor in whether a deal gets done.

The negotiations over Ocean Optics, a large photo-optics manufacturer, point to one of many creative solutions that angels and entrepreneurs can use in valuation. The company's founders and its would-be angels, a mid-Atlantic angel fund, had resolved all issues but were stuck on valuation. Everyone agreed on management, angel participation, and direction of research and marketing, but they couldn't see eye-to-eye on what the venture was worth. The entrepreneurs believed it should be valued at $10 million and the investors' $2 million stake worth 20 percent of equity. The angel fund disagreed and offered a compromise solution.

The angel-fund manager proposed that their investment be in the form of secured debt, not preferred stock, with rights to buy stock at a later date at the company's current price. In short, the angel investment would be a loan plus the chance to buy stock later. The angels were deferring their equity investment for a time when the company would have a better financial track record. It was a win-win proposal for both sides. The entrepreneur would receive his price, and the investors would receive proof in the company's financial performance that the $10 million valuation was realistic. If the entrepreneur didn't hit his numbers in coming years, the price would be adjusted downward. Half an hour after this proposal was voiced, the deal was done.

One of the last pieces of the valuation puzzle is the infamous exit strategy. Investors want to know when their rich rewards are coming, and the source. The entrepreneur's plans to pay back their money, and then some, within so many years, is predicated on where exactly this dough is going to come from. When will the company be ready to attract bigger investors, and who will these people be? Some of the possibilities: The company earns enough to buy back stock, another company buys stock, a stock swap, or the company goes public. We'll say more about exit strategies in chapter 7.

A word of caution about valuation formulas. While they can give the appearance of a cut-and-dried deal, we've found that the process can be quite pliable. Numbers can be flexible; people can be flexible. All the contractual safeguards in the world aren't going to reduce the risk involved. Whether someone's equity share is 30 percent or 33 percent has zero impact on whether a company is going to grow and thrive, or take a dive. *So don't get hung up on formulas, and keep the big picture in mind—to forge a win-win partnership.*

In all the haggling over numbers and a company's financial future, it's easy to lose sight of what's important in valuation. We began this discussion by talking about attitude, and at the end of the day, it comes back to attitude. The attitude that we believe in is basic fairness. The final valuation has to be fair for everybody, or it won't work. Sometimes getting to that point reminds us of kids' take-or-break method. You're on the playground, trying to figure out how to share something that's not cleanly divisible, like a large cookie. So one kid declares, "I'll break, you take," with one person doing the dividing and the other choosing first which half to take. It's a virtual guarantee that the halves will be fairly divided. This is what any valuation negotiation should strive for. Beneath the complex numbers and myriad unknowns, it's simply about fairness.

NEGOTIATING WITH A POSITIVE ATTITUDE

Negotiations are all about attitude. Sure, you're armed with facts and figures about costs and sales and future growth, and have persuasive arguments for why an angel group should invest at the level and terms you want. However, everyone in the room knows that eventually, numbers are going to be erased and new ones scratched in. What ultimately kicks the deal over the goal line is willingness—no, eagerness—on both sides to do the deal. Everyone has to want it. The people negotiating must want the deal more than they want to be right, more than they want to control the sequence of events, and more than they want to win a contest. This can-do attitude is especially helpful when the negotiations get stuck. Instead of banging their heads against a wall, intelligent negotiators set aside the contentious issues and keep pushing to agree on less thorny issues. Another part of this attitude is being flexible—not a pushover, but ready to listen to other ways of configuring time and money.

Here are some rules of thumb that may save you from negotiation headaches:

- As you begin to negotiate, tackle the big questions first—namely, the valuation. Leave the smaller but sometimes more emotionally charged issues, like compensation or adviser's fees, for later.
- Never criticize individuals. You can pick apart the numbers, the offer, and the terms, but not the people.

- Don't lose your temper. When the atmosphere gets tight, use the humor safety valve: self-deprecating remarks, silly asides, absurd observations, amusing stories. Anything to break the tension. If voices are raised, break off and reconvene later.

- Never look too hungry. Says Matt Mosman, the chief negotiator who acquires start-ups for Oracle, "If you come desperate, we're going to eat you up."

- Forget the bluff. Remember, you're talking to a future partner, and any tricks you use to seal the deal will come back to haunt you. Any sleight-of-hand will be revealed eventually.

- Remember that it's about more than money. Your goal should be not simply a hard-and-fast number but forming a partnership that builds a highly profitable company.

SHARING THE PASSION: GETTING TO A TERM SHEET

In this dating game, hashing out the term sheet is like rehearsing your vows for the wedding ceremony and negotiating a prenuptial agreement at the same time. A term sheet spells out your new partnership and is dedicated mostly to financial issues, but it can also include who does what through performance provisions, and looks ahead to how the relationship will be eventually dissolved.

Bear in mind that this is not the time for second thoughts—no leaving anybody at the altar. Minds should have been made up by the end of valuation (that was the proposal!). Coming to the term-sheet table with nagging doubts or feelings of unfairness will surely poison the relationship.

Cautions former PricewaterhouseCoopers senior partner Carl Grant, "If you're going to get an investor to the point of giving you a term sheet, you better be pretty darned sure what your options are and what you're looking for, and whether you want to go with that particular investor. I'm not a big fan of taking term sheets and shopping them around to others, saying, 'Can you give me a better deal?' You'll find that a lot of investors will walk away from those kinds of deals. You *are* getting into a relationship. They're not passive investors, especially on the angel side. They're people who, usually, share a passion for what you're doing."

FINANCING SOUGHT

DiamondBack is seeking $2.5 million to 1) establish and realize revenue as a video service provider, 2) develop our initial MPEG-4 encoder and incorporate it into our service bureau, 3) develop and distribute a freely available MPEG-4 encoder plug-in, and 4) develop and demonstrate a second-generation MPEG-4 video encoder.

The company will complement its current team of seven with an additional seven to ten members of the technical and marketing staffs. An additional round of capital formation will be necessary in eight to ten months to pursue aggressive marketing and sales objectives.

USE OF PROCEEDS

Salaries	$1,435,000
Other operating expenses	275,000
Capital expenditures	230,000
Facilities leases	215,000
Working capital	150,000
Marketing programs	120,000
Legal and accounting fees	75,000
Investor and marketing costs	5,000

The most important element of the term sheet is how a company's equity is parceled out, which can be one of three ways. It can be in stock, preferred or common. Angels usually want preferred because it's senior to common if there is a liquidation. Convertible preferred stock gives the investor the option of converting the preferred to common at a predetermined price. The second kind of equity is convertible subordinated debt—that is, a loan that usually includes interest payments, and the option to trade in the loan for stock at a predetermined price. The third color of money is long-term debt with warrants. Essentially, this is a loan with the added sweetener of the right to purchase stock sometime in the future at a predetermined price.

Arriving at the exact shade or combination of equity is a balancing act. Angels want a piece of the action but not so much that it dampens an entrepreneur's fire, and the entrepreneur wants to hold on to the baby but get the necessary help and funds to ensure its future. An angel with a group called the New Hampshire Breakfast Club, which prefers simple term sheets, declares, "We're stacking the decks to optimize the company's chance at success, not our recovery in the event of failure. We only pour a gallon of gas in the carburetor and get it off and going."

This same group presented an entrepreneur with terms on two five-by-seven-inch index cards. The first specified the company's incorporation and issuance of common stock—75 percent to the entrepreneur, 25 percent to the angels. The second card stated: $60,000 from the angels for 25 percent equity, money to be used to develop a product prototype, and the angels would lead the second round of financing and find $300,000 for the company.

While people have agreed to sketchier terms than these, we usually flesh out the picture somewhat. Here are the considerations besides equity that we like term sheets to address:

- Timing and next-round financing: When the company expects to need more money. When our angels can expect to see a return on their investment.
- Anti-dilution rights: Protecting first-round investors' equity share when later financing is brought in.
- Investor rights if a company goes public.
- Collateral and security (e.g., patents or equipment) when debt is involved.
- Representations and warranties: This guarantees that the investor and entrepreneur are who they say they are, that they've represented the status of the company accurately.

In deals that angels feel are high-risk, other stipulations are added to the term sheet. This is when a term sheet begins to resemble a prenuptial agreement. If an investor is worried about an entrepreneur becoming distracted by other ventures, or even leaving the start-up, his or her salary can be specified in the agreement and tied to stock options. In this way, if he or she sticks with the company and it prospers, the entrepreneur and the investors benefit. A vesting schedule, outlining when an entrepreneur's stock can be called his or hers or traded, is another way to hang on to someone. The term sheet can also include performance provisions for the entrepreneur and CEO.

Angels worried about an entrepreneur making bad decisions, hurling the company into risky ventures, or moving in a wrong direction can insist on a seat on the board. Furthermore, covenants or restrictions on a company's activities can force it to stick to its knitting. To protect their investment against an entrepreneur making financial mistakes, angels can dribble out their money and invest in stages. And tied to each stage can be a performance marker that, if it isn't met, brings a halt in payments.

Specific exit strategies are generally not spelled out in a term sheet, except occasionally broad references to what happens if a company goes public or is bought by another company. In this what-if case, angels may insist on piggyback or co-sale rights, giving them the opportunity to sell their holdings either in the public offering or to the buyer on the same terms as the majority stockholder. As entrepreneurs and angels negotiate term-sheet conditions, talking about exit strategies can smoke out widely different expectations for the nascent company. And these contrasting visions of a company's future may well signal whether or not the angel and founder should be in bed together at all.

When entrepreneurs or angels don't discuss all the possibilities, sometimes making assumptions about what the other side expects, trouble can erupt. For example, wrangling over exit strategies in the term sheet for Travel Guide Software Co. brought to light surprisingly incompatible aspirations. An early angel investor and board member was helping steer the young company through its first round of financing involving financial institutions. The software business already had secured funding from a couple of rounds with angels and was looking further afield. It managed to entice a big-time venture capitalist into leading a $5 million round of financing and so began term-sheet negotiations with the group. Like many venture funds, this group was aiming for hefty returns, in the neighborhood of ten times valuation, and so wanted the exit strategies to provide many belt-and-suspenders protections for its investment.

Travel Guide agonized over this term sheet. The exit-strategy protections demanded by the venture capitalists were all tilted toward it and hard to swallow. While the company was deliberating, Travel Guide received out of nowhere an overture from a competitor interested in acquiring it. The competitor planned to go public soon and wanted Travel Guide Software for extra window dressing. The terms for this deal were a lot less demanding—the competitor expected a mere 300 percent return, rather than 1,000 percent. Nevertheless, Travel Guide looked closely at the offer and informed the VCs that it was talking to another suitor.

News that Travel Guide was considering a much smaller, less restrictive offer brought the negotiations with the venture capitalists to a screeching halt. The group withdrew the term sheet, explaining that if Travel Guide's expectations were that small, then the partnership would never work. Everyone realized that by viewing the deal through the exit-strategy window, the company and VCs were looking at different horizons.

Your final term sheet will inevitably contain standard features and individual clauses crafted for your angels and your company. It will be as distinctive and special as a wedding ceremony, and when you sign it, you're saying, "I do." It may be reams of legal documents, a single-page letter of agreement, or, not unheard of, a handshake. The universe of term sheets is as diverse as people and companies.

But whether you sign or shake hands, you're not hitched yet. There's the delicate subject of consummation, which in investing is done a little less enthusiastically than in life! Consummation here is the handing over of the money, the closing, and entrepreneurs should push for it as soon as possible. This may be a delicate topic—asking for money is never easy, even when someone's promised it to you. Only when you have the check in hand is the deal done. So ask you must, especially before you run out of money. Otherwise, if the company bank account is empty, your pleas take on an unpleasant odor of desperation.

WHAT DO YOU WANT THE MONEY FOR?

An entrepreneur's plans for how he or she intends to use investment money can influence the tenor and success of valuation negotiations. For example, young companies that are looking for financing to pay off old debts, disperse as salaries, or buy out former partners aren't going to do as well in the valuation sweepstakes.

The story of David, an urban executive we know who became an angel investor, explains one reason why. In his forties, with twenty years in the mainframe-computer business, David wanted out of the big-city rat race and negotiated an investment with the two owners of a real-estate sales and management business. The entrepreneurs were seeking to grow their practice but also partially cash out after years of backbreaking ups and downs of business cycles. He received a minority share of the business and negotiated to pay the owners in multiyear installments. The initial valuation of the business was an arbitrary figure loosely based on national valuation standards for small businesses. The business owners agreed that outyear payments on the investment were to be based on the company's future sales and earnings. This angel investment enabled the two founders to partially cash out of their company, and gave them money that they could use elsewhere.

However, the experience for David's investment turned sour. The two founders pocketed their cash-out money and turned to other business activities, and lost interest in their real-estate concern. David had no role in the company or, as a minority stockholder, any say in its future direction. Within five years, David asked the two founders to buy him out or give him a substantial role in the company. He received a reluctant payment from them, fifty cents for every dollar he had originally invested, and he returned to the city. The entrepreneurs were distracted from their pursuit by the protracted negotiations and psychic energy burned dealing with their investor, and they wondered if in the long run this kind of investor was best for them and their business.

Financing intended primarily to give entrepreneurs liquidity or to cover past debts, like salaries or loans, isn't money that grows a business. Instead of fueling progress, this kind of investment may derail it. This is why angels look very closely at what an entrepreneur intends to do with the proceeds of financing rounds. An entrepreneur we dealt with, Bob Nelson, even prepared a chart (shown in Exhibit 6–3) detailing each round of financing he would be seeking, along with the whys and whens so that angels could see how their money was going to be used to build the company. All investors want to know if there will be an additional need for

Exhibit 6-3:

Start-Up Road Map (if you don't know where you're going, you're probably not on the right road.)

Date	Milestone	Burn to Next Milestone	Amount to Raise	Prospective Pre-money Valuation	Prospective Post-money Valuation	Shares to Issue	Price per Share
JUN-98	INCORPORATE	80K	100K	300K	400K	4MM FOUNDERS 2MM INVESTORS 2MM RESERVED FOR FUTURE EMPLOYEES	$0.05
DEC-98	ALPHA TRIAL 2 ACCOUNTS	200K	250K	2MM	2.25MM	1MM	$0.25
JUN-99	BETA TRIAL 4 ACCOUNTS	400K	500K	4.5MM	5MM	1MM	$0.50
DEC-99	RELEASE 1.0 2 PAID CLIENTS	3MM	3MM	10MM	13MM	3MM	$1.00

Exhibit 6-3 continues on page 140; pages 139–140 should be read as if they were side by side.

Spreadsheet courtesy of Bob Nelson, Nelson & Company.

Exhibit 6–3 continued

Start-Up Road Map (if you don't know where you're going, you're probably not on the right road.)

Date	Projected Upside (at 10/share)	Minimum Net Worth	Maximum Net Worth	Approaches	Man Hours Spent on Fundraising, Legal	Approx. Number of Full-time Employees	% of Company Owned by Founders & Team	Paper Worth of Founders' Stock
JUN-98	200x	2MM (5% OF NET WORTH)	40MM (5 X UPSIDE)	PERSONAL FRIENDS, FAMILY OR CREDIT CARDS	200 (5 WEEKS FULL-TIME, 10 WEEKS HALF-TIME, 6 MONTHS SPARE TIME)	2	75%	200K
DEC-98	40x	2MM (2.5% OF NET WORTH)	20MM (10 X UPSIDE)	50 INDIVIDUAL THROUGH INTRODUCTIONS	150	4	66%	1MM
JUN-99	20x	5MM (2% OF NET WORTH)	20MM (10 X UPSIDE)	25 INDIVIDUALS THROUGH REFERRALS	100	8	60%	2MM
DEC-99	10x	VC OR 20MM	100MM (6 X UPSIDE)	20 TARGETED VCs OR SUPERANGELS THROUGH REFERRALS OR INTRODUCTIONS	400	12	46%	4MM

Spreadsheet courtesy of **Bob Nelson, Nelson & Company.**

money and, if so, how soon. Demonstrating a realistic view of the ongoing financing needs will create confidence in your would-be partners.

WHO'S ON THE HOME TEAM? GETTING OUTSIDE HELP

In this section we will highlight when and what type of help entrepreneurs should seek from outside their inner circle of backers and employees. At times of rapid growth, crisis, or external threat, every business needs not only an angel but experienced outside advisers as well.

An entrepreneur building a business needs professional help—a lawyer to set up the company, prepare contracts and agreements, give advice on issues like intellectual property, patents, trademarks or securities law, and an accountant for tax advice and preparation. And, of course, there's the occasional ad-hoc adviser, like an insurance broker, real-estate broker, or headhunter. Some entrepreneurs bring in a management consultant to help write the business plan. While there's nothing magical about business plans that only consultants know the trick to, having an expert looking over your shoulder, checking your figures, and smoothing out your descriptions and explanations can help.

Most management-consulting firms and investment banks have someone, if not an entire division, who specializes in advising entrepreneurs on a smorgasbord of topics, from the initial structure of a company to financing techniques and finding strategic partners, to launching a public offering. And when the day comes when a company founder first goes looking for outside money, thoughts turn—like to baseball at springtime—to getting a pro to help. Whether you get someone to simply hold your hand as you knock on doors and cut deals or someone who leads the way depends on what you ask for and whom you talk to.

Carl Grant, formerly of PricewaterhouseCoopers, knows the start-up territory, having worked for a county economic-development authority and spearheaded business development for an Internet start-up. He describes how his firm helps founders find money.

"The goal in going out to get venture capital is to have somebody present you with a term sheet, because if you're without a term sheet, you're without a deal," he declares. "Entrepreneurs will often try to elicit our support and see if we're interested in working with the company early on, because we have a strong referral network. We don't tell investors whether or not they should invest in a company, but we can bring a company to an investor's attention.

"Certainly, if it comes in referred by PwC, it's going to raise their eyebrows and get their attention more than it would if it came in over the transom. Over and over again, you hear it said that a deal that just gets mass-mailed out, or comes in over the transom, if it's without a relationship or a referral, it usually gets ignored. So what we do is create some efficiency in the process."

In short, they open doors; you decide what that's worth. A danger lurks here: *Bringing in a big-time hired gun for a relatively small deal that's going to be conducted in an informal give-and-take is overkill,* and can raise caution flags in people's minds.

This sentiment is echoed by business lawyers. Michael Lincoln, a senior partner at the Cooley Godward law firm, has numerous Internet start-up clients and declares, "There's a sliding scale involved. It's not worth the effort for $50,000 to go to the trouble of having lawyers draw up gold-plated VC-like documents. It's more likely that for small amounts of money, the investor will sign a simple subscription agreement and buy common stock. No bells and whistles, almost a handshake deal, a simple subscription deal that says, 'Here's $50,000 for some common stock. I represent that I am an accredited investor, that I understand that this is risky, and that I could lose my entire investment.' That sort of thing. And the company will typically furnish to that investor some sort of disclosure document, usually in the form of a business plan."

"Everybody wants to talk about valuation—the big V word," says Grant. "Entrepreneurs often ask about valuation. They'll come to us hoping that we'll put some sort of valuation on their company, but we don't do that. We're not in the business of valuing companies. In fact, we're prohibited from doing that in situations when we may well one day be the auditor of that company."

If you need professional advice in valuation, a better source than an accounting firm would be an investment banking firm that has small business or start-up expertise. *Be forewarned, though, that most experts will demur assigning a value to your company.* It's too tricky a proposition, and loaded with potential liabilities and recriminations. At best, you may hear a broad range of the price tags on other, somewhat similar companies. Stuart Yarbrough of CrossHill Financial Group, a leading Washington, D.C., investment banker, is well versed in business plans and financing agreements. When going into valuation talks, he keeps his eye on the big picture.

"Too many business propositions are not at all clear as to what they want at the end of the day. Your business plan—indeed, all your documents—should really send a message as to what you're like to do business with as a partner. I think using a term sheet makes a deal move more smoothly, especially if you have a proposed valuation and general proposed terms in a business plan that you're distributing," he says.

You may want to bring in a professional adviser to help you negotiate values that you already have in mind. You know your numbers but may not feel equipped to persuade others that they're valid. This person can be a huge confidence booster, especially in situations where a founder has no one else to recruit for the negotiating team. No one likes to sit alone when bargaining over his or her company.

And a professional adviser may save you from making a disastrous mistake, as happened to a company we encountered. Jamey Harvey, the young CEO of Digital Addiction, a start-up that makes online video games, spent the early days of his company scrounging for money. He juggled expenses on his MasterCard and Visa, hit up his parents more than once, and at one point was reduced to holding pass-the-hat meetings with potential investors in cheesy hotels. Unfortunately, he hustled this money on his own, an economy that he would later regret.

His persistence and a win-at-any-cost attitude began to push his company into making money. Its first Internet game, Sanctum, had 10,000 user accounts in its second year, and the company generated revenues of $250,000. Expanding his horizon of financial options, he joined an incubator, received funding from its principal, and made a presentation at the

Mid-Atlantic Venture Fair. He started to get noticed by the big-money guys, and came away from his presentation at the fair with the business cards of twenty-five venture capitalists.

Yet when he sat down with the people who could lead Digital Addiction's first institutional round, which was for $4 million, VC after VC backed off. There were already too many angels in the deal. Harvey's whip-around among individual investors in the cheesy hotel had produced a snowstorm of agreements: twenty-five, to be exact. From the VCs' point of view, two dozen investors were too many interested parties, too many pieces of the pie to make it worth their while. A new term sheet would have to be submitted for everyone's approval, and the likelihood of all twenty-five agreeing to the terms was slim to none. Surely, someone would have a problem with clause 7b; someone else would object to section 3. A deal with VC money on top of so many angels would be almost impossible to structure. Harvey could have used a pro at his side during those sessions, someone who would have pointed out the danger of so many people in the money pool.

Fortunately, Jamey Harvey is one sharp tack, and came up with a creative solution. He went back to his original shareholders and said, "Instead of raising money in our existing company, I'm going to create a second company, which an outside venture fund is willing to finance. But because the basis for the new company will be technology, which now belongs to the existing company, in exchange for the technology rights, I'm going to give the original Digital Addiction and you, its shareholders, a 20 percent ownership in the new company."

This was an extraordinary solution for a couple of reasons. First, Harvey found himself with a company that possessed two different businesses, each quite valuable. He had the new technology venture and the original Internet game venture. And despite what he wanted, he had legions of shareholders who had strong ideas about where Digital Addiction should be headed. Second, Harvey was determined not to abandon anyone. He wasn't about to chase the perhaps more promising technology end of the business and leave his early angels high and dry. He wanted to do well by his investors. So his solution gave the angels who put their faith and money in him and his struggling game company a piece of the high-technology action.

Harvey did have advisers working with him throughout the evolution of the company. No one, however, had anticipated all of the twists and turns at the beginning of the fund-raising process. Once confronted with the VC's concerns, however, it was his legal advisers and the board members he had surrounded himself with who together created the structure that allowed him to both satisfy his original investors and raise new money for the technology company.

Sometimes professional advisers will help you avoid a problem down the road by creating appropriate legal and financial structures for your business. Sometimes they will help you by solving a problem that no one could have foreseen developing.

CONCLUSION

To wrap up, preparing yourself for the dance with a serious angel investor should be exhaustive. Building the best business plan—and several shorter, succinct versions of it—is essential. The backup appendices and documents supporting the plan are key to a smooth start to an in-depth due diligence. Having a well-reasoned and reasonable valuation for the company you bring to the negotiation will avoid the most common reason for failure: disagreement over how to divide the pie. The negotiation process we have described—dealing with allocating ownership, determining management and board control issues, and deciding exactly how much is needed to fund precisely which items—will lead either to a sadder-but-wiser experience or a successful closing. Many angels and venture capitalists will tell you that getting to this—a successful closing and the popping of the champagne cork—represents only one tenth of the way to getting to the finish line at the end of the relationship.

■ When negotiations drag, the reason could be a trivial holdup in exchanging documents, personal doubts, or a serious deadlock. Don't make assumptions about the reason for a delay—find out and confront it.

■ In arriving at a value for your company, try to establish a range instead of a single number. It's more realistic and shows flexibility.

■ To find an independent professional adviser to help you in negotiations, contact someone in an entrepreneurship program at a college business school, other CEOs who have gone through the process, or a venture trade association like the National Venture Capital Association in Arlington, Virginia.

■ Useful sources of information on industry multiples and ratios are publications issued by Standard and Poor's and Dun & Bradstreet, as well as numerous business education websites, such as that of the New York University Leonard N. Stern School of Business (www.stern.nyu.edu).

■ Negotiating should not be taken lightly or delegated to staff or advisers. Be prepared for give and take, be sure of your numbers and reasoning behind each key point, and be ready to horsetrade on nonessential points.

7

Guardian Angels: Good Investors Bring More Than Money to a Business

Angels come in all shapes and sizes, but ones who offer only money are a rare breed indeed. Most investors bring much more to the table than their checkbook. In this chapter, we'll explore some ways that angels can help your company beyond the initial investment, and we'll try to help you understand how best to use such diverse angels as the "executive recruiter," the "marriage partner," the "networker," and the "therapist." We'll also talk a little about how and why people become angel investors, so you'll understand more about what to expect from them.

Mostly, this chapter is about working together with your angel partner to achieve the most from this potentially very lucrative relationship. Finding the right angel is like being admitted to an exclusive club. Doors once closed now open. Important CEOs return your phone calls. People with money call you. Your business can now get a daily massage to work out the kinks and help it run more smoothly. Fancy clubs are more than squash courts and grill rooms serving fabulous fettuccine alfredo—they're a network of successful people who are a few rungs up the ladder from you and will gladly give you a hand up. So it can be with an angel.

MORE THAN MONEY—A SECOND TIME AROUND

The Dinner Club meeting was buzzing. As usual, members were angling to reach the bar, swapping notes about deals, and scanning executive summaries about the companies ready to make presentations. In the middle of this beehive was a tall blonde woman with a pleasant smile and a name tag announcing that she was with a company and not a club member. Like most of the outsiders at this gathering, she wanted something—but not money. She and the company where she worked as vice president for sales, VIPdesk, already had their funding. As she glided between groups of members, she handed a piece of paper to each. Kelly Christiano was in search of "guardian angels" from within her structured angel investor.

Months earlier (as we highlighted in chapter 4) the Dinner Club had made VIPdesk one of its headline companies, investing $460,000 in this Internet start-up—which offers online concierge services to large corporations—in its $3.5 million first round of institutional financing. The business was pulling in new clients every week—companies like Citibank, General Electric, and AOL—and USAir had asked it to make a presentation about offering its service to its premium flyers. VIPdesk was on a roll and wanted more, so Christiano returned to her angel group seeking names of contacts and references. She was not disappointed: The angels agreeably jotted down names and phone numbers and offered to make introductory calls.

The founder and other senior managers at VIPdesk are somewhat unusual in that they not only *listen* to their investors—they eagerly seek out their input. They have learned that their partners' value is limitless if the door is left open and constant communication is the rule rather than the exception.

The company sends out continual updates to its partners, keeping them informed as to progress and problems. As a result, the company has received a steady stream of referrals for open positions, leads to potential clients, and introductions to other financial sources who have actually ended up investing in the company.

GUARDIAN ANGELS OFFER "SMART MONEY"

The best business angels have been called guardian angels. Carl Grant, of PricewaterhouseCoopers, has witnessed dozens of angel-entrepreneur pairings and describes the ideal angel this way: "Not every million dollars is worth a million dollars. There's smart money, and there's dumb money. What you want to have involved with your company—unless all you need is cash because you're so brilliant that you can pull this off all by yourself—is smart money. You need people who are not just going to put money into your company, but are willing to take an active role in it."

An entrepreneur looking for angel financing should be casting around for a guardian angel—an individual or group who brings more than a checkbook to the deal. The distinction is between cash and what we call "warm money." There's the onetime payment, and then there's the months and, probably, years of expertise and experience that an angel willingly shares. Such a guardian angel is akin to a mentor not just for an entrepreneur but for the venture itself.

Some founders of new companies shy away from angels offering warm money, because they fear a bossy or controlling angel. They don't want anyone telling them what to do. Granted, there's the rare instance of an angel and other investors ganging up on an entrepreneur and wresting away control of the company or showing him or her the door. And the angel from hell isn't unknown. There are investors so anxious about their money that they want their hands held constantly. They may call an entrepreneur daily, even a couple of times a day, demand that the founder hire relatives of the angel, and expect royal treatment every time they meet. This is not warm money—it's scalding. The angel from hell is, fortunately, a rare creature, and when word about him or her hits the street, few entrepreneurs get in line to play again.

This is a misconception of how most angels work, even the most attentive guardian angel. Virtually all the angels we know have expressed the opposite sentiment. The last thing they want is to get back in the trenches and the day-to-day management of a company. They'd much rather offer their take-it-or-leave-it advice and leave their offices before six every evening. Remarks Dinner Club angel Steve Walker: "We get to offer advice but then don't have to make all the details happen. For me, for where I'm at, that's cool. I don't want to start another company."

AVOID "COLD-MONEY" ANGELS AND INEXPERIENCED ANGELS

Another extreme among angels is cold money. These are investors who show great enthusiasm for a deal and a company, then disappear when key documents need signing or the subject of reinvesting is raised. More unusual, but known to happen, is interference from a novice or inexperienced angel. This is, basically, someone who gives bad advice because he or she doesn't know the business or how to run a company. And a bad angel can rot the whole barrel. Remarks David Gerhardt, president of Austin, Texas-based Capital Network, which matches angels and entrepreneurs, about the effects of an incompetent angel, "I've seen cases where venture investors stayed away because they didn't want to be encumbered by an unsophisticated angel." Entrepreneurs can avoid this sticky situation by knowing something of their prospective angel's background and what motivates him or her.

Angel investments are rarely the only financing an early-stage company is going to receive. If the company is growing according to plan, then it is likely the founder will soon be back out looking for expansion capital. Later-round investors will always be interested in seeing whether the original angels are willing to participate in the next stage of financing. Subsequent investors will look for a strong reference from those angels already close to the company, so it is essential that the entrepreneur have a good relationship with these early partners. Without their ongoing participation, chances for future funding are nonexistent.

Since an uninterested angel can be deadly to the company at this point, you should perform your own due diligence on your potential partners. Interview other founders whom they have backed. Find out if the angels were willing to participate in future rounds, or if they were at least willing to provide a strong reference for the company.

We know of a case where lack of availability on the part of an angel was almost lethal to the fortunes of the start-up they originally backed. The angel had grown cool on the company's prospects and was busy with his other investments when new investors came calling. The new investors wanted feedback from the original angel and also hoped for his participation going forward. When phone calls went unreturned and meetings could not be arranged, it cast a pall over the entire proceedings.

Eventually a deal did get done, but the entrepreneur in this case was totally blindsided by the lack of support. Had there been better communication early on and had expected roles been better defined, the company probably would have had a much easier time raising money in the second round.

THE QUINTESSENTIAL GUARDIAN ANGEL

Steve Walker has had numerous encounters with new companies, originally as an entrepreneur himself and more recently as an angel investor. As we described in chapter 4, he sold his company, Trusted Information Systems, for $350 million and earmarked a portion of his 20 percent take for investment activities through Steve Walker & Associates. He meets lots of start-up jocks and especially remembers the eager entrepreneurs whose paths resemble his own early days.

When Walker had been first contacted by BioNetrix, he was well-known in his industry, Internet security systems. It was not unusual that he would get a call from the company founder, Pete Bianco, who was applying advanced technology to the highly specialized industry. Walker was especially curious because Bianco was trying to develop a new security concept, not simply manufacture a proprietary device. From Walker's point of view, building a model that could bring together many different products held much more promise than manufacturing another high-tech gizmo.

However, the address Bianco had written out for Walker gave him pause. It was a high-rent, glass-and-chrome business building in downtown Bethesda, Maryland, not exactly the kind of place he liked to see a struggling start-up situated. Walker's disappointment soon disappeared. When he walked into the office building and asked the receptionist for BioNetrix, she looked at him blankly. "Never heard of them," she said.

Minutes later, his cell phone chirped. It was Bianco, full of apologies. He explained that he'd faxed over the wrong directions, and half an hour later, Walker was entering the cramped, windowless space of BioNetrix. This was more like it. Walker had built his own company a decade earlier and could remember the chaos of the early days when time was a luxury and an undermanned staff performed at warp speed from project planning meetings to product development, from ordering Post-it notes to writing complicated software code.

Here were three gung-ho entrepreneurs, housed in a maze-like office. Thirty-six-year-old Pete Bianco was as enthusiastic and intense as a high-school kid about to go on a blind date with a beauty queen. He again apologized to Walker for the wrong directions, thinking to himself, "Of all the times to make such a stupid mistake! How can I convince this guy to invest in me if I can't even get the directions right?"

Walker, fortunately, was so intrigued by the business that he quickly forgot about the extra thirty minutes spent en route. Looking over BioNetrix's operation, he flashed back to 1983, when he was in the same position, a virtual puppy in the dog-eat-dog business world. He laughs now to think how naive he was when he launched Trusted Information Systems with his savings from a twenty-one-year career building security computer systems for the U.S. Department of Defense. When he left the government, all he had was a half-dozen wall plaques for his distinguished career, expertise in building state-of-the-art security systems, and a lot of moxie. There were no Yahoo!s, AOLs, or eBays to fuel Walker's dream back then—nor many angels to tap for investment help. He was fueled only by his own vision of rags-to-riches or, in his case, bureaucrat-to-business-tycoon. The young entrepreneur before him seemed similarly jet-propelled.

Walker's investment style is deceptive. He comes across as grand-fatherly—white-haired, easygoing, a listener more than a talker or debater—but he insists on meeting key executives and studying the books. His quiet demeanor disguises a sharp business mind, and every now and then, Walker makes an insightful observation or asks a perceptive question.

Attracted by Bianco's infectious intensity, Walker quickly immersed himself in BioNetrix's cutting-edge technology, which controlled computer access for network systems with voice scans, fingerprints, and digital photos. Walker immediately saw the promise in the technology—its software had viable commercial appeal for the thousands of giant companies concerned about protecting access to employee workstations. Yet Walker was assessing not only the technology but the people behind the company. He could identify with Bianco, who possessed an abundance of vision and drive but, as a newly minted entrepreneur, lacked experience in the field and needed lots of "adult supervision."

Walker was also pleased that Bianco was candid with his would-be angel. He confided to Walker that he was worried about competitors and the pace of his company's development. He was afraid someone would get wind of BioNetrix's technology and slip into the market earlier. Only an infusion of cash, he believed, would enable the company to get production up and running and a marketing plan in place before the window of opportunity shut for good.

Like many angels, Walker is willing to take risks but also feels a young company needs to learn to walk before it can run. And he also makes investment decisions, after all the questions are answered and the uncertainties aired, on instinct and personal chemistry. Since he's willing and wants to get involved in the start-ups he backs, he needs to respect the founder, enjoy working with him, and believe the story the founder spins about where his company is headed. Walker won't talk himself into a deal or go against his gut feelings.

Steve Walker decided to help BioNetrix and, in his classic style, started small. His first check was for $350,000, then he waited to see how the firm performed. Bianco wasted no time and immediately geared up development and marketing plans. Months later, Walker invested another $400,000 in the young firm. Such an investment is larger than many angel checks, but Walker was clearly comfortable with how Bianco was proceeding. The eager entrepreneur was recruiting top-notch executives, signing up customers, and forging partnerships with other companies. Walker was also reassured, and he became an active partner in planning the business' next stage. He met with Bianco to map out marketing strategies and share his knowledge of the industry network. He was available for advice and to make a phone call to establish new connections. He agreed to serve as chairman of the board (in exchange for stock warrants) to lend credibility and stature to the company, as well as attract other investors. "When I was starting out, I struggled to get venture capital and never succeeded," Walker says. "I can identify with these companies. BioNetrix was going to get blown away without some help."

Before Walker's involvement, BioNetrix couldn't get attention if it yelled "IPO!" in a crowded bar of investment bankers. The company was too risky, one more minnow in the shark tank of new businesses; it was undercapitalized and inexperienced. But adding Walker suddenly made BioNetrix a noteworthy prospect.

He was especially helpful in protecting BioNetrix's groundbreaking technology. He helped Bianco hire patent lawyers who quickly went to work protecting the company's intellectual property, which was the heart of its pioneering network-security software and the key to its future prosperity in a world where bigger rivals can steal ideas that aren't protected. Although there is heated debate among entrepreneurs in the high-tech community about whether patent protection is helpful—in some cases it can backfire and alert rivals to your secrets—investors generally look at patent protection as a minimal insurance policy.

"You need to take the part of the operation that is unique and protect it," Walker told Bianco. "Without intellectual-property protection, you have nothing. Even with it, someone else can always come along and do what you do better, but at least this way you have some legal recourse if they copy you too closely."

Walker and his colleagues also helped BioNetrix assemble a credible marketing plan, which immediately showed results. The young tech company signed up the World Bank, Johns Hopkins University, and Ernst & Young as customers. Now BioNetrix was no longer, in the euphemism of the industry, "pre-revenue." In other words, it was bringing in money—not much, but some.

Walker had added business backbone to the skeleton company. Within six months, BioNetrix had fifteen employees, a marketable product, and investors beating down the door to take part in a second round of financing. Smitten by a presentation the firm made in Chicago, telecom giant Ameritech decided to invest $2 million. And our angel group, the Dinner Club, voted to invest another $573,000, in part because Walker's active participation in the project gave members confidence in the company's chances of success. In the commercial equivalent of a heartbeat, the company's value rose from less than $2 million to $13 million. Whether BioNetrix will one day be acquired, sold in an IPO, collapse in a heap of unfulfilled dreams, or join the legions of "living dead"—a company that survives but doesn't thrive—one thing is certain: Its path forward would have been a lot more rocky without Walker's seed capital and savvy help.

He approached BioNetrix the way a grandfather would a grandchild. He took pride in the accomplishments and felt keen disappointment at its setbacks, but he did not feel personally responsible when things went wrong. At the end of the day, he went home to his family without worrying about cash flow, landing a big client, or an operational nightmare cropping up. It wasn't his baby to run, just to advise.

"I can offer advice, and then it is up to the child to take it or leave it," he reflected. "I don't have the same responsibility as a parent, but I get the same thrill if they succeed."

And like a grandparent, Walker was forgiving of the small missteps, like when he was given the wrong directions for the first meeting. Another investor might have driven away and left BioNetrix without a second thought. Walker did not let the trivial things distort his perspective. He was so impressed with the company's vision, and how it paralleled his younger days, that he forgot the snafus and listened. It turned out that he and Bianco were a good match—smart, practical experience meets youthful, enthusiastic energy.

And Walker got more than money from the deal. Like many angels, he was deeply invested financially and emotionally in the company. "It's more than the initial $350,000 investment. Actually, a lot more," he says. "What is more important is helping get them going. I've never had more fun in my life. It's a joy to see someone listen, take action, and win."

Walker is a good example of how, in the high-tech economy, business angels lend invaluable expertise to start-ups. With his fifteen years in the industry, he gave BioNetrix critical advice and insight. Even such famous angels as Steve Case at AOL, Howard Schultz of Starbucks, and Paul Allen of Microsoft have provided similar services to the entrepreneurs they've backed. And when angels band together, like the members of the Dinner Club or Silicon Valley's Band of Angels, their smorgasbord of advice and strategic services frequently makes the difference between life and death for a start-up.

TYPES OF GUARDIAN ANGELS

The role of a guardian angel is often misunderstood because it varies—it depends on the angel. A savvy guardian angel is often exceedingly useful in a couple of arenas, and she usually knows it. Judging from the partnerships that have come out of our angel groups, we have found that an angel can function in several ways.

Marriage partner. This angel has fallen in love with your business and wants to do everything to help it succeed. He's in for the long haul, through good times and bad, and brings to the alliance the experiences of someone who has weathered the ups and downs of a venture trying to get off the ground. This angel is supportive, not domineering, and gently steers the entrepreneur toward the right moves.

Networker. This angel often has a long history in your industry. She knows where the land mines are, where the bodies are buried, and where to find the best pickings. She may be on a nickname basis with your competitors and her e-mail list packed with the names of potential clients, customers, suppliers, and strategic partners. Best yet, the networker angel enjoys acting as go-between for an entrepreneur and her legions of contacts.

Executive recruiter. This angel is a management specialist, excelling at identifying the holes in an entrepreneur's executive team and recruiting someone to fill it. He may have extensive contacts with industry headhunters and been in the same business himself for many years. In any case, he knows how to find people and how to assess them. He's great to have along during interviews of key personnel and for sharing impressions of prospective employees.

Therapist. This angel brings to the partnership years of experience with many young companies or a few companies with dramatic fortunes. She may be a turnaround artist and revived more than one near-dead enterprise. Or she may be the quintessential bootstrapper who scrapped, struggled, and clawed her way to success. What makes this angel shine is a lifetime of experience that has given her a big-picture perspective that many beginning business owners lack. Nothing surprises her; nothing rattles her. She offers the entrepreneur an anchor in rough seas. From experience, she knows that an entrepreneur's outlook and decisions determine a company's fortunes, so she spends a lot of time talking to him. The therapist angel offers the calming voice that doesn't overreact when things go badly and doesn't get squeaky with excitement when things go stupendously. She's a steadying influence that helps an entrepreneur keep an even keel and not get distracted by insignificant squalls.

Strategic partner. This angel's specialty is an area of the business, like marketing or production, that can benefit from alliances with complementary firms. Years of experience have given this angel a knack for seeing possible synergies and collateral advantages from joining forces with outsiders.

General utility player. This angel can hit, field, and run. He's equally knowledgeable about management, financing, operations, marketing, and competitors. He knows enough about each area of a company's operations to recognize potential problem areas and offer workable solutions. We've known general utility-player angels who are on the phone daily with an entrepreneur, helping him sort through a smorgasbord of problems.

Fund-raiser. This angel is a master in financing and knows where the money is. She's learned from experience that a shortage of capital will deep-six a company quicker than a crashed website. She'll bust her butt to help a company produce a positive cash flow and show some earnings, no matter how modest. Sometimes a former CFO, if not a successful entrepreneur in her own right, she has connections with venture capitalists, investment banks, and superangels. She's always looking ahead to a new venture's financing needs and casting about for likely sources.

There is no way for us to recommend which type of angel will be right for you. It's a matter of style. You and your angel both need to understand the role that will be played. Perhaps you already have the necessary staffing in place, so hooking up with an executive-recruiter-type angel will probably result in frustration for both parties. Perhaps what *you* need most is a networker to help acquaint you with potential strategic partners in your chosen industry. The important point to take away here is that there is a *right* type of partner for every deal. Knowing there are differences should help you in picking the right one for your given needs.

FOLLOW THE MONEY: FIND OUT HOW PEOPLE BECAME ANGELS

As attractive as guardian angels sound to a budding entrepreneur, it's admittedly difficult to know what type of angel you're talking to. It's usually the company founder or CEO who is on the hot seat, answering all the questions, not the angel. This raises the delicate subject of checking out your future angel—in essence, doing due diligence on the angel or angel group. It's delicate because no one likes other people poking into his background, especially when it's aimed at the origins of his money. Nevertheless, *doing research on an angel's business and financial history will tell you volumes about why someone is in the angel business.*

Angels are like everyone else. They stick to what they're good at, the ballparks where they've cleared the fences before. A history of financial success in one field, be it as a start-up whiz, a loyal lieutenant for a high-tech phenom, or a king of software code, is strong motivation for staying in that arena. So if you want to know where guardian angels are going to direct their attention and energy in your fledgling enterprise, check out how they made money in the first place, because that's what they are going to try to do for you.

For example, Michael Rowny, an angel with the eMedia Club you read about in chapter 3, certainly fits this mold. He came into angel investing from the telecommunications industry, having been an executive with MCI when it was an upstart challenging the AT&T behemoth. As a senior vice president in charge of the long-distance phone company's international acquisitions, Rowny knew how a company could accelerate its growth by swallowing smaller fish. So when eMedia jumped in to back Mark Merrick and his venture, Step 9, which offered back-office technical and managerial services to local phone companies, Rowny became a heaven-sent guardian angel. In the short time that Rowny has been overseeing Step 9 operations, his role has intensified from someone Merrick telephoned occasionally to daily adviser. His advice has become so integral to the fortunes of Step 9 that he has taken an office in the company's suite.

When the time came that Step 9 needed another round of financing, it was Rowny who identified the best source of that money and helped negotiate the term sheet. In doing so, he helped to boost the company's valuation to $25 million, at least four times higher than the first round just a year earlier. Rowny's expertise is knowing how to build a business. That's the source of his good fortune, and he's sharing his wisdom with the entrepreneurs he takes under his wing.

The following paragraphs describe some of the ways that other angels made their money.

Self-made millionaires. An informal survey of our clubs, as well as superangels we know, reveals that angel bucks and business experience spring from all over the map. There are the self-made millionaires who fit the classic mold: hard-driving, aggressive, and absolutely determined to be successful. Whether they came from a family business, a franchise operation, or a from-the-ground-up triumph, their wealth stems from their own sweat. Making money is hard work, and self-made millionaires know firsthand the value of a dollar. As a result, they're shrewd, thoughtful investors, never handing over money without knowing what they want it to accomplish. There's nothing spontaneous or dilettantish about their investing, and any entrepreneur they select to support gets their full attention.

High-tech options angels. These angels were once a small cadre of pioneers in the early days of mainframe computers and electronics, but they are becoming as common as cappuccino bars. Usually younger, with a highly prized skill such as designing websites or solving network security issues, they emerge most often from a single, celebrated company, having garnered their fortunes by being in the right place at the right time. They devoted mind-numbingly long days to young companies, often staking their careers on a charismatic CEO with a brilliant idea. When the founder's pipe dream became an IPO, or was purchased by an even bigger dreamer, their risk paid off, and the options they received in lieu of a higher paycheck catapulted them into angeldom. Although known for their 90-hour workweeks and the sacrifice of a home and personal life, they made their fortunes in a relatively short period of time compared to the self-made millionaire. These roots are obvious in the ways they handle angel investing.

These multimillionaires probably ran only a department or were product managers or incredibly successful salespeople. Consequently, they tend to be masterful in dealing with certain areas of business, and offer the best help and advice when focused on their specialty. They have never operated a business or made a payroll but possess the stamina for hard work and may expect others to be equally dogged. They are totally confident that backbreaking hours coupled with high risk can knock the cover off the ball.

Professional angels. This term refers not to full-time, paid angels but to those who come from the professional ranks of doctors, lawyers, accountants, and management consultants. Their careers have happily spun off not only hefty fees but bonuses or royalties large enough to elevate them to angel status. Some of these professionals are dabblers, making numerous small investments ($5,000 to $50,000) in a cats-and-dogs portfolio that may include such diverse enterprises as the restaurant of a football star and a better-mousetrap invention. Historically, these individuals have formed the core group of angels known as family-and-friends. They sometimes have only a passing familiarity with business, and their judgment is frequently clouded by personal friendships, peer-group influence, and well-meaning philanthropic intentions.

Another breed of professional angel are serious students of the investment world, who eagerly educate themselves on the latest business developments and practices. They seek out experts in any field they're interested in, are voracious readers of the general and specialized business press, and enjoy the prospect of receiving a hands-on education from their investment.

Company executives. This is yet another class of angel: upper management from *Fortune* 1,000 companies who have dedicated their careers to an industry and want to parlay their lifetime of knowledge into a savvy investment. They have high salaries, good option plans plus bonuses, discretionary income, and many friends with the same qualities, and pocketbooks. These people not only know their industry's markets, competitors, and technology, they know the gossip—who's making money, who's losing it, who's in, who's out. They offer an entrepreneur an insider's perspective that's hard to find anywhere else. The young companies that catch their eye are often on the periphery of their industry and have an exciting scheme for slipping into some highly lucrative niche. The budding company is very early stage, barely off the kitchen table, and gives the executive angel a chance to flex his industry connections and know-how.

Old money. A long tradition in American venture investing is the support of wealthy, multigeneration families. The industrial titans of the nineteenth and early twentieth centuries dutifully plowed their multiplying millions into the next generation of merchants and builders. Many early venture funds were established with money from pools of wealthy family investors, and as the American economic boom took hold in the 1990s, wealthy families created family enterprises and foundations dedicated to managing their holdings.

A common scenario among wealthy families is for a younger member to acquire a business and financial education, gain firsthand experience in a family business, then turn his or her attention to overseeing investments. Frequently these families have access to large sums and become superangels to start-ups. Another element to this sketch is that they may prefer to invest in ventures involved in causes and social issues important to the family. As angels, they may stay well in the background of a new venture, offering advice and support when asked but preferring to give the entrepreneur free rein to develop his dream.

Real-estate developers and property owners. A singular species of angel has come out of one segment of the economy: real estate. The boom in U.S. real estate that began in the 1980s, abated slightly, then came roaring back, has spawned enormous wealth among developers and property owners. While some fortunes languished in later years as the returns on investment in technology vastly outstripped those in real estate, many individuals whose fortunes have come from property have managed to hold on to their winnings and apply them to venture-capital investing. As an angel, a former real-estate king brings a keen understanding of financing and debt structures, as well as of the gyrations of economic booms and busts.

"Lucky" angels. Probably the quirkiest and least predictable of angels is the lucky angel. These are the lottery winners, large lawsuit beneficiaries, divorcées with huge settlements, children of wealthy deceased parents, and portfolio-rich widows and widowers. Professional athletes with fat contracts and entertainers with star-studded fees and royalties can also be lumped in this category. These people may know little about investing or

the world of entrepreneurial capital. However, more than one lucky angel has hired sophisticated financial advisers to help guide their investments and educate them in the ways of venture-capital investing. And the commitment to excellence they have shown in their particular field may well be transferable to the world of angel investing. Beyond the fact of their wealth, it's impossible to make generalizations about how involved in or distant they are from their investments.

Superangels and archangels. As the world of angel investing expands, it's bound to produce subspecialties and refinements. Superangels are investors with enough financial muscle to create what looks like a VC fund. Superangels dip from bigger coffers, have deeper pockets, and are usually in a deal for more than one round of financing. They also help an entrepreneur find additional funding, lead added financing rounds, and have a well-cultivated network of venture capitalists. Experienced superangels may also have staff support. But unlike venture capitalists, superangels are tossing in their own money, not someone else's, and may demand an active role, like a board seat, in a company.

Archangels are rarer birds. They're the point of the flock, providing guidance, direction, and leadership. In structured angel groups, they may be called managers and be responsible for managing the flow of business plans, monitoring due-diligence activity, and tracking investments. Usually founding members of the group, they have enormous influence over where and how the group invests.

The term "archangel" has also been used to refer to a hybrid type of angel group that backs start-ups by combining the hands-on investment style of guardian angels with the VC approach of spreading out and diversifying an investment pool. For example, a Silicon Valley group called Angel Investors consists of highly successful technology entrepreneurs, who each put in $300,000 to $500,000 and want an active part in their investments, providing advice and mentoring to entrepreneurs. But unlike other structured angel pools, the group has a kitty of over $100 million and, in the first nine months of 1999, invested in eighty start-ups.

AN ADVISORY BOARD FOR VITAL CARE AND FEEDING

Sure, many guardian angels have terrific talents that can be used to give a start-up a boost, but entrepreneurs sometimes struggle to figure out the best way to tap into their angel's expertise. A practical solution is to *include your angel on either an advisory board or, for a stronger voice, on the board of directors.* Before you do so, however, have a clear picture of how this is going to play out.

A company advisory board has a number of distinguishing features. For starters, it has no legal authority or operational power. It doesn't set policy, determine salaries, hire or fire, or enter into agreements. But it isn't entirely toothless, and entrepreneurs should strive to give members as much authority as they can handle. An advisory board's bite and influence comes from an entrepreneur who listens to it and follows up on its suggestions. Guardian-angel advisers are great idea people—they've been around your track many times before and have seen things you have yet to experience. Ideas for mergers, strategic alliances, marketing campaigns, ways to beat the competition, how to find a new CFO, the best ways to secure a line of credit—there's no limit to the scope of their suggestions.

If you're going to really listen to your advisory board, it's important to select good people. Everyone has heard stories about advisory boards whose sole function is to sit on the company letterhead and impress outsiders. Take your time assembling an advisory board, inviting people who have something to offer other than fame, who know the reality of their position with your company, who can offer useful advice, and whom you respect enough to listen to. This is your kitchen cabinet, so pick people whom you feel comfortable going to with any issue. A good combo for an advisory board is a mixture of insiders and outsiders: senior managers from the company, plus outsiders such as your lawyer or accountant, experts from industry, influential investors, and other entrepreneurs from similar stage companies.

Entrepreneurs may be tempted to skip forming an advisory board, perhaps feeling it's an unnecessary formality, and instead designate individuals as "advisers to the president" or whatever. The flaw with this approach is that the adviser's role is so vague as to gradually fade and vanish, and all you will have accomplished is annoying someone with an ill-conceived gesture. Another pitfall is an advisory board that rarely meets or has no designated functions. A paper advisory board is worse than worthless, because word will get out to others in your business that you don't know how to use advice. This could come back to haunt you when you're trying to raise money.

Most of the advisory boards we're familiar with began as relatively informal gatherings. They usually met quarterly, sometimes at the CEO's home, where, after dinner, they chat about the company, what it's doing, and where it's going. We've found that such informal boards are most helpful in a company's early days, when the entrepreneur is encountering a barrage of new situations and problems, and needs a steady stream of sage advice. But over time, as a CEO grows more confident and successful, he or she calls on the advisory board less. Loosely arranged advisory boards, especially if they're composed of more friends and family than experienced business-people, can easily evaporate.

At this point in a company's growth, you need a more formal advisory board. There's an old saying that applies here: "Advice is worth what you pay for it." While this is not an absolute truism, we've found that entrepreneurs listen more and advisers participate more when something other than goodwill is at stake. To give this body heft and real influence, a founder may set aside a small percentage of the company's equity, for instance 5 percent, to give to the advisory board as compensation and incentive. In addition, *advisory board members should receive a fee for attending meetings, even if a nominal amount, and perhaps an equity bonus if they're an active member of the advisory board for a certain number of years.* You want these people to have a vested interest in your company's future.

Even fractions of percentages can keep an advisory board's interest. Many businesspeople are familiar with the story of Ken Brody, the former Goldman Sachs director and onetime head of the Export-Import Bank, who agreed to serve on the advisory board of a start-up called Yurie Systems, founded by the promising Korean-American entrepreneur

Jeong Kim. Brody received a small percentage of Yurie Systems stock for his participation, and six months later, when the fledgling enterprise was sold to Lucent for $1.1 billion cash, his symbolic compensation was worth millions.

CEOs determine how often an advisory board meets, although we'd caution against too few meetings, like one a year, or too many, like every month. The regularity really depends on what the CEOs need, and may well change as they gain experience. When it meets, an advisory board can split its time between micro and macro issues. The micro items involve the company's daily dealings—personnel issues, office space and leasing questions, contacts with customers. These questions are pretty light fare for an advisory board, though they may vex a CEO who's too close to the situation, and they can usually be dispensed with by simple, quick answers. The meat-and-potatoes of the meeting are questions surrounding a company's core operations and direction.

The CEOs we know are under constant pressure to re-examine their company's mission and consider additional or alternative ways to achieve it. Debates about whether to build or buy key technology, the nature of strategic alliances and who the company should be targeting as a potential partner, positioning itself for a particular exit strategy, and the never-ending dilemma of where to find additional financing are the main course of advisory-board meetings.

In its finest hour, an advisory board can do for a company what one did for a Gaithersburg, Maryland, outfit called ScienceWise. The board, after much deliberation, advised relaunching the company as a more modern Internet-based enterprise. Before bringing in an advisory board, ScienceWise, originally called Research and Management Systems, was a sleepy information-publishing organization. It had revenues and a steady operating history but few prospects for growth, namely because its sole customer was the federal government. Around 1999, its co-founder and CEO, John Rodman, decided it was time to rethink his venture, especially as he glanced around and saw what was happening to other information-resource companies that were jumping on the dot-com bandwagon. While technically not a start-up, Rodman was going to treat his decade-old company like one and see if, with the help of a smart advisory board, he could relaunch it into another sphere. Its primary service had been as a bulletin board for the government. Rodman wanted to discard the bulletin board and build a fabulous interactive research library for technical professionals around the globe using the most modern delivery technique available: the World Wide Web.

Rodman created a three-person advisory board, consisting of: an expert in financing and technology start-ups, Chuck Stein, an experienced technologist and manager, who had been CEO of a public company; Jeff Weiss, a serial Internet entrepreneur himself; and one of the authors of this book, John May, who brought years of knowledge about entrepreneurial technology companies. At first, their assignment was unclear. There were conflicting expectations about whether the advisory board was brought in mainly to open doors to additional financing or to tackle broader company issues. It took a couple of meetings with top management for everyone to agree on the advisory board's role.

Then their task was clear: Rodman asked them to help him turn the company into a viable Internet enterprise with a revenue stream coming from many sources, not just the federal government. Rodman wanted to build his company into a premier engineering and scientific information resource. He knew he would need capital to do this, and so he had to configure a company that had not only inherent value but the prospect of a highly profitable future.

The advisory board suggested that Rodman concentrate on three areas: the product, the customers, and the company story. The success of Internet information sources had vividly demonstrated that Web users would pay for research and information. Scientists and engineers would pay to learn about jobs, research grants, scholarships, fellowships, and avenues for collaboration with other professionals, and for professional articles. Subscribers would also pay for enhanced services, like individualized literature searches and e-mail alerts on special events. With an enhanced, targeted service product, ScienceWise would appeal to thousands of scientists and engineers. Changing the company story meant changing its image from a staid private adjunct to the federal bureaucracy to a Internet-based, technology-driven marketer of information services.

The advisers suggested that Rodman shift the company's customer base, first by working with existing government customers, explaining the company's expanding focus and offering an improved product, then aggressively seeking out customers in the private sector.

The advisory board's ideas transformed ScienceWise into Science-Wise.com and, even more dramatic, into a company that soon attracted the attention of venture capitalists. Within a year of the creation of its new identity, ScienceWise.com received $7 million in first-round funding, and now boasts a customer base of more than 150,000 scientists, engineers, and health-care providers. One of its advisory members became so essential to the company that he was asked to join the board of directors.

ANGELS CAN HELP PULL MONEY TOGETHER FOR SECONDARY FINANCING

Angel investors, especially guardian angels who become immersed in a company's fortunes and future, can provide yet another service beyond financing and advice. It is common for them to act as syndicators by pulling together various sources of money for follow-on financing. Think of a circus master, bringing into the ring different-size creatures to perform and then slip backstage. As angel club manager, we play this role frequently with the companies we support.

What happens is that a juicy-looking company comes to one of our angel groups looking for financing, but it wants, or needs, more than we alone can bankroll. We don't want to turn them away empty-handed but can't support the company on our own, so we enlist other funding sources. We bring in the elephants and tigers. Our relationship with a new company called DiamondBack Vision happened this way. You might remember from chapter 5 that DiamondBack, which has developed new technology in the field of Internet video compression, was shopping for $2.5 million when it made a presentation to the eMedia Club.

The angels in eMedia quickly realized that this company had a great future ahead and would need more than $2.5 million—closer to twice that—and their wallets were not that fat. Assuming the role of syndicator, the group first cast about for a lead investor, a heavy hitter, probably from the venture-capital community, who shared our vision for this up-and-comer. We enlisted the participation of a regional venture firm that specializes in technology enterprises, Novak Biddle Venture Partners II. Other venture-capital funds showed interest, but Novak Biddle had experienced, highly trained tech people on their staff, which gave them the edge. They also created a snowball effect for the syndicate, drawing in other sources of venture capital—namely, ABS Ventures, a wing of the investment banking firm Deutsche Banc Alex. Brown, and a publicly held consortium of Internet technology companies, CMGI Ventures. And adhering to the universal philosophy of syndication, More Is Always Better, we also enrolled a superangel in the project.

At the end of all this orchestrating, DiamondBack Vision got more than angel backing—it got a syndicate behind it, which invested $5 million so it could boost its technology and grow the company.

ANGEL HANGOUTS AND ANGEL NETWORKS

As angel investing has come of age, it has developed an infrastructure. This consists of the numerous services and sources that link entrepreneurs with individual angels and with angel groups. Entrepreneurs looking for guardian-angel-type advice, as well as angel dollars, can turn to online services, a matching service, or placement agents.

Probably the best-known online service is Garage.com. Created in 1998 by former Apple executive Guy Kawasaki, it aims to help entrepreneurs rev up their companies by providing help with financing and management structure, as well as helping polish the company for angel and VC consumption by offering advice on presentation, negotiation, and valuation techniques. Garage.com also maintains a roster of active investors (what it calls "Heaven" on its website and is accessible only to qualified subscribers) shopping for a start-up to invest in.

The website doesn't do any of the middleman stuff that structured angel groups do—it doesn't target start-ups or likely investors, help with decision-making, or get into negotiation. Member investors of Garage.com make their own decisions and strike their own deals. The website aims to serve start-ups looking for between $500,000 and $10 million, and also offers to help with follow-on financing for even larger deals. Of course, you're asking, "Does it work?" We think it's too early to tell, but what we've seen looks sound. (Guy Kawasaki also offers his own fund-raising tips, which we've included here.)

WORDS OF WISDOM FROM GUY KAWASAKI ON HOW TO FIND FINANCING

Guy Kawasaki is one hip entrepreneur, having parlayed his years at Apple Computer into a start-up that—get this—sells advice to other start-ups. Garage.com sure looks like a home run—its list of partners and backers reads like a tombstone page in *The Wall Street Journal*. He's on the mark with these ten tips, taken from his website, for entrepreneurs looking for financing.

1. Don't outsmart yourself. Refrain from reinventing securities law with sophisticated financing schemes. This game is simple. You find believers, they give you money, you build the company, and everyone gets rich.

2. Don't be paranoid. You don't want money from anyone dumb enough to sign a nondisclosure agreement. If you have a good idea, five people are working on it. If you have a great idea, ten people are working on it. Thus, the key is implementation, not protecting the secrecy of an idea. So talk it up, find your believers, and get on with it.

3. Be brief. One-page e-mail. Twenty-page business plan. Fifteen PowerPoint slides. One-hour meeting.

4. Acknowledge an enemy. When you say, "No one else is doing this," investors are thinking: "Then there's no market," or "These guys are clueless." Both are not conducive to getting funded. Competition at least validates that there's a market. Focus on proving how you have an unfair, sustainable competitive advantage.

5. Look for value, not valuation. True or false: The holy grail of entrepreneurship is preventing dilution. Answer: False. The holy grail of entrepreneurship is finding high-value investors who help you create a high valuation company. Look beyond the money to see what kind of recruiting, business development, and expert advice the investor can give you.

6. Eat when served. When people are offering to invest in your company, take the money. I've never seen a company go out of business that still had money. I have seen many companies go out of business who thought they could always raise money later.

7. Build the team. How do you think the system works: Get the money, then hire the team; or, hire the team, then get the money? This is not a chicken-and-egg problem. The order is, without question, get the team, then you get the money.

8. Ask for less than you need. This is counterintuitive, but the reason you ask for less than you need is so that you can quickly declare victory ("We're fully subscribed!") and get more money. If you can't declare victory right away, some of the people who were committed may lose interest because hot deals are always oversubscribed.

9. Avoid blood and sex. Maybe your grandmother and grandfather worked together for thirty years at the family dry-cleaning business. That's wonderful. But if you want to start a venture-capital-funded company that's going public on NAS-DAQ, don't do it with relatives or spouses. When you have to hire a CFO to take your company public, who's going to tell your husband that he has to go?

10. Keep burn rates low and cash balances high. No matter how much money you raise and how much pressure you're under to expand and scale, conserve your cash. Most companies have to change their business models on their way to success. Suffice it to say that it's a bad time to try to raise more money when your old business model is failing.

Keep in mind that the angel matching services make the phone calls and set up the date, but it's the entrepreneur who knocks on the front door and does the wooing. We believe angel investing is an intensely personal interaction. It will be interesting to see how these matching sites weather the eventual downturn in start-up activity around the country. Angel investing grew out of informal referrals from friends and associates. Today it has become more structured through investment groups like our Dinner Club, but we're not sure it's ready for automated search engines online. Time will tell.

While Garage.com may be the highest-profile Web-based matching service, there are many others that offer to connect investors and entrepreneurs. While not all deal with entrepreneurs and investors mostly through cyberspace, they share common characteristics. Most charge a processing or "membership" fee, offer seminars and forums on start-up operations, financing and business-plan preparation, and consulting for individual firms. They usually have paid staff who may be mostly administrative, managing inquiries and the flow of business plans, or who are knowledgeable and experienced entrepreneurs themselves. Some matching firms screen the new companies that come to them, usually applying criteria related to size and point in development, industry segment, and amount of money sought.

There are hundreds of angel matching services, databases, and firms specializing in providing help, and sometimes financing, to entrepreneurs and start-up ventures. We have a directory that lists 138 such outfits, not to mention 1,167 venture capitalists. Entrepreneurs looking for angel-like financing resources should consult one of the venture-capital textbooks or do an online search. Databases sound fairly unsexy but can be very attractive, especially those developed by venture-financing firms that include exhaustive information about investors. For instance, International Capital Resources, a venture-capital resource firm in San Francisco, has a database containing profiles of more than 8,200 high-net-worth investors. The company spends thousands each month maintaining this list and providing information services to investors. What entrepreneur wouldn't like to get hold of ICR's passcode?

Even the federal government has gotten into the act. The U.S. Small Business Administration sponsors the Angel Capital Electronic Network, a listing service that provides information about small, growing companies to venture capitalists, institutions, and accredited individual investors via a secure Internet database. It's for companies looking for between $250,000 and $5 million. To be listed on the ACE-Net, a company must complete a Small Company Offering Registration, U-7 form, which looks a lot like the prospectus a company files before an IPO. In essence, this listing is like a mini-exchange for start-up IPOs. (It's at www.ace-net.sr.unh.edu.)

ANGELS AND ADVISERS IN A BOX: INCUBATORS

Yet another route for entrepreneurs looking for the kind of tender loving care that guardian angels provide is to join an incubator. In case you've been living in a cubicle for the last year, incubators are centralized office spaces (renovated warehouses and seedy strip malls are popular) housing clusters of individuals, each toiling on his or her own start-up venture and supported and advised by the incubator owner/manager, who's often an entrepreneurial guru and a cashed-out former business owner as well. Incubators have sprung up as a result of the flood of new companies being formed and the thousands of entrepreneurs looking for help. Of course, they already have their own trade association, the National Business Incubation Association, which reports that the number of incubators has leapt from 12 in 1980 to around 850 today.

The early incubators were offspring from universities and regional business-development agencies. One of the first Silicon Valley incubators was created by the National Aeronautics and Space Agency in 1993 and is still going. Private enterprise has taken over the incubator business bigtime, with blue-chip tech companies, high-flying venture-capital firms, and big-bucks individuals leading the parade. One of the more famous private incubators is idealab!, founded in Pasadena, California, by former Lotus exec Bill Gross, and which has hatched at least three companies that have gone public: eToys, NetZero, and GoTo.com.

Here's how incubators work: An individual or company, usually bankrolled by a successful entrepreneurial venture, rents a large chunk of office space and offers start-up whizzes a place to develop ideas and create a company. The incubator takes care of the messy, distracting stuff of running a business, like buying furniture, answering phones, supplying office equipment, and making lattes, and, more valuable, help in conceptualizing their idea and bringing it to market. The people running an incubator help entrepreneurs with business plans, marketing, finding financing, and all the peripheral issues of running a company, like legal and accounting advice. Incubator owner-managers sometimes invest in their fledglings, although usually not at an angel level, and may introduce them to other sources of financing. Naturally, all this nurturing comes with a price tag—usually a chunk of a new venture's equity. Entrepreneurs commonly have to cough up between 10 and 60 percent.

An incubator we work closely with, ASAP Ventures in Alexandria, Virginia, provides physical and strategic support and helps a start-up with fund-raising, but it doesn't write checks. Its relationship with a young company, Star Remote, which moved into its facilities when it consisted of three founders and a draft business plan, illustrates how some incubators work. Star Remote, which develops software for wireless communication between a PDA or phone and computer, had made a presentation at the Dinner Club. (The company may sound familiar to you—its original name was UWapIT, which we wrote about in chapter 2). The presentation didn't go over well. The three founders were engaging enough, but club members felt the venture was too young for angel financing. They concluded that Star Remote was just three guys and a business plan, and that it needed to bulk up before any angel investing took place.

So they joined the ASAP Ventures incubator, which offered to help them raise enough money to develop a bankable business plan and introduce them to likely providers of bridge financing, but not invest in them. The company found money at Toucan Capital, an early-stage venture fund that's a little like superangels but somewhat more formal. Toucan provided Star Remote with a $500,000 bridge loan, which paid interest and would convert into equity in the Series A financing round, when the first institutional financiers joined in. Later, the incubator managers helped arrange additional financing from Zilkha Capital Partners in New York.

An incubator generally won't let a company attempt to hatch itself indefinitely. Many have deadlines—a set number of years in which they have to break out and fly on their own. It's like living at home after college, with your parents doing your cooking and laundry and giving you job-hunting advice (and maybe a small loan to tide you over)—and then kicking you out of the nest when you land a job.

Incubators can be picky and not let in any old hatchling. Since the incubator will be investing time, resources, and often money in a venture, it wants entrepreneurs who can deliver on their dreams. Some incubators even have waiting lists of eager entrepreneurs who are eager to join that coop and no other.

Incubators can't take the place of guardian angels, but they can plug some huge holes in an entrepreneur's knowledge base. Digital Addiction's Jamey Harvey, the entrepreneur who first rounded up a couple dozen angels and later had to restructure his company to enable a VC firm to invest (whom we talked about in chapter 6), came out of an incubator called Phase 1, which is run by Doug Humphrey and Lisa Losito. Humphrey's wherewithal came from his stake of the sale of his Internet service-provider company, Digex, for $150 million. Instead of using the money to buy himself a quaint bed-and-breakfast and the Life of Reilly, he created Phase 1 in a warehouse in Laurel, Maryland, on the edge of the Washington, D.C., metro area.

The companies that come into Phase 1 have two years to learn to fly on their own. Phase 1 gave Digital Addiction a comfortable nest; it enabled Harvey to move out of his mother's attic and to bring together his employees. One of the first things Humphrey did for the young man was help him reincorporate his company, create stock, and set up accounting books. The Phase 1 leader also kicked in $150,000 and, even more precious, gave him expert advice in how to make a presentation before an investment group. The incubator paid off for Harvey: Digital Addiction was able to attract angel capital—and subsequently spun off a technology that led to the creation of another start-up, iKimbo. As of this writing, iKimbo has attracted over $10 million in venture capital and has excellent prospects. For Harvey, his guardian angel turned out to be an incubator.

Regardless of whether your angel support comes from an experienced business executive, an incubator staff, or angels found through a matching service, it is essential that you work with your backer to obtain more than money to grow your company. Our club members have shown over and over again that they want to mentor their entrepreneurs. The psychic reward received by angels complements the entrepreneur's "leg up" received from warm money.

■ Try not to burden your guardian angel with dreary, mundane concerns that you can resolve with a little thought and effort. Save your chips for when the stakes are higher.

■ Due diligence on an entrepreneur's part—getting to know your angel and his or her investment style—is the best way to avoid an angel from hell or cold money.

■ Try the straightforward route in doing due diligence on your angel's background: Take him or her to dinner and ask.

■ Superangels are often headliners. To find them, follow local news about venture investing, noting the individual names as distinct from company names.

■ If your guardian angel is going to help secure financing, talk about that arrangement and what he or she expects in return. Some angels will insist on compensation, such as cash paid as a percentage of funds raised, or stock options. Others do it gratis. Raise this subject before your angel begins to approach prospective investors or follow-on angels.

■ In picking an incubator, look at the other companies working there and the track record of the owner/manager. Find out if the incubator knows enough about your kind of business to add value besides desks, chairs, and Xerox machines.

■ If you deal with a structured angel group, try to establish a close relationship with one or more angel members.

■ Learn about the many types of guardian angels, and match your needs with the right type.

8

Bye, Bye Angel:

Establishing Exit Strategies for Your Investors

In this chapter, we will discuss how to position businesses for sale, and we will evaluate the various merits of such investor exit strategies as acquisitions, management buyouts, and IPOs.

Mention the words "exit strategy" to anyone even vaguely familiar with investing and the first thing that pops to mind is IPO—yippee, we're going public!

If that's all you want to read about, we're going to disappoint you. In fact, it's pretty far down our list of exit strategies that entrepreneurs need to know about. An IPO is to an exit strategy what a royal flush is to a poker hand. It's a rare event, happening to less than 1 percent of new companies. In an average year, only a few hundred companies become publicly traded, out of tens of thousands being started. To say it's a long shot is an understatement. Furthermore, we've found that many angel investors don't like to hear entrepreneurs spinning grand plans about taking their company public. Unless these entrepreneurs have done it before (in which case they've got a great track record and people throwing money at them), it reveals not just naiveté but a lack of realism. Marc Seriff, an angel and co-founder of AOL, offers this perspective on the illusion of thinking about an IPO too soon: "If you've raised kids, you don't tell your seven-year-old to go play Little League baseball so he can turn pro." When we hear promises for a stellar public offering and astronomical valuations, we wonder if the founder is a couple of cards short of a full deck.

WHEN TO START LOOKING FOR THE DOOR

The irony of exit strategies is that angels and entrepreneurs need to think about them from the first day of their partnership, long before anyone thinks about making a move toward a door. A good exit strategy is founded on a good operating strategy. If a business is built and run well, there will be exit strategies galore to choose from.

For example, the rise of a company called Preview Travel, an online travel-information and reservations site, which went from a handful of angel investors to partnering and eventual merger with a major publicly owned company, shows how sound decisions about growing a company naturally lead to a profitable exit for investors. The company's first angels began investing in the company in the early 1990s, when it was a brand-new venture selling travel packages to consumers via an 800 number and TV infomercials. The idea of planning an exit strategy or flipping an investment was foreign to most investors at this time. The entrepreneurial climate emphasized building a company and the slow creation of wealth, not quick returns. The angels intended to be with the company for many years.

Preview Travel went out of the gate fast and within a few years was swamped with more phone inquiries and orders than it could handle. Its founder, Jim Hornthal, huddled with his investors, pulling ideas and suggestions from them. As a consequence, he decided in 1994 to try various marketing methods, and gradually the company's primary business tool, phone sales, evolved into Internet sales.

This was a gutsy decision, since Web-based sales were more a gleam in a few people's eyes than much of a reality. Adding to the risk was the shift in Hornthal's business concept. By offering people travel packages they purchased as a result of television advertising, Hornthal was acting as a travel agent. In switching to an e-commerce model, he was going to let people act as their own travel agents by making their own arrangements. Hornthal would provide the pieces, but individual customers would have to put them together.

From an investor's point of view, Hornthal's decision could also be viewed as a delay in their exit plans, if not an outright danger to them. But even without the benefit of today's hindsight, we can say it was the right decision. This is because Hornthal was thinking first and foremost about how to expand his company and build a brand. If an exit-strategy mentality had been the driving force, he might have tried to handle the growing phone business by adding more lines and beefing up those revenues rather than looking further ahead to a larger potential marketplace.

His angels were right behind him, pushing not for a quick return but for a company with legs. His decision proved prescient. One of Preview Travel's early angels was Ted Leonsis, who had founded his own company, Redgate Communications, which eventually he sold to Steve Case, who was in the middle of shaping America Online. Leonsis joined AOL, and by becoming a senior manager there, he was immediately in a position to make introductions between the online travel company, Preview Travel, and the online service provider, AOL. It was a serendipitous turn of events, with Leonsis as the pivot point. Hornthal and Case began to talk and explore the possibility of a partnership, and in 1994, AOL bought 20 percent of Preview Travel, which made its debut with the online service months later as Preview Vacations Online.

The AOL investment in Preview Travel elevated it to another level, giving the company cachet, credibility, and clients. It also enabled Hornthal to take his company public, which he did in the mid-1990s at around $10 a share. Many of the original angels were still with Preview Travel, and rode their stock from their original price of $2 a share to as high as $50 a share. Early investors were able to cash in their holdings for a return twenty-five times greater than their original investment.

After the AOL investment and the subsequent public offering, Preview Travel continued to evolve. In 1999, its main competitor, Travelocity, offered to buy the company, and the angel investors who were still holding their original investment received shares of the now-dominant online travel provider. Along the way, Preview Travel's investors have had more exit opportunities than they could have imagined.

The lesson for investors is a simple one. By choosing a solid company with a CEO who takes the long-term view, exit options will become available. Too many investors are looking for the quick hit and, given that opportunity, may cash in their chips too soon.

Every entrepreneur should be guided by a dream but also a realistic sense of how long and in what form that dream will exist over time. Leonsis and Hornthal both realized that their dream could grow best in the bosom of another company, in this case AOL. To prepare your company for every eventuality, you must first come to grips with your own ability to be flexible and open-minded to growth options. Entrepreneurs with successfully executing companies will constantly be presented with choices relating to both the interim direction and eventual sale of their enterprises. Good communication between founders and investors is essential to gaining consensus on exit choices.

TALK ABOUT EXITS EARLY AND OFTEN

Exit-strategy discussions need to be raised early and often. We've found that when the subject isn't discussed, the fault may lie with either party, investor or entrepreneur. One endearing angel quality is patience. We generally have longer timelines than venture capitalists, and it's not unusual to find an angel who's content to stay with an investment for many years. This makes sense, given that so many angels finance start-ups not solely or primarily for the financial reward but for the sheer fun of staying in the entrepreneurial arena. As long as they're enjoying themselves—wheeling, dealing, and making connections—they stay with a new venture.

This was surely the thinking for some of the angel investors in Preview Travel—they held on even when Preview looked as though it was permanently grounded. Says one angel investor, "During those years, if anybody had offered me the price I paid originally, I would have happily taken it.

Eight years into the investment, it felt like the company was going nowhere. But we had never planned an exit. Then all of a sudden, the AOL deal happened, and our share value jumped five times. The day before that, I would have sold out for a fraction of my investment." As the Preview Travel angels discovered, sometimes an extraordinary event can provide the booster rocket to launch an exit.

On the other hand, entrepreneurs may avoid talking about exits for a variety of reasons. They may not want to give investors the appearance of getting ahead of themselves, of building castles in the sky before they have constructed a rocket to get there. And a company founder who dwells on the pot at the end of the rainbow can alienate an angel who's more interested in nurturing a start-up. Bobby Ray Inman, a well-known Texas businessman who was an early investor in Dell Computer and Oracle, says, "For those who are purely interested in how they can make how much money, I simply pass. When I hear the dialogue where they're calculating how quickly they can do an IPO, I wish them good luck and refer them to other people."

Uncertainty can also tongue-tie an entrepreneur, especially a first-time CEO who's unsure how the business is going to develop. Not knowing all the possible options and detailed permutations of those options may prompt an entrepreneur to sidestep the subject entirely. It's like the novice gambler sitting down to a craps table at Atlantic City for the first time, and letting his chips ride because he has no idea of other ways to configure his bet.

Exit strategies in general should be discussed when the initial term sheet is being negotiated, and regularly from that time forth. A compelling reason to bring it up during negotiations is that legal groundwork must be laid that can accommodate an entrepreneur's plans for his company. Both the entrepreneur and angel want to structure a deal that offers the most options and flexibility when it comes time to exit, years down the road. For example, consider the implications of the class of stock an angel accepts. Angels like preferred stock, because it confers more rights if a company is liquidated. Frequently, the stock clause in a term sheet speci-fies a convertible security, meaning that the type of stock that a company gives to an angel can later be traded in or converted to another class of stock. Unlike venture capitalists, many angels (or friends and family) do take common stock, but getting out is harder.

Other clauses in term sheets that refer to liquidity—how easy or difficult it is to turn a company asset, like stock, into cash—influence the how and when of an exit. Thus, provisions for stock options, conversion timetables, warrants, follow-on financing, dilution, redemption rights, sale of stock to a third party, rights of first refusal if an owner decides to leave the start-up, default events, and any covenants about a company's financing or operations all become ingredients in the exit stew. Exhibit 8–1 lists some of the key provisions included in a term sheet that pertain to exit strategies.

EXHIBIT 8–1:
EXIT SIGNS IN THE TERM SHEET

These clauses or provisions set forth in the term sheet lay the path for an angel's exit route from an investment. Here's how they affect what happens when an angel wants out.

Covenant: A promise added to a term sheet, like a founder agreeing to meet certain financing landmarks or an investor agreeing not to sell shares before a certain time.

Convertible debt: An interest in a company, like preferred stock, that can be converted into another form of interest, like common stock or cash. There's usually a rate or an amount attached to it, which can be part of an exit payoff.

Dilution: What happens to the value of an investor's stock when new money comes in and more stock is handed out. If an angel's investment is diluted, he or she has less say about the exit and receives less.

Exploding preferred: Preferred stock that pays substantial dividends after a certain number of years, forcing a company to raise more money, sometimes through a liquidity event like going public.

Full ratchet: A protection against dilution, specifying that when new money comes into a company, the value of an angel's investment is ratcheted or adjusted to the new value.

Fully diluted outstanding shares: This is a company's total number of shares, with everything factored in—warrants, convertible stock, the whole ball of wax. It's the final number that will determine company ownership and its liquid value.

Liquidity event: Investment jargon for any activity that turns an asset other than cash into usable money.

Pay-to-play: The term used for a participating anti-dilution clause, meaning that an investor has to pay more money into a company to keep playing and participating in the company's promising future at the same level.

Piggyback rights: Investors' right to include their shares in a public offering at no cost to the investor. They piggyback on top of the company selling the shares, which picks up all the costs. This clause is for investors with IPO stars in their eyes.

Redemption: A company's right to buy back stock from an investor at a specified time. This is akin to an automatic or forced exit for an investor.

Registration rights: Investors' right to include their stock at the same price as the owner's share as part of a general pool of stock a company offers for sale in a public offering. Investment bankers, the people who arrange IPOs and the sale of stock, sometimes balk at getting into an IPO if there are many individual investors holding registration rights.

Rights of first refusal: The right of investors to have the first say in whether they want to purchase additional company stock that's being offered to new investors.

Tag along: Investors' right to also sell their shares if the founder or another investor is selling.

Voting rights: Rights given to stockholders to vote on a company's operations and financial transactions, including its repurchase of stock, mergers, and seeking more money. These give investors a loud say in a company's future, including exit events.

Warrants: An option given to an investor to buy stock in a company at a predetermined time and a predetermined cost. Or, a warrant may have no expiration date. Outstanding warrants can postpone an investor's exit, enabling him or her to become more, not less, involved with a company.

Figuring out the ramifications of each of these is like trying to solve Rubik's Cube. So as they say on TV: Don't try this at home! Leave it to professionals, and *bring in a lawyer familiar with corporate law and investing to help you sort through term-sheet provisions.* Let them educate you quickly.

Mike Lincoln, a senior partner with Cooley Godward, law firm to the Internet stars, has seen entrepreneurs' and angels' ignorance or unfamiliarity in drafting a term sheet come back to haunt them. People can be in such a hurry to seal a deal that they ask him to draw up a bare-bones agreement. "It's a document without any bells and whistles—things like preferred stock, liquidation preference, dividend rights, redemption rights, registration rights, information rights, and right of first refusal or co-sale right." Without many of these provisions spelled out in advance, an entrepreneur is begging for trouble come time for an exit.

On top of legal advice, an entrepreneur should also bring in an accountant fairly early. Any business, no matter how green or how small, needs standardized financial controls and an accounting system acceptable to the entire business industry. Instituting creative, original methods for keeping track of your money may doom its future. Angel Bobby Inman cautions, "Make sure from day one you can account for the way you've spent the money you've raised." Otherwise, when outside money people come calling on your company, they're going to take one whiff of your books and head for the door.

Talk of an exit should be not a onetime event but discussed as a company grows. People, circumstances, and the business climate are going to change. Entrepreneurs decide they want to retire, angels discover an immediate need for money, customers want a company to go into a new line of products, an unexpected new market opens up. The possibilities are endless, and every upheaval in a company's, entrepreneur's, or angel's life can dramatically alter the path to the exit. The story of a rising new golf-club company presents a vivid illustration of this lesson.

In the mid-1990s, Terry Koehler approached Cal Simmons, who was managing a pool of angel capital, about a new company he wanted to create. Koehler had quit his job as a senior executive with the Ben Hogan Co. and designed what he believed was a revolutionary golf club. It was a wedge featuring what he called a "dual bounce sole," meaning that a golfer could use it to hit off of either tight, smooth grass or fluffy, rough grass. This wedge could be used by a player on a parched course in Oklahoma or on the lush turf of Atlanta.

Cal met with Koehler a number of times to talk about his vision but hesitated over investing. What won him over was Koehler's passion for his invention and his extensive experience in the golf business. The golfing executive had even patented his inventive new club, which increased its value in Cal's mind. Koehler's smart marketing strategy was also persuasive. He intended to market and sell the special wedge not as a tool to improve everyone's game but to the best golfers, the single-digit handicappers. Koehler felt that the golf boom was ignoring top-flight golfers who played two or three times a week and spent a lot of money every year on clubs.

Cal introduced Koehler to other investors and the group negotiated a term sheet. The angels invested about $500,000 for Koehler to launch his wedge and position his company for later stages of growth. The entrepreneur and investors also discussed an exit strategy. Everyone agreed to Koehler's plan, which was to design and sell a line of wedges in the first year and, if that was successful, produce and sell a line of irons the second year, then on to a line of woods. Around the time the irons were introduced, the company would look for a larger company to acquire it. The financing agreement also specified that some investors would sit on the company's board and together own 60 percent of the company, a portion of which Koehler could buy back once his company hit certain milestones. As a final piece of insurance, the investors attached a lien to Koehler's patented design. In the unlikely event that there was some kind of company blow-up, the investors would own certain rights and royalty streams from the patent.

It was a sound, thoughtful exit strategy. The young company would concentrate on marketing its wonderful wedge and not need to make a large investment in manufacturing or production, because those functions would be provided by the bigger fish that was going to take it over.

The wedge was a huge hit. The sports press gave it great reviews, the best players around the country started hitting with it, and the premier golf country clubs, like Pebble Beach and Greenbriar, stocked it. Emboldened by success, Koehler told his angels that he wanted to move the company ahead faster. He wanted to raise more money to put into heavy promotion. The board members reminded Koehler that rapid growth wasn't the plan, and they wanted to stick to the original idea. The founder chafed at and resisted the board's reining in of him. Nevertheless, he made forays into other lines of business, trying to take the company in a new direction. After months of wrangling, with everyone growing increasingly frustrated, Koehler announced that he wanted to bring in new investors to buy out the original angels.

Although this wasn't the exit plan anyone had envisioned, the investors sensed that it was fruitless to attempt to adhere to the original blueprint. The board agreed, and now Koehler launched a search for fresh investors. But as he made the rounds of venture capitalists and investment bankers, the company faltered and sales slipped. By the time the second round of investors replaced the original investors, the company fortunes had dimmed. The first-round investors received half of their original amount, notes for the balance, and a promise for future royalties.

The company had a new team but continued to stumble. Koehler quickly found himself at odds with his new board on key issues, and within months, the second-generation investors pulled the plug on the venture and withdrew their support. The company was disbanded, leaving the original investors with only 50 cents on the dollar, worthless notes, and a patent that could not be easily monetized.

The moral of this story, to paraphrase Robert Burns, is that even the best laid plans of investors and entrepreneurs can go awry. Even with a great product, a skilled entrepreneur, and eager investors, a company can falter if the main players can't work together toward the same goal. When investors and entrepreneurs disagree, everyone loses. The investors even thought they had protected themselves against just the kind of implosion that happened by taking ownership of the patent on the wedge. But without the founder, whose vision and drive had created it, the patent wasn't worth much. Without a harmonious working arrangement, even legal rights aren't going to protect people.

The point we're trying to make here is that entrepreneurs should think through and be sure about how they want to manage and grow their companies. And they should be truthful about sharing that information with their investors, so that their plans don't blow up in everyone's face a few years down the road. In the golf-club company example, everyone turned out a loser. That happened either because Koehler didn't really consider how he wanted to grow his business, or because he misrepresented that to his angels, or because he changed his mind along the way. Probably the last.

Our advice here comes back to something we have tried to emphasize repeatedly: the importance of good communication and striving for win/win relationships between entrepreneurs and their investment partners. Everyone realizes that circumstances can change along the way and that a founder may want to go off in a different direction. That's OK—but *only* if there is consensus between management and investors. Treat your investors as true partners—that's what they are. Once they have written the check, you're all in the same boat, so be sure to do whatever is necessary to keep everyone rowing in the same direction.

There are five ways investors can typically get their money out of a new venture. Various finance experts have been collecting data, which is why we've included a range for some figures, in Exhibit 8–2. These are the routes for professional angels or VC-backed companies. The next sections discuss each exit strategy in more detail.

EXHIBIT 8–2:
FIVE TYPICAL EXIT STRATEGIES

Route	Frequency
Trade sale or acquisition	27–43 percent
Sale of shares back to the company	5–26
Sale of shares to other early investors	16
Initial public offering for large VC-backed companies	13–27
Liquidation	1–32

EXIT STRATEGY 1: PREPARING YOUR SHOWCASE FOR A TRADE SALE OR ACQUISITION

Planning for a company to be bought by a competitor or a larger player in the same industry is probably the most realistic exit plan. Acquisitions have much to recommend them. The best ones involve companies who complement each other and together produce a synergy that enables the younger sibling to flourish. And contrary to the popular idea of a company sale, the entrepreneur isn't necessarily out in the cold with a wad of cash and nothing to do. A frequent scenario is for the founder to stay on with the new entity, sometimes with enough autonomy so that it feels like the same old business. Of course, plenty of entrepreneurs choose to bail out at this point, because they are, after all, entrepreneurs. They don't fancy punching someone else's time clock or having to learn to negotiate corporate politics.

Each acquisition is a unique partnership between two companies. It's just like a marriage (we're back to *The Dating Game!*), with all the potential promise and pitfalls. But unlike a marriage, which is judged by its longevity among other things, a successful acquisition for entrepreneur and angel is one that pays off. Start-up artists, and their angel advisers, should always be thinking about how to enhance the value and attractiveness of their company to an admirer. Showcasing a feature of a young company that draws second glances is a sure way to attract a buyer.

There are reasons a competitor or larger firm buys a start-up:

- The new venture owns patents, proprietary technology, intellectual property, or market share that the buyer can't get any other way.
- The new venture is firmly lodged in a lucrative niche that the buyer wants into.
- The new venture has managerial expertise, like great marketing skills, that it needs to fill a hole in its operations.
- The new venture has a dependable cash flow a buyer wants to tap into.
- The new venture has a star performer, like the founder, whom it wants on its team.

Young companies that plan to be sold or purchased eventually by a richer company often tailor their operations to enhance their appeal. *To prepare your company for shopping itself, make sure all its valuable, proprietary assets are in good shape, and have all the necessary paperwork up to date.* This may include completing applications for patents, trademarks, and licenses or hiring a patent attorney to show you how to protect your name, identity, technology, or unique formulas. If your company has an especially strong management team—perhaps even a star in your industry—think about arranging for key man insurance and asking people to sign employment agreements. Freeing the company from any encumbrances, such as pending lawsuits or audits, also makes it look better.

A CEO should review company operations, looking for strengths and weaknesses, shore up the thin spots and emphasize the strong, unique elements. Preparing a written plan—be it a marketing strategy, a phased move into a new product line, or an idea for developing a new service—can highlight what's special about a company.

Angels can be a big help to a business looking to be acquired by a larger firm. Their industry network may extend far beyond the entrepreneur's, and they may have a clear sense of the kind of company, and even individual names, looking to acquire another. Angels also know what it is about a young venture that might appeal to an outsider, and can help an entrepreneur spit-shine that facet of the company.

Although there are two ways a company can be sold—either its stock or assets—most acquirers prefer to take on the entire corporate entity and so want to purchase stock. The kind of money buyers use varies, too. Cash is always king, and so the purchaser who offers all cash probably has the best deal. Another form of money is stock, particularly if the acquirer is a public company. Cash and stock can be combined, and notes can be thrown into the pot.

The young Cambridge, Massachusetts, firm e-Niche Inc. discovered the value of a purchasing company's stock as it was accelerating its business. Formed by a former management consultant, Stig Leschly, and a technology expert, Sridhar Rao, e-Niche merged their two talents into an online service offering a marketplace for people wanting to buy or sell rare, hard-to-find, and secondhand books and collectibles. It moved into a corner of the huge marketplace occupied by online sellers like

Amazon.com and Barnes & Noble. The company created an online matching service, putting together, for instance, a consumer looking for an autographed first edition of Tom Wolfe's *The Right Stuff* with a bookseller in Vermont who wanted to sell a copy.

Clearly a brilliant idea coupled with a pair of entrepreneurs who could bring it off, e-Niche brought in $6 million in its first round of financing. Seven months later, the company scored a second round of financing, $10 million from venture capitalists, and earmarked the money to improve and expand its website and beef up its technical and administrative staff. To mark the occasion and emphasize its premier service, the company changed its name to Exchange.com.

The principals rededicated themselves to what was important. The company took on new board members who were technology and industry experts, like Mitch Kapor, the founder of Lotus Development Corp. Its venture-capital backers obviously felt that Exchange.com was on the fast track and headed for either an IPO or a strategic acquisition. Paying attention to business paid off. Only months later, Amazon.com announced that it was acquiring Exchange.com in an all-stock transaction valued—at the time—at $645 million.

Accepting another company's stock for your promising venture has risks, the most obvious being the fluctuating value of the stock. Usually when a company pays with its stock, those shares come with restrictions. The entrepreneur now falls under the watchful eye of the SEC as a company insider and so is limited as to when he or she can sell the stock. The lock-up period attached to a stock acquisition generally runs from six months to a year. A stock purchase, as well as a cash acquisition, also delivers a hefty tax bill to an entrepreneur and other company owners.

Acquisitions are not all a bed of roses. They can be acrimonious, especially when board members disagree about whether to sell out, want to shop for a better offer, or wait for the IPO brass ring. We've heard of instances in which the company founder or major investor, unhappy with the prospective acquirer, has gone looking for a better match. This can thoroughly muddy the waters, and not infrequently, the company that's trying to juggle and evaluate more than one bidder ends up losing both. The bird-in-the-hand-or-two-in-the-bush dilemma can be very costly.

A board needs to agree ahead of time, before a company starts shopping itself, about who to solicit and who the ideal purchaser would be. Acquisitions rarely happen by chance. *A young company that wants to hook up with a larger strategic partner would do well to initiate the search, in order to control events as much as possible and target whom to go after, and it should realistically allot sufficient human and financial resources to execute the search well.*

A HIGH-STAKES ACQUISITION

In some circles, acquisitions have a tainted reputation because some experts say that most of them don't work out. People frequently say that more than half of them don't end well, with executives and operations unable to mesh. However, the acquisitions we're talking about—involving small, privately held companies—aren't generally tracked and entered into a data base. As an exit strategy for both angels and even entrepreneurs, they can make people very happy. This certainly was the case with the purchase of Accipter, a young North Carolina company.

Accipter is a software company that enables websites to deliver targeted advertising to specific visitors to a site. Its founder, Chris Evans, had created one successful e-mail company before launching Accipter, and he recruited two experienced executives, including Paul Rasmussen, who also had built a successful technology company before and was an angel investor with TriState Investor Group (TIG). Naturally, TIG invested in the software entrepreneurs, along with a handful of venture-capital firms. The investors and principals didn't have a specific exit strategy in mind but knew the options, especially the fair odds for acquisition and long odds for an IPO.

Around this time, the late 1990s, a consortium of Internet companies based in Boston and operating under the umbrella known as CMGI was acquiring Internet start-ups. (We first introduced this investment innovation in chapter 2, when CMGI acquired Ben Lilienthal's company, Nascent Technologies.) CMGI was especially eager to purchase companies like Accipter that had developed technology to refine and strengthen Internet advertising. When CMGI approached it, Accipter was still a youngster and not thinking much about exits. It was less than three years old and had just two rounds of angel and venture-capital financing. But CMGI was hungry, especially when it came to technologically endowed companies like Accipter. The young company agreed to an all-stock acquisition, and investors received shares of the publicly traded CMGI representing a value of four times their original investment.

Normally, at this point in an acquisition, all the finagling and uncertainty is over. But not in this case, for one reason. CMGI's stock was extremely volatile, and the lock-up agreement prohibited investors from selling any stock for a year. An acquisition that uses locked-up stock for its currency always generates risk and uncertainty, and with CMGI stock, investor nervousness was heightened by the company's huge price swings. In 1998-99, the price (adjusted for splits) had swung between $5 and $85, and in the following year, from $85 to $160.

Some TriState investors wanted to hedge their stock and had located an investment banker willing to give them an option that guaranteed an upper and lower limit of the stock's price, about 10 percent less on the downside and 20 percent more on the upside. In this way, they were certain that in a year's time, they'd receive at least the current value of their stock minus 10 percent or, at most, the value plus 20 percent. All together, the angels had put about $320,000 into Accipter, which included the club's pooled investment and side-by-side investments by individuals. This original investment at CMGI's then-current price was worth fifteen times their investment. Club members debated heatedly about whether to go for the hedge. Even though some members had more at stake than others, the group's rules were one-person-one-vote, regardless of the size of individual investments.

The angel club voted not to hedge, and let the stock ride. The market would decide whether their exit was profitable or not. A year later, when the lock-up expired, the CMGI stock was worth sixty-four times the angels' original investment. One side-by-side angel investor risking $20,000 converted it into $1.2 million of cold, hard cash. This was one small-company acquisition that defied any and all odds.

EXIT STRATEGY 2: BUY-BACKS AND BUYOUTS

The absence of a market for the shares of a start-up, even when it's showing plenty of flash and dash, limits possible exit routes. Anyone wanting to retrieve his or her investment and cash in on gains in the company's value must look around for possible purchasers of a company's stock. After testing the interest of possible buyers outside the company, an obvious place to look is *inside* the company. The purchase of investor's stock by the company itself is one of the exits that can be predicted and planned for. Given enough preparation and foresight, this is an exit everyone can count on.

The groundwork for a buy-back of stock can be laid in the term sheet. It can specify that a company create a sinking fund. A sinking fund is a special account that a company funds for the sole purpose of retiring a bond or, in this case, purchasing its preferred stock. The provision includes the amount of money a company has to put in every year, which can be a fixed amount or tied to company sales or earnings, and a time-table for when it's ready to start buying preferred stock. Naturally, a sinking fund can impose a heavy load on an aspiring new company, which is why many founders balk at the idea. Frankly, its purpose is for investors' benefit, not a company's. But when a major angel or investment group insists that a sinking fund be established or the check doesn't get written, a company may have no choice.

EXIT STRATEGY 3: SALE OF STOCK TO EARLY INVESTORS

Another buy-back scenario is when an individual, be it board member or outsider, offers to purchase the stock of early investors and even those of the founder. This can be a white-knight scene, with the outsider saving the day by acquiring the stock of an investor eager to exit, or a black-knight scene, when the new purchaser is seeking to oust controlling shareholders.

Not all exits are anticipated or planned. In the case of one company, Color Me Beautiful, neither the founder nor the CEO expected a buy-back to change the company management and direction. Color Me Beautiful began life as a best-selling book written by Carole Jackson. The self-help book offered makeup and clothing advice based on the idea that people's skin tones matched one of the four seasons and that women should wear colors that complemented their season. For instance, a woman whose skin was considered a "spring" would look best in various pastel shades. The book stayed on bestseller lists for more than a year.

Two years after publication, Jackson hired former McKinsey & Co. consultant Steve DiAntonio and formed the company. The product: a packet of swatches for each season that women would take shopping with them to help select clothing best suited to their complexion. Within a few years, company sales hit $6 million, then stalled out. The problem was that women bought the swatches only once, so the market for growth was limited. DiAntonio suggested that they reposition the company, and convinced Jackson that they needed to raise money to finance their new direction.

Three venture-capital funds stepped forward, and Color Me Beautiful had $2 million. This infusion cost Jackson part of her equity, reducing her ownership to less than 50 percent, with the rest held by DiAntonio and the venture capitalists. However, the question of who held the most shares wasn't an issue for anyone, because no single individual or group had majority ownership. The subject of control and ownership wasn't part of the financing discussion or growth plans.

Shortly afterward, the fabric of Color Me Beautiful started to tear. DiAntonio wanted to expand the idea into cosmetics and different ways of marketing, Jackson did not, and they could not agree. DiAntonio tried another avenue and approached the venture capitalists on the board to enlist their support for his ideas and, if necessary, vote as a bloc to force Jackson to go along with him. The venture capitalists sided with DiAntonio, and together they outvoted Jackson on important decisions. Jackson became a founder with little influence over what the company was doing. Frustrated with her new position as a minority owner with no control over the company, Jackson eventually sold her shares to DiAntonio, who assumed the biggest share of company stock.

Sometimes exits happen by accident, and entrepreneurs should expect the unexpected. When Jackson and DiAntonio raised venture funding, their thoughts were on growing and building the company, not changing ownership. However, this exit became more precisely a management buyout, a tool for dislodging an owner or founder. *Every entrepreneur should realize the inherent risks in terms of his or her control and ownership when enlisting the financial backing of outsiders.* DiAntonio's buyout was financed by the venture capitalists, but it could have been bankrolled by a variety of sources. Although this story sounds a bit sad from the perspective of Carole Jackson, it actually wasn't all bad. She was ready to pursue other plans at this stage in her career, while the CEO, Steve DiAntonio, was still eager to build the company. In essence, he became the "founder" of the company in its new incarnation. This creative financing allowed the original entrepreneur and early investors to be bought out and an entirely new group of owners to move the company forward. Remember our words at the beginning of this chapter: Founders and management must be flexible—times change, markets change, companies change. There are very few examples of companies that were launched, funded, and then liquidated all according to the original plan. But new plans can be good for everyone involved.

EXIT STRATEGY 4: THE IPO

As we wrote in chapter 2, the company webMethods, a northern Virginia software business founded by Phillip Merrick, is a stunning example of the outer limits of a spectacular initial public offering. It's stories like that of webMethods, which went from brilliant idea to a stock offering that ended opening day at six times its opening price, that inspire entrepreneurs to keep pulling the one-armed bandit hoping to see a row of cherries and a jackpot.

Many companies that go public come from outside our domain—relatively young entrepreneurial businesses originally financed by angels and venture capitalists. The National Venture Capital Association reports that only half of the 544 IPOs in 1999 were backed by venture money. However, the trend is upward—in 1998, only 20 percent of the IPOs were venture-backed companies.

An IPO is a rare event among start-up companies—fewer than one new company in a thousand gets to an IPO—for a couple of reasons. To begin with, they're expensive to pull off; any company wanting to enter that arena needs substantial resources. Before a company can even daydream about going public, it needs to have a history of revenues and earnings, annual audited financial statements with "clean" opinions, and a sufficient percentage of stock owned or controlled by the company. A company has to be worth at least $50 million, at a bare minimum, to attract an underwriter and then shareholders. Usually by the time a company is ready for an IPO, it's been through repeated rounds of institutional financing or is generating profits that it can plow back into the company.

Access to more money is one of the motivators for going public. While the rags-to-riches stories of entrepreneurs becoming gazillionaires when their little software company went public get the most ink, there are numerous other, even more compelling reasons for a company to go public. Reasons for going public beside liquidity and fabulous fortunes include:

- Substantial capital can be raised at one time.
- The offering gives a company access to additional capital.
- The creation of a company currency that can be used to acquire other companies.
- Proceeds from the offering are true gains and, unlike other kinds of financing, do not have to be repaid.
- The company becomes more attractive to potential employees and potential buyers.

Finding an investment banker willing to underwrite an offering is one of the most difficult hurdles a company will face. Underwriters assume financial, legal, and regulatory risks when they agree to lead a public offering, so they do so very carefully. Naturally, their vetting and due diligence of a prospective company is exhaustive—and exhausting. An underwriter isn't even going to talk to an entrepreneur unless it's familiar with the company through a professional connection, like an accountant or lawyer, from other deals, or it comes with a respected reference.

When an underwriter assesses a company it's considering handling, it wants a business that has a substantial valuation and the promise of growth. A profitable company on its own holds little appeal, unless it can show that its prospects in the coming years are even better. An underwriter also looks for a company in an industry that people understand and want to get into. It doesn't necessarily have to be a sector with stratospheric growth, like some Internet niches, but it does have to be a segment that the underwriter will not have a hard time selling to other institutional investors. Every now and then, a sector becomes decidedly unglamorous or even tarnished, and this can give an underwriter cold feet. Exhibit 8–3 lists the type of investment bank that might handle different IPOs, depending on the valuation of the company going public.

EXHIBIT 8–3:
IPOs LARGE AND SMALL

Not all initial public offerings are mega-deals involving hundreds of millions of dollars and a frantic opening day. Many are much more modest. This table shows the ranges of capital received in IPOs, along with the type of investment banks or underwriters that manage them.

Capital Raised	Type of Investment Bank
$50 million and up	Major banking firm (e.g., Goldman Sachs)
$15 million to $75 million	Specialty firm (e.g., BancAmerica Robertson Stephens)
$12 million to $50 million	Regional firm (e.g., Friedman Billings Ramsey)
$5 million to $20 million	Boutique (e.g., Allen & Co.)

(Adapted from *Where to Go When the Bank Says No: Alternatives for Financing Your Business* © by David R. Evanson. Reprinted by permission of Bloomberg Press.)

Taking a company through an IPO is like a tango, an intricate dance involving a series of set pieces as well as some small individual flourishes, little dramas, and, at times, a fabulous finish. The dance begins with filing a registration statement and preliminary prospectus (the notorious red herring) with the Securities and Exchange Commission, and then filing the final prospectus when the registration has cleared the SEC. Next, the underwriter decides whether to form a syndicate of other financial institutions to help purchase the company stock. Whether a syndicate is needed depends on the size of the offering—smaller ones worth between $5 million and $20 million are often handled by a single underwriter. In most underwriting situations, an investment-banking firm makes a firm commitment to the company about how many shares it will purchase; if these share aren't sold, the investment banker still pays.

If all goes smoothly for the entrepreneur, the IPO machinery cranks steadily through the underwriter's due diligence, the SEC, the road show when the company's CEO talks up the issue with institutional investors, setting the final price, and—a day or two later—the first day of public trading. Alas, many IPOs don't go smoothly, and therein lies more risk. The SEC can hold up paperwork, pushing back timetables that were precisely set to take advantage of a good market. The market can turn and the underwriter decides to hold off until the climate improves. The road show can be a disaster and not gin up the interest or market needed to launch the stock. But when everything is in place—paperwork filed, investors eager, the company's future looking golden—it's a great ride for everybody.

With the webMethods IPO, for instance, the underwriters first fixed the offering price at $13. But there were so many pledges to buy blocks of shares that hours before the opening bell, the offering price was lifted to $35. At the end of that first day of trading, which began at $35, the price rocketed to $212. By the time this happened, the stock owned by founder and CEO Phillip Merrick had been chipped away to a little over 10 percent, which translated into 3.3 million shares. It was still not a bad payday—you do the math.

An IPO isn't cheap. The cost of filings is in the neighborhood of $200,000, and this doesn't begin to cover the underwriter's fees. The firm leading the charge gets a discount on the offering price of the stock, which covers its fee for managing the deal, plus a general fee that represents its profit on the deal, and another fee for the cost of placing the issue with brokerage firms. The final price tag, which is routinely in the millions, depends on the spread (the difference between the discount price you give the underwriter and the offering price) as well as the fixed fees.

As we stated at the beginning of the chapter, IPOs are not the likeliest exit route for every angel-backed deal. However, for many it is not only appropriate but sometimes the *most* likely vehicle. If that is the case, then this should be clearly communicated to prospective investors right from the beginning. Some companies are more capital-intensive than others. They need access to large pools of capital to realize their plans for growth. For some angels or venture capitalists, this is not a game they want to be a part of, and they will quickly pass on the opportunity. But that's OK. Why waste time courting partners who will be at odds with you down the road? There are other angels and VCs who want to "swing for the fences" and be part of the IPO roller coaster. Investors who have had experience with this exit vehicle can be invaluable in making introductions to investment bankers and advising you in other ways that require prior knowledge of the IPO game.

In the case of webMethods, the earliest angels may not have known just how big the potential really was, but they certainly knew that this was going to be a publicly funded company if it was to be successful ultimately.

EXIT STRATEGY 5: A COMPANY YARD SALE— ASSET LIQUIDATION

A company yard sale—selling off a company's assets—is not an exit strategy that anyone plans for. A company contemplating an asset sale doesn't necessarily have one foot in the bankruptcy grave; the value of its assets may far exceed its liabilities. The trouble may be that the entrepreneur has a sinking feeling that the business is hopelessly stalled. The revenue base may be eroding and prospects for growth dried up. Stopgap measures—like finding more funding to revive the company's marketing, product, or service—may not pan out. And sometimes, entrepreneurs run out of gas. The years of chasing money and assembling a going concern may have exhausted their resolve; their heart may not be in it anymore.

One of the bright spots of this country's entrepreneurial boom and the thousands of people who have started a business is that failure is no longer considered a cause for shame. It's almost a badge of honor these days. We've seen more than one set of credentials that practically *brags* about the number of ultimately failed ventures that a person has launched. A failed business today, be it through a sale of assets or even bankruptcy, rarely reflects on the individual involved. Some people even believe it's a good experience—a baptism by fire, if you will. Failures happen, and, if managed right, investors can recoup some of their original money, and the entrepreneur can escape pretty much unscathed.

The possibility of a liquidation, no matter how remote it seems at the time, is why angels insist on receiving preferred, not common, stock. In the queue waiting for receipts from an asset sale, preferred shareholders are ahead of common stockholders. Sometimes entrepreneurs balk at putting investors' interests before their own. Before objecting, they should realize that unhappy investors are unlikely to step forward in any future deals. Many an entrepreneur has walked away from one failed venture to embark on another enterprise that will need venture capital. Alienating sources of start-up money is never a good idea.

The sale of the assets of a magazine company that published *The Journal of NIH Research* shows that a liquidation doesn't have to be a total bust for angels and entrepreneurs. Recovering part of an investment is better than recovering nothing at all. In this example, two experienced magazine executives sold a group of investors—angels and magazine publishers—the idea that a scientific publication dedicated to the massive research community connected to the federal government's health and scientific efforts would be a winner. A partnership was formed, and millions of dollars were raised and invested in the launch of a slick, news-filled magazine for the tens of thousands of scientists in and around the National Institutes of Health. For several years, a dedicated staff and active angel-led board tried various approaches to subscriptions, ads, and other revenue sources. The publication continually got close to breaking even, but there were always setbacks. Eventually, the investor leadership group realized that they didn't have the depth of pockets and capacity to figure out the solution to the journal's problems. So they sold the publication to a large publishing concern, on a gradual payment plan, over several years. The employees and founders moved on to the new owner, the publication was modified and continued, and small payments, representing a fraction of the angel investors' exposure, were made in the first few years of the buyout timeframe. However, within two years, the acquiring company reevaluated the upside for this type of publishing asset and decided to pull the plug. The staff was let go, the final receivables were collected, the lawyers were paid off, and final, small liquidation payments were made to the founding investors of the journal. The entrepreneurs got nothing, the investors got a fraction of their out-of-pocket exposure, and everyone learned a key investment lesson—you win some, you lose some.

BEWARE OF THE LIVING DEAD: NO EXIT

As an exit strategy, an asset sale may be preferable to an even more painful situation, which is a company slipping into operational limbo, what's known as the land of the living dead. The name says it all—this isn't an exit but, rather, perpetual purgatory for an entrepreneur and angels. Of course, no one plans to join the living dead. They end up there by accident, not knowing how bad things truly are. Instead of reading the signs that indicate the company isn't breathing, the entrepreneur keeps slugging but with little to show for it. Angels suffer, too. Their business sense tells them not to invest any more until the company can broaden its appeal and investor base. So they can only watch as a fledgling struggles without success to lift off.

What makes the land of the living dead especially harmful, financially and psychically, is that it can be hard to recognize. Companies don't realize they are there. Here are some signs we have found that point to a company in entrepreneurial limbo:

- Company begins to isolate itself from current and potential investors, perhaps afraid that the subject of results and exit strategies may come up.
- Company focus has shifted away from growth activities, like finding additional financing, new markets, or strategic partners, and turned inward. Under the guise of "let's stick to our knitting," a company draws a circle around itself and holds off ideas for expansion.
- Company cuts back in staff and expenses with little thought as to how these actions affect its business plan. The instinct to save money or curtail spending dominates all decisions.
- Company loses key clients or customers, with no replacements in sight.
- The entrepreneur stops thinking about making money and producing a good return for investors. The profit motive and ideas about great exits have faded, or been deferred so far into the future as to be out of sight.

Our advice to both entrepreneur and investor is that if you find yourself involved in a project that resembles the "living dead," cut your losses and run. Sell the company, merge it with a competitor, turn it over to a hired president (if it is self-sustaining), or close it down. In the long run, a fresh start will probably be better for all involved.

HALLELUJAH, IT'S A HOME RUN

We don't want to conclude on a sour note, especially since, in our experience, many exits turn out well for all involved. Ultimately, the proof is in the pudding. For investors, this means a substantial return on their investments, and figures show that this happens often. According to a variety of sources and people who specialize in tracking seed-stage investing, the return on angel investments over the years is an annualized 30 percent. Angels have throughout history been a source of funding for new businesses, sometimes on a grand scale, such as Queen Isabella's staking Columbus in his journeys to the New World! Many of today's entrepreneurs are no less ambitious as they seek funding for their own discoveries in the new worlds of information technology, communications software, and the bio-tech sciences. We hope entrepreneurs reading this book will now be armed with the information they require to successfully find and negotiate with their own personal angels. Good luck.

- Be patient executing an exit strategy, and remember that angels usually have a longer time frame in mind than do venture capitalists. We'll stay in as long as the prospects stay healthy. Remember that angels, unlike VCs, aren't in it solely to make money. Don't feel rushed to pull off a fabulous exit before the company is ready.

- Don't stint on quality legal and accounting advice for setting up your corporation and your books. Also, arrange to have an audit according to generally accepted accounting practices done annually, if not quarterly.

- Before you go looking for a buyer for your company, spruce it up. Organize company records. Make your office space look established and businesslike, not like a fly-by-night boiler room. Fill important management slots, and make sure your board is active and involved. Bring all licenses, policies, and contracts up to date.

- Never burn bridges. Regardless of how a deal ends, go out of your way not to alienate investors, employees, consultants, and institutional players. Being an entrepreneur is often a way of life, and many founders roll from one new venture to another.

- Be up-front with funders about your exit intentions from your first term sheet negotiation onward.

Epilogue

Much has happened in the world of private equity investing and new business start-ups since late 1999, when we conceived of a book on angel investing and flew to New York City to pitch our concept to Crown Business. We have expanded our work with angel venture groups to 7 clubs in more than 4 cities, we have grown our pool of investors to over 350, and our clubs have made more than 20 investments in early-stage private companies.

The field of angel investing has exploded, just as the public stock markets and nascent world of dot-com companies have had their first shakeouts. More angel investors than ever are plying their money and time, partnering with hundreds of thousands of entrepreneurs. Dozens of magazine articles have covered this national phenomenon. Clubs, networks, and forums are springing up in smaller and smaller communities. The entrepreneurial spirit is alive and well in the nation, as well as internationally.

Small is beautiful. Democracy in application of private equity is profitable. Wealth creation via small-business growth is alive and well, as ever, in the North American continent. What is different from earlier decades is that the level of sophistication and hands-on activity of the holders of capital is growing. We believe that this bodes well for economic development, job creation, and wealth generation in our nation, because hands-on monitoring of one's wealth is better in the long run than passive, blind delegation of money management to "professionals" in such risky endeavors as venture capital.

Institutional venture capital is at an all-time high—measured by money raised and rate of return to investors. Individual activity in early-stage private investing is close behind, in large part because of the growth of structured angel groups and thousands of guardian angels who are providing warm money to individual businessmen and -women. We hope that this book of insights, stories, and tips helps to cement that trend. Our fun and personal wealth comes from monthly—no, daily—contact with the men and women who now take in their own hands the risky but lucrative world of venture capital in the twenty-first century—angel investing.

Small-business people and entrepreneurs have never had a better support system for the growth of their dreams. When individuals like Steve Walker, Steve Case, Jeanette Lee White, Phil Gross, and Michael Rowny risk their capital to create products, jobs, and wealth, they bring resources that no bank or venture firm can bring. Hundreds of thousands of you will prosper because of this relationship. We wish you well in seeking and finding your unique source of "warm" money.

Appendix A:

Recommended Reading

Bartlett, Joseph W. *Fundamentals of Venture Capital.* Lanham, Md.: Madison Books, 1999.

———. *Venture Capital: Law, Business Strategies, and Investment Planning.* New York: John Wiley & Sons, 1988.

Benjamin, Gerald A., and Margulis, Joel. *Angel Financing: How to Find and Invest in Private Equity.* New York: John Wiley & Sons, 1999.

———. *The Angel Investor's Handbook: How to Profit from Early-Stage Investing.* Princeton, N.J.: Bloomberg Press, 2001.

Bloomberg, Michael, and Winkler, Matthew. *Bloomberg by Bloomberg.* New York: John Wiley & Sons, 1997.

Card, Emily, and Miller, Adam. *Business Capital for Women: An Essential Handbook for Entrepreneurs.* New York: Simon & Schuster, 1996.

Cohen, Ben, and Greenfield, Jerry. *Ben & Jerry's Double-Dip: How to Run a Values-Led Business and Make Money, Too.* New York: Simon & Schuster, 1997.

Covey, Stephen R., and Merrill, A. Roger and Rebecca R. *First Things First: To Live, to Love, to Learn, to Leave a Legacy.* New York: Simon & Schuster, 1994.

DePree, Max. *Leadership Is an Art.* New York: Doubleday, 1989.

Evanson, David R. *Where to Go When the Banks Say No: Alternatives for Financing Your Business.* Princeton, N.J.: Bloomberg Press, 1998.

Gardner, David and Tom. *You Have More Than You Think: The Motley Fool Guide to Investing What You Have.* New York: Simon & Schuster, 1998.

Gates, Bill. *The Road Ahead.* New York: Viking, 1995.

Gladstone, David. *Venture Capital Handbook.* Rev. ed. Englewood Cliffs, N.J.: Prentice Hall, 1988.

Gladwell, Malcolm. *The Tipping Point: How Little Things Can Make a Big Difference.* New York: Little, Brown, 2000.

Hagel, John III, and Armstrong, Arthur G. *Net Gain: Expanding Markets Through Virtual Communities.* Cambridge, Mass.: Harvard Business School Press, 1997.

Hagstrom, Robert Jr. *The Warren Buffett Way: Investment Strategies of the World's Greatest Investor.* New York: John Wiley & Sons, 1994.

Kawasaki, Guy, et al. *Rules for Revolutionaries: The Capitalist Manifesto for Creating and Marketing New Products and Services.* New York: HarperBusiness, 1999.

Lowenstein, Rodger. *Buffett: The Making of an American Capitalist.* New York: Random House, 1995.

Mackay, Harvey. *Dig Your Well Before You're Thirsty: The Only Networking Book You'll Ever Need.* New York: Doubleday, 1997.

Maddox, Rebecca. *Inc. Your Dreams: For Every Woman Who Has Ever Considered Business Ownership.* New York: Viking Productions, 1995.

Makower, Joel. *Beyond the Bottom Line: Putting Social Responsibility to Work for Your Business and the World.* New York: Simon & Schuster, 1994.

Mancuso, Joseph R. *How to Prepare and Present a Business Plan.* New York: Prentice Hall, 1992.

———. *How to Write a Winning Business Plan.* New York: Prentice Hall Trade, 1992.

Martin, Michael J. C. *Managing Innovation and Entrepreneurship in Technology Based Firms.* New York: John Wiley & Sons, 1994.

McCormack, Mark. *What They Don't Teach You at Harvard Business School: Notes from a Street-Smart Executive.* New York: Bantam, 1984.

McQuown, Judith H. *Inc. Yourself: How to Profit by Setting Up Your Own Corporation.* 9th edition. New York: Broadway Books, 1999.

Morgan, Anne. *Prescription for Success: The Life and Values of Ewing Marion Kauffman.* Kansas City, Mo.: Andrews & McMeel, 1995.

Osnabrugge, Mark Van, and Robinson, Robert J. *Angel Investing: Matching Start-Up Funds with Start-Up Companies.* New York: Jossey-Bass, 2000.

The Portable MBA in Enterpreneurship. 2nd edition. Edited by William D. Bygrave. New York: John Wiley & Sons, 1997.

Pratt's Guide to Venture Capital Sources 2000. 24th edition. Edited by Stanley E. Pratt. New York: Venture Economics, 1994.

Rickertsen, Rick. *Buyout: The Insider's Guide to Buying Your Own Company.* New York: AMACOM, 2001.

Sherman, Andrew J. *Mergers and Acquisitions from A to Z: Strategic and Practical Guidance for Small- and Middle-Market Buyers and Sellers.* New York: AMACOM, 1998.

Stevenson, Howard H., and Amis, David. *Winning Angels: The Seven Fundamentals of Early-Stage Investing.* New York: Prentice-Hall, 2001.

———. *Raising Capital: Get the Money You Need to Grow Your Business.* Washington, D.C.: Kiplinger Books, 2000.

Stanley, Thomas J., and Danko, William D. *The Millionaire Next Door: The Surprising Secrets of America's Wealthy.* Atlanta: Longstreet Press, 1996.

Wolff, Michael. *Burn Rate: How I Survived the Gold Rush Years on the Internet.* New York: Simon & Schuster, 1998.

Appendix B: Venture Fairs

Arizona Venture Capital Conference
Phoenix, December
www.azventurecapitalconf.com
(602) 495-6470
twasley@phoenixchamber.com

Capital Connection
Washington, D.C., spring
www.mava.org
(410) 560-5855
julie@mava.org

Crossroads Venture Fair
New Haven, Connecticut, May
www.Crossroads–CVG.org
(860) 644-5988
GwennMitchell@aol.com

Early Stage East
Wilmington, Delaware, June
www.earlystageeast.org
(302) 239-6334
info@earlystageeast.org

Early Stage Investor Conference
Chicago, September
www.csa.org
(847) 358-0567
csahq@csa.org

Florida Venture Capital Conference
Florida, January
www.flvencap.org/conference.shtml
(305) 446-5060
forum@flvencap.org

Golden State Entrepreneur Expo &
Venture Capital Conference
Northern California, April
www.goldencapital.net
(530) 893-8828
karen@goldencapital.net

Great Lakes Venture Capital Conference
Chicago, June
www.glvcc.com

Invest Midwest
Kansas City, May
investmidwest@stlrega.org
(314) 444-1151

Investors Choice West Equity Capital
    Conference
Salt Lake City, February
www.venturecapital.org/ICWInv.html
(801) 595-1141
jnathe@venturecapital.org

Mid-Atlantic Venture Fair
Philadelphia, October
www.midatlanticventurefair.com
scarney@gpcc.com

New Jersey Venture Fair
Jersey City, N.J., March
www.njtc.org/events/vf/index.html
hlevy@njtc.org

Innovest
Cincinnati, Ohio, May
www.innovest.org
rsimpkins@edinc.org

New York City Venture
    Capital Conference
New York City, June
www.srinstitute.com
(212) 967-0095
info@srinstitute.com

Research Triangle Venture
    Capital Conference
Research Triangle Park, N.C., April
www.cednc.org/venture/2001
hrice@cednc.org

Southern California Venture Forum
Los Angeles, April
www.theventureforum.com
info@theventureforum.com

Texas Venture Capital Conference
Austin, May
www.thecapitalnetwork.com
(512) 305-0826

Venture Capital in the Rockies
Denver, February
www.vcac.net/rockies.html
(303) 831-4133
maita@amanagementgroup.com

Venture Oregon
Portland, October
www.oef.org/oefventure.html
shonnaw@oef.org

Venture Downtown
New York City, May
c/o New York New Media Association
www.venturedowntown.org
(212) 785-7898
eventreg@nynma.org

Appendix C:

Representative Structured Angel Investment Clubs and Networks

Organization:	**Band of Angels**
Address:	4450 Capitola Road, Suite 103
	Capitola, CA 95010
URL:	www.bandangels.com
Phone:	N/A
Fax:	N/A
E-mail:	N/A
Objectives:	The Band of Angels is a formal group of 150 former and current high-tech executives and entrepreneurs who provide counsel and capital to start-up companies. Prior to the monthly meeting where three start-ups are considered, many companies are vetted with a thorough diligence process that taps the special skills, knowledge, and experience of the Band's seasoned membership. Companies that receive investment also receive the benefit of contacts and mentorship from the same people who helped build Silicon Valley.
	Institutional support for portfolio companies, such as bridge financing and follow-on rounds, is provided by the Band of Angels Fund, L.P., a venture capital fund made up exclusively of institutional partners, and by the numerous venture capitalists with close ties to the Band. To date, more than $300M has been placed in Band portfolio companies in such follow-on investments.

Method:	With 150 well-networked members located in the Silicon Valley, the deal flow considered by the Band of Angels comes exclusively from our membership. There is no mechanism for considering unsolicited deals and entrepreneurs are asked not to submit their proposals directly to the Band administration or the Band Fund managing directors. Our members are well known in the community and the best approach is to discover and solicit one of them. That being said, plans of interest are generally early stage, Series A or B high-technology deals, located in the Silicon Valley.
Structure:	Band Members have founded companies such as Cirrius Logic, Symantec, National SemiConductor, and Logitech, and have been executive officers at Sun Microsystems, Hewlett Packard, Intel, 3Com and Intuit.
Meetings:	Monthly

Organization:	**Capital Investors**
Address:	Potomac Tower 1001 Nineteenth Street North Arlington, VA 22209
Phone: Fax: E-mail:	(703) 469-1082 (703) 469-1063 kirstin@thecapitalinvestors.com
Objectives:	To provide seed capital to technology-related businesses in the Greater Washington, D.C., area. To perpetuate the vitality of the region's high-technology community by finding, cultivating, and supporting entrepreneurial companies. To offer access to key relationships acquired and cultivated through personal experiences in building successful companies.
Founded:	1997
Preconditions:	Only invest in seed-stage technology-related businesses located within the Greater Washington, D.C., area.
Method:	Entrepreneurs submit 2–5 page executive summary. Each month, two companies are selected to present for funding. The partners vote on the

investment immediately, and if approved, begin due diligence. If the company meets certain due-diligence criteria, the company is funded in the range of $100,00 to $300,000, although it is possible to increase the investment size if individual members determine that a larger investment is warranted.

Structure:	Partners include entrepreneurs that have founded and managed some of the country's most successful companies.
Meetings:	Monthly

Organization:	**The Dinner Club**
Address:	402 Maple Avenue West Vienna, VA 22180
URL:	www.thedinnerclub.com
Phone:	(703) 255-4934
Fax:	(703) 255-4931
E-mail:	info@thedinnerclub.com
Objectives:	To make early-stage private equity investments into promising new ventures that have the prospect of achieving a high rate of return.
Founded:	1999
Preconditions:	Accredited investors
Method:	Entrepreneurs send executive summaries to the Dinner Club's managers, who may then request further information, including a business plan, and afterwards will notify entrepreneurs if their plans have been selected for presentation to the Dinner Club. If the Club votes to consider the plan for an investment, the managers will contact entrepreneurs to conduct further due diligence, including discussing terms of any investment, before the Club votes to make an investment.
Structure:	Dinner Club members are regional angel investors.
Meetings:	Monthly

Organization:	**The eMedia Club**
Address:	402 Maple Avenue West Vienna, VA 22180
URL:	www.emediaclub.com
Phone:	(703) 255-4934
Fax:	(703) 255-4931
E-mail:	info@emediaclub.com
Objectives:	To make early-stage private equity investments into promising new ventures that have the prospect of achieving a high rate of return.
Founded:	1999
Preconditions:	Accredited investors
Method:	Entrepreneurs send executive summaries to the eMedia Club's managers, who may then request further information, including a business plan, and afterwards will notify entrepreneurs if their plans have been selected for presentation to the eMedia Club. If the Club votes to consider the plan for an investment, the managers will contact entrepreneurs to conduct further due diligence, including discussing terms of any investment, before the Club votes to make an investment.
Structure:	EMedia club members are regional angel investors.
Meetings:	Monthly

Organization:	**Maryland Angel Council**
Address:	3060 Washington Road, Rt. 97, PO Box 160 Glenwood, MD 21738
URL:	www.stevewalker.com
Phone:	(301) 854-6850
Fax:	(301) 854-6235
E-mail:	alan@stevewalker.com
Objectives:	The Maryland Angels Council (MAC), LLC is a limited liability company organized to provide participants an opportunity for active

involvement in a diversified venture capital process. The group provides equity capital to early-stage entrepreneurial companies based primarily in Maryland and the Mid-Atlantic region that are in the new media, e-commerce, telecom, software, Internet, bioscience, or health markets.

Founded: 2000

Method: Interested in presenting: E-mail a summary of your business plan to Alan Burk at Steve Walker and Associates.

Structure: Investors who desire to participate in a private equity investment vehicle and to promote entrepreneurship in technology-based business in Maryland.

Meetings: Monthly

Organization: **Private Investors Group (Philadelphia)**

Address: 610 York Road
                Suite 107
                Jenkintown, PA 19046
                www.ppig.com

Phone: (215) 884-9300 ext. 140
Fax: (215) 884-9528
E-mail: rich17400@aol.com

Objectives: The PPIG is dedicated to providing a forum for entrepreneurs to present their business plans to investors for the purpose of obtaining financing.

                PPIG is not an investment pool. The members make their own investment decisions and negotiate terms of their investment directly with the companies.

Founded: 1990

Method: Please send an e-mail with your executive summary attached to submit@ppig.com.

Structure: The members of PPIG are sophisticated individual and institutional investors who invest in small, privately held, early-stage companies.

Meetings: Monthly

Organization:	**Washington Dinner Club**
Address:	402 Maple Avenue West Vienna, VA 22180
URL:	www.washingtondinnerclub.com
Phone:	(703) 255-4934
Fax:	(703) 255-4931
E-mail:	info@washingtondinnerclub.com
Objectives:	To make early-stage private equity investments into promising new ventures that have the prospect of achieving a high rate of return.
Founded:	2000
Preconditions:	Accredited investors
Method:	Entrepreneurs send executive summaries to the Washington Dinner Club's managers, who may then request further information, including a business plan, and afterwards will notify entrepreneurs if their plans have been selected for presentation to the Washington Dinner Club. If the Club votes to consider the plan for an investment, the managers will contact entrepreneurs to conduct further due diligence, including discussing terms of any investment, before the Club votes to make an investment.
Structure:	Washington dinner club members are regional angel investors.
Meetings:	Monthly

Organization:	**WomenAngels.net**
Address:	1054 31st Street, NW Suite 110 Washington DC 20007
Phone:	(202) 342-1627
Fax:	(202) 342-1203
E-mail:	info@womenangels.net

Objectives:	WomenAngels.net is a new angel investment club designed to help women investors capitalize on the explosive growth in entrepreneurial activity and venture financing in the Mid-Atlantic region. Women Angels.net is a manager-led Limited Liability Company organized to provide participants an opportunity for active involvement in a diversified venture capital process. The club's goal, first and foremost, is to enhance the wealth creation of its members by investing in young, high quality, high-growth companies in the Mid-Atlantic region.
Founded:	January 2000
Method:	Submissions are accepted in two ways:

1. E-mail your executive summary to info@womenangels.net. All executive summaries submitted must be two pages or less. Or

2. You can complete the online executive summary form.

Upon submission of your executive summary, the club manager will review the opportunity. Typically, you will be notified within three weeks as to the club's level of interest. If WomenAngels.net is interested in proceeding further, you will be required to submit a copy of your business plan, including full financials.

Structure:	WomenAngels.net is a group of highly successful women who have invested their money and will contribute their talent, expertise, and experience in selecting investments and in assisting in the growth of the Club's portfolio companies. The member profile includes women with a variety of professional and private equity experiences—entrepreneurs, venture capitalists and angel investors—as well as women from financial and professional service industries.
Meetings:	Monthly
Organization:	**Chesapeake Emerging Opportunities Club**
Address:	5094 Dorsey Hall Drive, Suite 104 Columbia, MD 21042
Phone:	(410) 442-2521

Objectives: The primary focus of the Club is to invest in early-stage companies with significant growth potential that operate in large markets and are run by talented management. The target return for an investment, in most cases, is three to five times initial investment over a three- to five-year period. Obviously, no assurances can be given that this target will be met. The Club plans to co-invest with established venture capital firms, other New Vantage Network clubs, and other sources of capital when practical and to take a lead in an investment at other times. The Club will endeavor to provide its interested individual Investor Members the opportunity to participate in side-by-side investments on the same terms as the Club itself.

Founded: 2001

Method: For further information contact: Steve Dubin at (410) 442-2521 or Rick Kohr at (410) 997-6000.

Structure: The Club provides equity capital to early-stage, non-public technology-based companies and other companies with the potential for rapid growth.

Meetings: Monthly

Organization: **Common Angels**

Address: One Cranberry Hill
Suite 6
Lexington, MA 02421
URL: www.CommonAngels.com

Phone: (781) 274-9124
E-mail: info@commonangels.com

Objectives: Boston's source for "Mentor Capital." Named after the city's historic public meeting grounds, CommonAngels[SM] is a group of fifty leading private investors and three dozen limited partners in our co-investment fund. Our members and limited partners have founded, co-founded, or run high-tech companies. They work closely with early-stage software, information technology, and Internet companies in the Northeast to build successful profitable businesses.

Founded:	1997
Method:	If you have an opportunity, please complete the Common Angels screening questionnaire, located on the Web page, and return it by e-mail to deals@commonangels.com. Business plans are *only* accepted by e-mail.
Structure:	Common Angels are private investors who have founded, co-founded, or run high-tech companies. They include some of Boston's most successful entrepreneurs and leaders in the software, information technology, and Internet business communities.
Meetings:	Monthly

Organization:	**TechCoast Angels**
Address:	23011 Moulton Parkway, Suite F-2 Laguna Hills, CA 92653
URL:	www.TechCoastAngels.com
Phone:	(949) 859-8445
Fax:	(949) 859-1707
E-mail:	techcoastangels@earthlink.net
Objectives:	Tech Coast Angels is a network of individual investors whose mission is to fund early-stage technology companies in Southern California and to accelerate them to financial and market leadership.
Founded:	1997
Method:	Most investment opportunities come from TCA members, or from a recommendation by an investor, entrepreneur, or professional who knows one of the members. The best way to contact them is by a personal referral. You may also submit a proposal from the website.
Structure:	Members are founders, CEOs, venture capitalists, and business leaders who have funded and built world-class companies. They mentor and coach the entrepreneurs they invest in, serve on their boards, provide contacts, and assist with team building, strategic planning and fund-raising.
Meetings:	Monthly

Organization:	**Tri-State Investment Group (TIG)**
Address:	405 Tramore Drive
	Chapel Hill, NC 27516
URL:	www.tignc.com
Phone:	N/A
Fax:	N/A
E-mail:	or@unc.edu
Objectives:	TriState Investment Group (TIG) is a group of investors dedicated to providing equity capital to early- and mid-stage entrepreneurial companies that are based in Virginia, North Carolina, and South Carolina. TIG IV is the group currently making investments in new companies.
Founded:	1989
Method:	To be considered for an investment by TIG, forward a copy of your company's business plan to inbox@tignc.com. Consideration is generally limited to companies based in the Carolinas.
Structure:	Members of TIG have extensive expertise in biotechnology, medical devices, consumer goods, computer hardware and software, telephony, and in manufacturing, marketing, and finance. Many members are or have been senior managers of *Fortune* 1,000 companies, entrepreneurs, and venture capitalists. TIG members make this expertise available to portfolio companies.
Meetings:	Monthly
Organization:	**Rockies Venture Club**
Address:	190 East 9th Avenue, Suite 440
	Denver, Colorado 80203
URL:	www.rockiesventureclub.org
Phone:	(303) 831-4174
Fax:	(303) 832-4920
E-mail:	maita@rockiesventureclub.org

Objectives:	The Rockies Venture Club (RVC) is a nonprofit, volunteer organization that celebrates the spirit of entrepreneurship in the Rocky Mountain region. Founded in 1983, RVC is the only networking organization that connects entrepreneurs, service professionals, investors, venture capitalists, and other funding sources.
Founded:	1983
Method:	Submit business plans to the following address:

RVC
190 East 9th Avenue, Suite 440
Denver, Colorado 80203

You can also call the RVC main office at (303) 831-4174, or fax us at (303) 832-4920.

Structure:	Potential investors can learn of growing businesses through the RVC's presentation series and monthly forums.
Meetings:	Monthly

If you have any corrections or additions please forward them to our website.

Appendix D:

Sample Term Sheet

Newco Inc.

Summary of Terms for Proposed Private
Placement of Convertible Preferred Stock

Issuer:	Newco Inc. (the "Company")		
Investor:	Venture Capital Partners I ("VCP") or its assignees and certain other investors to be determined (including $150,000 for six individuals to be named by the Company) (together with VCP the "Investors") for an amount up to $5 million with an initial closing of $4 million. The Company shall have the right to approve all members of the investment syndicate, and such approval shall not be unreasonably withheld.		
Securities Purchased:	4,000,000 shares of Series A Convertible Preferred Stock ("Preferred") at $1.00 per share ("Original Purchase Price") at the first closing and 1,000,000 additional shares thereafter at the option of the Investors.		
Post Closing Capitalization assuming 5,000,000 shares are purchased: (Assuming a 15.514 for 1 stock split to be consummated at the closing.)		# Shares	At Close
	Investors	5,000,000	45.45%
	Founders (Common Stock and Granted Options)	3,500,000	54.55%
	Option Reserves for Future Hires	2,500,000	—
	Total	11,000,000	100%
Option Grant	After the Closing, the Founder shall be granted options to purchase 100,000 shares of Common Stock at fair market value. Such options will be granted from the Option Reserves.		

Rights, Preferences, Privileges and Restrictions of Preferred	(1) *Dividend Provisions:* A cumulative dividend on the Preferred will accrue at the rate of $.08 per share per annum ("Accruing Dividends"). Accruing Dividends will be payable only (a) if, as and when determined by the Board of Directors ("Board"), (b) upon liquidation or winding up of the Company, or (c) upon redemption.
	No dividend will be paid on the Common, and no shares of Common will be repurchased by the Company except (a) for shares repurchased from former employees (other than the Founders) at their original purchase price and (b) as set forth under "Stock Restriction Agreements" below.
	(2) *Liquidation Preference:* In the event of the liquidation or winding up of the Company, the holders of the Preferred will be entitled to receive in preference to the holders of Common an amount equal to the Original Purchase Price plus (i) any dividends accrued on the Preferred but not paid plus (ii) the amount they would have received had they converted the Preferred to Common immediately prior to such liquidation or winding up until the Preferred have received four times their Original Purchase Price. Thereafter, all remaining assets shall be distributed pro rata to the holders of Common. A consolidation or merger of the Company or sale of all or substantially all of its assets or any substantial portion of the assets of the Company will be deemed to be a liquidation or winding up for purposes of the liquidation preference.
	(3) *Redemption:* At the election of the Preferred, on each of December 20, 2004, December 20, 2005, and December 20, 2006, the Company will redeem one-third of the Preferred originally issued by paying in cash the Original Purchase Price plus any dividends accrued, but not paid, on the Preferred.
	(4) *Conversion:* A holder of Preferred will have the right to convert the Preferred, at the option of the holder, at any time, into shares of Common. The total number of shares of Common into which the Preferred may be converted initially will be determined by dividing the

Original Purchase Price by the conversion price. The initial conversion price will be subject to adjustment as provided in paragraph 7 hereof.

(5) *Automatic Conversion:* The Preferred will be automatically converted into Common, at the then-applicable conversion price, in the event of (a) an underwritten public offering of shares of the Common at a public offering price per share that would value the Company at not less than $5 per share in an offering of not less than $25,000,000 ("QPO") or (b) the vote of a majority of the outstanding Preferred.

(6) *IPO Shares:* In the event of an underwritten public offering, the Preferred or their designees will have the right to purchase up to 5% of the publicly offered shares, and the Company shall use its best efforts to obtain the approval of the underwriters of such public offering to this right to purchase.

(7) *Antidilution Provisions:* If the Company issues additional shares (other than the shares described under "Reserved Shares" below) at a purchase price less than the applicable conversion price, the conversion price of the Preferred will be reduced on a weighted average formula basis to diminish the effect of such dilutive issuance on the Preferred. However, sales of additional shares at or below the purchase price during the first 9 months after the investment shall receive full ratchet anti-dilution protection.

(8) *Voting Rights:* Except as provided by law and with respect to election of directors and certain protective provisions, the holders of Preferred will have the right to that number of votes equal to the number of shares of Common issuable upon conversion of the Preferred. Election of directors and the protective provisions will be as described under "Board Representation and Meetings" and "Protective Provisions," respectively, below.

(9) *Protective Provisions:* Written consent of the holders of at least two-thirds of the Preferred will be required for

	(i) any sale by the Company of substantially all or any substantial portion of its assets, (ii) any reorganization, consolidation, or merger of the Company with another entity or other transaction or series of transactions in which more than 50% of the voting power of the Company is transferred, (iii) any liquidation or winding up of the Company, (iv) any amendment of the Company's charter or by-laws that is adverse to the Preferred, (v) authorization or issuance of any equity securities other than Reserved Shares, (vi) authorization or issuance of any debt securities or agreements causing the Company to incur debt, (vii) any redemptions or payment of any dividends, (viii) any material change to the Company's business or future prospects, and (ix) certain other actions (to be listed in the definitive agreements) materially affecting the Preferred. The definitive agreements shall contain such other protective provisions as are appropriate for this transaction. In addition, the consent of both of the directors selected solely by the Preferred shall be required for the Company to license or sell any of its intellectual property. The Board, including both of the Preferred Directors, shall approve the annual budget. The consent of the Board, including both of the Preferred Directors, shall be required for expenditures in excess of $50,000 (individually or in the aggregate) not contemplated by the annual budget.
Information Rights:	So long as any of the Preferred is outstanding, the Company will deliver to each Investor holding at least 100,000 shares of the Preferred annual, quarterly, and monthly financial statements, a business plan containing an annual budget at least 30 days prior to the start of each fiscal year, and other information reasonably requested by an Investor.
Registration Rights:	(1) *Demand Rights:* If, at any time after the earlier of (a) the date 180 days following the effective date of the Company's initial public offering and (b) the date three years from the purchase of the Preferred, Investors holding at least two-thirds of the Common issued or issuable upon conversion of the Preferred request that the Company file a Registration Statement covering at least

20% of the Common issued or issuable upon conversion of the Preferred (or any lesser percentage if the anticipated aggregate offering price would exceed $5,000,000), the Company will use its best efforts to cause such shares to be registered.

The Company will not be obligated to effect more than two registrations (other than on Form S-3) under these demand right provisions.

(2) *Registration on Form S-3:* Holders of Common issued or issuable upon conversion of the Preferred will have the right to require the Company to file unlimited Registration Statements on Form S-3 (or any equivalent successor form), provided the anticipated aggregate offering price in each registration on Form S-3 will exceed $1,000,000.

(3) *Piggyback Registration:* The Investors will be entitled to "piggyback" registration rights on registrations of the Company, subject to the right of the Company and its underwriters to reduce in view of market conditions the number of shares of the Investors proposed to be registered to not less than one-third of those to be registered. No stockholder shall be granted piggyback registration rights superior to those of the Preferred without the consent of the holders of two-thirds of the Preferred.

(4) *Registration Expenses:* The registration expenses (exclusive of underwriting discounts and commissions) of all of the registrations under paragraphs (1), (2) and (3) above will be borne by the Company.

(5) *Transfer of Registration Rights:* The registration rights may be transferred provided that the Company is given written notice thereof and provided that the transfer is (a) in connection with the transfer of at least 20% of the securities of the Company held by the transferor, (b) of at least 100,000 shares of Preferred, (c) to affiliates of a stockholder, or (d) to partners of a stockholder who agree to act through a single representative.

	(6) *Other Registration Provisions:* Other provisions will be contained in the Investor Rights Agreement with respect to registration rights as are customarily reasonable, including cross-indemnification, the Company's ability to delay the filing of a demand registration for a period of not more than 90 days in certain circumstances (or 60 days for S-3 registrations), the agreement by the Investors (if requested by the underwriters in a public offering) not to sell any unregistered Common they hold for a period of 180 days following the effective date of the Registration Statement of such offering, the right to obtain more favorable registration rights in the event that such rights are granted to persons other than the Investors, underwriting arrangements, and the like. (7) *No Registration of Preferred:* The registration rights set forth herein apply only to the Common, and the Company will never be obligated to register any of the Preferred.
Use of Proceeds:	The proceeds from the sale of the Preferred will be used for working capital.
Board Representation and Meetings:	The charter will provide that the authorized number of directors is seven. The Preferred (voting as a class) will elect up to three directors, the Common (voting as a class) will elect one director, and up to the remaining three directors (the "Independent Director") will be elected by the Common and subject to the approval of the Preferred (whose consent shall not be unreasonably withheld). Directors shall be elected annually, and the approval process set forth above for the Preferred Directors and Independent Directors shall apply for each election. The Board will meet at least bimonthly. Initially, the Board will meet monthly. The Company shall permit each Investor or its designee to have one representative attend each meeting of the Board and each meeting of any Committee thereof and to participate in all discussions of each such meeting.
Compensation and Audit Committees:	The Company shall maintain and establish Audit and Compensation Committees, which each shall consist of

	not more than three directors, two of which shall be designated from the Preferred Directors.
Key Person Insurance:	Up to $1,000,000 on each Founder, with the proceeds payable to the Company, provided the annual premiums are reasonably acceptable to the Board of Directors in its good-faith judgment.
Right of First Offer for Purchase of New Securities:	So long as any of the Preferred is outstanding, if the Company proposes to offer any shares for the purpose of financing its business (other than Reserved Shares, shares issued in the acquisition of another company or shares offered to the public pursuant to an underwritten public offering), the Company will first offer all such shares to the Investors. Investors may assign such offer to their affiliates. If the Investors (or their affiliates) do not respond within 25 days to the Company's notice of such offering or if the Investors decline to purchase all of such securities, then the Company may offer the securities to other parties on terms no less favorable than those described in the notice to the Investors for a period of 90 days. Such right of first offer will terminate upon a QPO of the Company's securities.
Stock Restriction Agreements:	The Founders will execute a Stock Restriction Agreement with the Investors and the Company pursuant to which the Investors will have a right of first refusal with respect to any shares proposed to be sold by the Founders (other than gifts and other transfers for purposes of estate planning of such Founder's stock as of the Closing Date ["Excluded Transfers"]). The Stock Restriction Agreement will also contain a right of co-sale providing that before any Founder may sell any of his or her shares (other than Excluded Transfers), he or she will first give the Investors an opportunity to participate in such sale on a basis proportionate to the amount of securities held by the seller and those held by the Investors. The Stock Restriction Agreement will also give the Company the right (the "Repurchase Right") to repurchase a portion of such Founder's shares ("Unvested Shares") at a price equal to the lesser of cost or the fair market value of such shares (as determined in good faith by the Board of Directors) in the event the

Founder voluntarily terminates his employment with the Company or is involuntarily terminated for cause. Such right shall not apply to (a) 35% of shares held by the Founder and 25% of such other Founder's shares as of the closing or to (b) an additional 1/36th of the balance of such Founder's shares (i.e., 2.0833%) on the first day of each succeeding month or (c) upon the death or total disability of the Founder.

If, in connection with the sale of substantially all the Company's assets or the merger of the Company with another (a "Sale Transaction"), a Founder becomes party to a one-year or longer employment agreement with the acquiring company (the "Acquirer") which (a) provides compensation to such Founder equal to or in excess of the compensation such Founder was receiving from the Company immediately prior to such sale or merger and (b) provides that such Founder's employment may not be terminated by the Acquirer without "cause" (a "Satisfactory Employment Agreement"), then (x) the Repurchase Right shall terminate as to 50% of such Founder's remaining Unvested Shares and (y) the Repurchase Right shall convert into a right to repurchase at such Founder's cost with respect to the other 50% of the remaining Unvested Shares ("Other Remaining Shares") in the event that the Founder's terminates his or her employment with the Acquirer voluntarily or is terminated for cause within one year after the Sale Transaction. If a Satisfactory Employment Agreement has been entered into by such Founder, and provided that such Founder has not terminated his or her employment voluntarily or been terminated for cause by the Acquirer, such Founder's Other Remaining Shares shall vest in a single installment one year after the Sale Transaction. If no Satisfactory Employment Agreement is entered into by a Founder in connection with the Sale Transaction, then 100% of such Founder's Unvested Shares shall vest immediately prior to the closing of the Sale Transaction.

The sale or exclusive licensing of all or a substantial portion of the intellectual property assets of the Company which does not include the sale of the Company's business as a going concern or the continued

	employment of the Company's employees by the Acquirer shall be deemed to be a (a) liquidation or winding up of the Company under "Liquidation Preference" above and (b) a Sale Transaction for purposes of this section. The Stock Restriction Agreement will terminate after ten years or, if earlier, with an underwritten public offering of the Common in an amount of at least $25,000,000.
Reserved Shares:	The Company may reserve up to 2,500,000 of its Common shares for issuance to directors, officers, employees, founders, and consultants and for the exercise of warrants issued to lenders and other creditors (the "Reserved Shares"). The Reserved Shares will be issued from time to time under such arrangements, contracts, or plans as are recommended by management and approved by the Board, provided that without the unanimous consent of the directors elected solely by the Preferred, the vesting of any such shares (or options therefore) issued to any director, officer, employee or consultant shall not be at a rate in excess of 25% per annum from the date of issuance. Unless subsequently agreed to the contrary by two-thirds of the Preferred, any issuance of shares in excess of the Reserved Shares will be a dilutive event requiring adjustment of the conversion price as provided above. Holders of Reserved Shares who are officers or employees of the Company will be required to execute Stock Restriction Agreements generally as described above.
Non-Compete Agreement:	Prior to Closing, each Founder will enter into a noncompetition agreement with the Company in a form reasonably acceptable to the Investors that will include two-year noncompetition and nonsolicitation provisions.
Nondisclosure and Developments Agreement:	Each officer and key employee of the Company will enter into a nondisclosure and developments agreement in a form reasonably acceptable to the Investors.

Advisory Board:	Upon request, the Company shall establish a Technical Advisory Board subject to the approval of the Board of Directors.
The Purchase Agreement:	The purchase of the Preferred will be made pursuant to a Series A Convertible Preferred Stock Purchase Agreement drafted by counsel to the Investors. Such agreement shall contain, among other things, appropriate representations and warranties of the Company and the Founders, covenants of the Company and the Founders reflecting the provisions set forth herein and other typical covenants, and appropriate conditions of closing, including, among other things, qualification of the shares (or exemption from registration thereof) under applicable Blue Sky laws, the filing of the Company's charter to authorize the Preferred, the incorporation of the Company in Delaware, satisfactory patent due diligence, and an opinion of counsel. Until the Purchase Agreement is signed by both the Company and the Investors, there will not exist any binding obligation on the part of either to consummate the transaction.
Closing:	At their option, the Investors shall have 45 days from the date of the first closing on 4,000,000 shares of Series A Preferred to purchase the remaining 1,000,000 shares of Series A Preferred on the same terms and conditions as set forth in the Purchase Agreement. At the option of the Founders, the Investors shall have an additional 45 days (90 days from the date of the first closing) to purchase the remaining 1,000,000 shares of Series A Preferred on the same terms and conditions as set forth in the Purchase agreement if no such purchase has been previously been consumated.
Legal Fees and Expenses:	The Company and the Investors will each bear their own legal and other expenses with respect to the transaction (except that the Company will pay the fees and expenses of (a) counsel to the Investors; (b) patent counsel to the Investors; and (c) consultants to the Investors, subject to a maximum of $25,000.)
Exclusivity	Upon the acceptance hereof, the Company, its officers, and shareholders agree not to discuss the sale of any equity or equity-type securities, provide any information

	to or close any such transaction with any other investor or prospective investor, unless the Investors are unable to close this transaction under similar terms to those contained herein on or before 30 days after the execution of this Summary of Terms, or the Investors waive their rights under this provision in writing.
Non-Disclosure	The Company, its officers, and shareholders agree not to discuss, disclose, or otherwise transmit this Summary of Terms to anyone other than officers, shareholders, and legal counsel to the Company.
	The undersigned agree to proceed in good faith to execute and deliver definitive agreements incorporating the terms outlined above and such additional terms as are customary for transactions of this type. This Summary of Terms expresses the intent of the parties and, except for the paragraphs entitled "Exclusivity," "Legal Fees and Expenses," and "Non-Disclosure," is not legally binding on any of the parties unless and until such mutually satisfactory definitive agreements are executed and delivered by the undersigned.

AGREED AND ACCEPTED:

Newco Inc.

By: _____

Date: _____

Venture Capital Partners I

By: _____

Date: _____

confidential

Appendix E:

AOL Investment Pitch

Presented at 1988 Mid-Atlantic Venture Capital Conference
Tysons Corner, Virginia

Company: **Quantum Computer Services, Inc.**
8619 Westwood Center Drive
Vienna, Virginia 22180
(703) 448-8700

Business: Online services and communications for personal computers

Established: 1985

Presenter: Philip J. Gross, Senior Vice President—Finance & Administration

Executive: James V. Kimsey, President and Chief Executive Officer

Financing Sought: $5,000,000

Summary: Quantum Computer Services, Inc. is the nation's fastest growing
provider of online services to personal computer owners. The online
services include communications (electronic mail, real-time chat,
message boards), computer enhancement (free software, answers to
hardware/software questions) and entertainment (multi-player
nationwide games). Quantum also offers general and financial
information (news, stock quotes), education (electronic encyclopedia,
online classes) and transactions (make airline reservations, order
products, transmit securities orders to discount brokers). The most
popular services—communications and computer enhancement—are
generally developed and owned by the company itself. Most other

services are developed by third parties such as USA Today, American Airlines and Lucasfilm.

Quantum's initial product, Q-Link, was introduced in November, 1985 and is designed for Commodore 64 and 128 owners. Q-Link members log more than a quarter million connect hours per month, earning Q-Link the distinction of being the second most-widely used online service in the country.

AppleLink—Personal Edition, a joint effort between Apple Computer and Quantum, was launched in May 1988 for the owners of Apple II and Macintosh personal computers. An MS-DOS based service will be available later in 1988.

Financing sought is $5 million in equity capital to develop new business opportunities. In addition, Quantum is seeking to develop relationships with investment bankers in preparation for an initial public offering.

Acknowledgments

FROM US

We wish to heartily thank all the members of all of our angel investment clubs for their insights, laughs, and time devoted to investment activity of our funds.

We wish especially to give thanks to the key staff of New Vantage who perform the research, work with Club's companies, put on the meetings, and have made it possible for us to spend the time it took to chronicle our experience and prepare this manuscript—Anne Lord, Sean Kish, Sinclair Dunlop, Chuck Easley, Karen Cristiano, Karen Edwards, and Sravant Lavu.

We'd also like to thank several individuals who assisted us in the research, writing, and editing of this book: Kerry Hannon, John Greenya, Lisa Berger, and Lauren Chambliss, with special thanks to John Mahaney and Ruth Mills at Crown Business and copy editor Matthew Budman.

Truly, every business needs an angel. And for this book project it was Gail Ross, our agent. Gail not only provided constant encouragement, but it was she who helped conceive the book and provided us with its title. Thanks, Gail.

FROM CAL

I believe that individuals are the sum of their experience—so I would like to acknowledge and thank all those wonderful friends, teachers, co-workers, clients, teammates, competitors, and collaborators who have enriched my life. Special appreciation to my lifetime partners—my wife, Sally, my children, Charlotte, Jeremy and Amanda. The book is done, it's okay to play in my den now.

FROM JOHN

There is no way to express in a few public words the deep personal appreciation I feel toward my wife of twenty-five years—Ann—and my rapidly maturing "little ones," Courtney and Scott. The experiences I've had and insights I've gained are in large part because they allowed me the space and time to be more than a husband or father—to explore new ways to ply my trade and to expand the community of private investors I've met over the past two decades. You're the best!

Index

About the Authors

JOHN MAY

John May was a founder in 1997 of New Vantage Group, a firm that innovatively mobilizes private equity into early-stage companies and provides advisory services to both funds and angel "clubs." For over ten years, he has participated in private equity funds and networks. John is managing general partner of Calvert Social Venture Partners, LP, a Washington, D.C.–based venture capital firm specializing in providing early-stage capital and assistance to emerging growth companies. He is also an adviser to and a member of the Investment Committee of the Women's Growth Capital Fund, LP, a Washington, D.C.–based $30 million fund. New Vantage Group is also the mid-Atlantic office for Solstice Capital, a $23 million venture fund headquartered in Boston. In 1999, he co-founded the Dinner Club with Cal Simmons.

In 1991, he co-founded the Investors' Circle, a national nonprofit group of 150 family and institutional investors. Additionally in 1996, he co-founded and became executive director of the Private Investors Network, an angel network sponsored by the Mid-Atlantic Venture Association, which has grown to over 130 investor members. He sits on several boards of directors of nonprofits, such as Students for Responsible Business, the Institute for Educational Leadership, First Tuesday of Washington, D.C., and two university incubators.

A native Washingtonian, he and his wife, Ann, reside in McLean, Virginia, with their teenage son and daughter.

CAL SIMMONS

Cal Simmons is a highly successful business executive and a longtime angel investor. He founded Cal Simmons Travel, which he sold after twenty-two years in 1997 to Navigant, the fourth-largest public travel company. He is co-founder and manager of the Dinner Club, eMedia Club, and Washington Dinner Club, early-stage venture funds that leverage the capital, expertise, and relationships of angel investors to identify, invest in, and grow promising young technology companies.

Cal has extensive experience in early-stage private equity. He has run an early-stage venture fund and is an experienced angel investor. He has invested in some thirty early-stage companies, and is repeatedly asked by CEOs to mentor them as a board member and adviser. He is a current member and past chairman of the Washington-area chapter of the Young Presidents Organization (YPO). A nationally ranked tennis player and active supporter of area charities, he and his wife, Sally, reside in Alexandria, Virginia, with their son and two daughters.